DATE DUE

DEMCO 38-296

The North African
Environment at Risk

STATE, CULTURE, AND SOCIETY
IN ARAB NORTH AFRICA
Series Editors
John P. Entelis, Fordham University
Michael Suleiman, Kansas State University

The states and societies of Arab North Africa have long been neglected in the scholarly literature dealing with the Arab world, the Middle East, and Islam, except in the context of dramatic international events. Yet this region has a rich historical and cultural tradition that offers important insights into the evolution of society, the complexity of cultural life, forms of social interaction, strategies of economic development, and patterns of state formation throughout the developing world. In addition, as the region has assumed more importance in geopolitical terms, both the United States and Europe have become more directly involved in its economics and politics. Few books of a scholarly or policy nature, however, analyze and interpret recent trends and changes in the constellation of relations between regional and global powers. This new series—the first in English to focus exclusively on North Africa—will address important conceptual and policy issues from an interdisciplinary perspective, giving special emphasis to questions of political culture and political economy.

Books in This Series

The North African Environment at Risk, edited by Will D. Swearingen and Abdellatif Bencherifa

State and Society in Algeria, edited by John P. Entelis and Phillip C. Naylor

Polity and Society in Contemporary North Africa, edited by I. William Zartman and William Mark Habeeb

Port Sudan, Kenneth J. Perkins

The North African Environment at Risk

EDITED BY

Will D. Swearingen
and Abdellatif Bencherifa

WestviewPress

A Division of HarperCollins*Publishers*

State, Culture, and Society in Arab North Africa

Copyright © 1996 by Westview Press, Inc., A Division of HarperCollins Publishers, Inc.

Published in 1996 in the United States of America by Westview Press, Inc., 5500 Central Avenue, Boulder, Colorado 80301-2877, and in the United Kingdom by Westview Press, 12 Hid's Copse Road, Cumnor Hill, Oxford OX2 9JJ

Library of Congress Cataloging-in-Publication Data
The North African environment at risk / edited by Will D. Swearingen,
Abdellatif Bencherifa.
   p. cm.
   Includes bibliographical references and index.
   ISBN 0-8133-2127-1
   1. Environmental degradation—Africa, North.   2. Environmental
risk assessment—Africa, North.   3. Man—Influence on nature—
Africa, North.   I. Swearingen, Will D. (Will Davis), 1946- .
II. Bencherifa, Abdellatif.
GE160.A35N67   1996
333.73'137—dc20   95-39919
                                                                          CIP

The paper used in this publication meets the requirements of the American National Standard for Permanence of Paper for Printed Library Materials Z39.48-1984.

10   9   8   7   6   5   4   3   2   1

Contents

Tables and Figures

Acknowledgments

Many institutions and individuals deserve thanks for helping make this publication a reality. I would particularly like to thank Dr. Edward Murdy of the National Science Foundation and Dr. Gilbert Jackson of the U.S. Agency for International Development for their early confidence in this undertaking. Dr. Greg Johnson, head of the Entomology Department at Montana State University, generously provided funds for manuscript preparation. Genevieve Gwynne has been involved with the editing, layout, and preparation of this manuscript from the very beginning; her cheerful and skillful assistance has been much appreciated. I also wish to thank Janet Petroff and Jennifer Swearingen for their editorial help and Niki Jefferies for drafting or redrafting several of the figures. Jeanne Mrad, Resident Director of the Centre d'Etudes Maghébines à Tunis (CEMAT), has been extremely helpful in facilitating communications with the Tunisian contributors. Dr. I. William Zartman, President of the American Institute for Maghrib Studies, has been a strong supporter of this book project from the beginning. Theresa Simmons, of the African Studies Program at the School for Advanced International Studies, Johns Hopkins University, also deserves thanks for her invaluable assistance at many critical steps along the way. Thanks are also due to Cambridge University Press for allowing me to use material from my chapter in their publication, *Drought Follows the Plow* (1994), edited by Dr. Michael H. Glantz, and to John Wiley and Sons Ltd. for kind permission to reprint the map in the Sutton and Zaimeche chapter, previously published in these authors' article in *Land Degradation and Rehabilitation*. (Unless otherwise noted, all other figures used in this volume are original.) Finally, my warm thanks to my co-editor, Dr. Abdellatif Bencherifa.

Will D. Swearingen
Bozeman, Montana

About the Contributors

Abdelmalek Benabid, Professor at the Ecole Nationale Forestière d'Ingénieurs, Tabriquet-Salé, Morocco, is a plant ecologist who studies human impacts on Mediterranean vegetation formations.

Abdellatif Bencherifa, Professor and Vice President for Student Affairs at Al Akhawayn University, Ifrane, Morocco, is a geographer whose current research focuses on labor migration, drought impacts, and agricultural change in Morocco.

Mohamed Berriane, Professor in the Département de Géographie of the Faculté des Lettres et des Sciences Humaines, Université Mohammed V, Rabat, Morocco, is an economic geographer who conducts research on international labor migration and the impacts of tourism on Morocco.

Zitouni Boutiba, Professor at the Institut des Sciences de la Nature, Université d'Oran, Oran, Algeria, is a biologist concerned with biodiversity in North Africa's marine and coastal ecosystems.

Sadok Bouzid, Professor in the Département des Sciences Biologiques of the Faculté des Sciences, Université de Tunis, Tunis, Tunisia, specializes in plant morphogenesis, micropropagation of tree seedlings, and strategies to combat desertification.

Pamela Chasek, who received a Ph.D. in international relations at the Paul H. Nitze School of Advanced International Studies, Johns Hopkins University, Washington, D.C., in May 1994, consults on international environmental policy and is an editor of *Earth Negotiations Bulletin*.

Belgacem Henchi, Directeur Général, Secrétariat d'Etat à la Recherche Scientifique et à la Technologie, Tunis Mahrajène, Tunisia, is an ecologist specializing in natural resource management and environmental protection.

Douglas L. Johnson, Associate Professor in the Graduate School of Geography, Clark University, Worcester, Massachusetts, has conducted extensive research on pastoral nomadism and land-use practices in North Africa and the Middle East and is currently investigating intensification of pastoral systems in Morocco.

James A. Miller, Associate Professor in the Department of History at Clemson University, Clemson, South Carolina, is a geographer specializing in land use and cultural change in Morocco's mountain and desert environments. He is currently conducting research on ancient land-use practices in the Tafilalt Oasis.

Barbara Parmenter, Lecturer in the Community and Regional Planning Program of the School of Architecture at the University of Texas, Austin, is a geographer whose studies of environmental history and environmental perception focus on wetland ecosystems in the Middle East and North Africa.

Christopher S. Potter, Senior Research Scientist with Johnson Control World Services, NASA Ames Research Center, Moffett Field, California, specializes in global computer simulation of greenhouse gas fluxes in terrestrial ecosystems using remote sensing, ecosystem models, land-use change information, and GIS databases.

Dah Salihi, National Expert with the Projet de Lutte contre l'Ensablement et Mise en Valeur Agro-Sylvo-Pastorale of the Ministère du Développement Rural et de l'Environnement, Nouakchott, Mauritania, is a rangeland specialist involved in fighting desertification and promoting sustainable land-use practices in Mauritania.

Allan T. Showler, Assistant Professor at the University of Missouri and Senior Technical Advisor to the Africa Emergency Locust/Grasshopper Assistance (AELGA) Project of the Africa Bureau, USAID, Washington, D.C., is an entomologist who specializes in emergency responses to pest outbreaks and related problems, particularly in Africa.

Keith Sutton, Senior Lecturer in the Department of Geography at the University of Manchester, Manchester, England, has conducted extensive research on economic development and rural settlement in Algeria and has recently focused on electoral geography and environmental degradation in Algeria.

Will D. Swearingen, Associate Research Professor, Earth Sciences Department, and Director of the Africa Grasshopper/Locust Biocontrol Program, Montana State University, Bozeman, Montana, explores the political, economic, and environmental dimensions of agricultural development in North Africa.

Lynn Wagner, Ph.D. candidate in international relations at the Paul H. Nitze School of Advanced International Studies, Johns Hopkins University, Washington, D.C., specializes in negotiation processes and conflict resolution.

Salah Zaimeche, Honorary Research Fellow at the Department of Geography, University of Manchester, Manchester, England, is a historian whose recent research focuses on environmental degradation in North Africa.

I. William Zartman, Professor of international politics and Director of the Africa Studies Program at the Paul H. Nitze School of Advanced International Studies, Johns Hopkins University, Washington, D.C., is an expert on political systems in North Africa and the founding president of the American Institute for Maghrib Studies (AIMS).

The North African
Environment at Risk

2

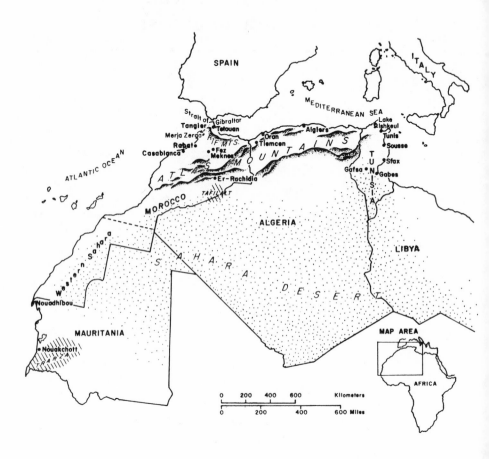

FIGURE I.1 North Africa

Introduction:
North Africa's Environment at Risk

Will D. Swearingen and Abdellatif Bencherifa

This book focuses primarily on the North African countries of Morocco, Algeria, and Tunisia. These three countries are the heart of the Maghreb, or western part of the Arab world.[1] They share many characteristics that distinguish them from other North African countries, including their complex natural environment, French colonial legacy, and distinctive blend of Arab, Berber, and European cultures. Their distinctive regional character gives coherence to the present study.

However, despite its specific focus on Northwest Africa, this book has much wider relevance. It provides insight into environmental problems occurring throughout North Africa and the Middle East—indeed, throughout the developing world. Nearly everywhere in the developing world, the underlying causes of environmental deterioration are the same. These include environmental constraints, rapid population growth, rampant urbanization, and poorly regulated industrialization. This introduction presents an overview of these root causes of environmental deterioration. It begins with a sketch of the Northwest African environment.

The Northwest African Environment

The Northwest African environment consists of three major environmental zones: the southern Saharan deserts, the mountain highlands, and the arable northern coastal plains and plateaus (Figure I.1).[2] Of these, the southern deserts comprise by far the largest zone, accounting for roughly

70 percent of the total territory of the three countries. Mountain highlands account for roughly 20 percent, and the arable northern lowlands for 10 percent.

However, these proportions vary greatly from country to country. Nearly 90 percent of Algeria consists of desert, as opposed to around two-thirds of Tunisia and half of Morocco (including the Western Sahara). Mountainous highlands cover roughly a third of Morocco's national territory, but only about a tenth of that in Tunisia and Algeria.[3] Arable coastal plains and plateaus comprise around a fourth of Tunisia's national territory, a fifth of Morocco's, and less than 5 percent of Algeria's.

Morocco, Algeria, and Tunisia are clearly distinguished from the rest of North Africa by their extensive mountains and relatively well-watered coastal lowlands. Mountain highlands extend for more than 2,000 kilometers (km) from west to east, and form a barrier that varies from 200 to 400 km in width (Figure I.1). Elevations range from more than 4,000 meters (m) in the west, for the highest peaks in the Moroccan High Atlas, to around 1,500 m in Tunisia's Dorsal to the east.

This highland barrier intercepts storms arriving from the Atlantic and Mediterranean during the autumn-spring cool season, triggering precipitation. Rainfall throughout much of the northern coastal lowlands is sufficient for rainfed agriculture. Generally heavier rainfall in the mountains (or snowfall on higher peaks) gives rise to permanent streams that are extensively exploited for irrigation. However, Northwest Africa's mountainous barrier also casts a long "rain shadow." Beyond the mountains, desert abruptly begins.

Owing to the beneficent moisture-capturing effect of its mountains, the northern tip of Northwest Africa is a relatively lush island rising from the world's largest desert. The boundary of this island extends from slightly south of Agadir in Morocco to Gabes in Tunisia. South of this boundary, where watercourses drain into the desert or subsurface water is available, intensive oasis agriculture is practiced. Nevertheless, such areas are rare: these oases are mere scattered pinpoints on a map of the Sahara. Though much diminished in importance, pastoral nomadism also persists in the southern deserts. However, despite these desert-based activities, all but a tiny percentage of Northwest Africa's population lives north of the Agadir-Gabes line.

Just as water shortages limit population in the southern deserts, lack of level land is the major limiting factor in the mountains. Most of the highland population is concentrated in a relatively few well-watered valleys, where terraces are commonly used to create fields. Cereal and vegetable crops are grown for subsistence needs, and flocks of sheep and goats are maintained for sale to lowland urban areas. Settlements in many mountain valleys also supplement their incomes with small-scale market-oriented production of tree crops such as olives, apples, figs, cherries, apricots, and walnuts.

To an impressive degree, Northwest Africa's deserts and mountain areas have maintained their traditional character. Compared to the northern lowlands, they have benefited relatively little from economic development. As a result of population growth and limited opportunities, both zones have long been major regions of out-migration. Emigrants have settled in urban areas in the northern lowlands.

Due to relatively higher rainfall, better soils, level terrain, and the availability of irrigation water, most of Northwest Africa's arable land is concentrated in the northern plains and plateaus. Arable land is relatively extensive by North African/Middle Eastern standards. Morocco has approximately 8.4 million hectares (ha) of arable or permanently cropped land, Algeria has 7.5 million ha, and Tunisia has 4.6 million ha (FAO 1988). Despite this, arable land is a minor percentage of the national territory. Only around 3 percent of Algeria's total national territory is arable or permanently cropped, as opposed to 13 percent in Morocco (counting the Western Sahara) and 29 percent in Tunisia (FAO 1988).

Since the initial colonial takeover (in Algeria in 1830, Tunisia in 1881, and Morocco in 1912), modern economic development has been focused almost exclusively on the northern coastal lowlands. Desert and mountain regions —traditional hearths of North African culture—have increasingly become marginalized. Today, most of Northwest Africa's population, urban areas, industry, tourist developments, modern agriculture, and perennially irrigated areas are concentrated in the environmentally more-favored coastal lowlands.

However, the relative lushness of the northern coastal lowlands is deceptive. Occasionally, this lushness seems as fleeting as a mirage. Northwest Africa's destiny is constrained by its geographic location astride the Sahara Desert, on the extreme margins of moisture-bearing storm tracks. The only truly humid areas are in the northern mountains along the Mediterranean, where average rainfall exceeds 1,000 millimeters (mm) in certain locations. In most of the coastal lowlands, average rainfall varies from only around 600 mm in the north to as little as 200 mm in the south. These rainfall levels are only marginally adequate for rainfed agriculture. In the more southern lowlands, such as the Haouz or Souss plains in Morocco, irrigation is essential.

In addition to their generally low rainfall levels, Northwest Africa's arable lowlands are subject to high rainfall variability and recurring drought. "Normal" rainfall is largely an average of extreme rainfall conditions — too much or too little. Both the timing and total amounts of rainfall fluctuate dramatically from year to year. Flash floods following brief downpours are a periodic hazard. Occasionally, Northwest Africa's

mountains trap storms for extended periods, resulting in days of uninterrupted rainfall. For example, in 1969, more than 1,700 mm of rain fell in the
central Rif during a 17-day period. That same season, the Rifian station of
Ktama registered an astounding 3,173 mm of precipitation (Maurer 1985).

However, drought is a more common natural hazard. Usually, 400 mm
of annual rainfall is considered the minimum for viable rainfed agriculture
in semi-arid lands. Most of Northwest Africa's arable lowlands receive
only 300-500 mm of rainfall in an average year. In short, even in higher
rainfall areas, the margin of error is precariously lean. The risk of drought
is high in most of Northwest Africa. During the present century, for
example, drought in Morocco has occurred, on average, about one year out
of every three.[4]

Poor soils are another major environmental constraint in Northwest
Africa. Soil formation is impeded by the region's extreme aridity during
summer. Cool winter conditions in much of the region also inhibit chemical
reactions needed for soil formation. As a result, Northwest Africa's soils
are generally thin. In addition, some of its best soils were formed during
warmer, more humid periods in the past. These soils are not renewable
under present climatic conditions.

Northwest Africa's generally arid character, its thin soils, and the often
intense nature of rainfall make this region naturally vulnerable to land
degradation. Erosion and desertification are major hazards. Intense
rainfall rapidly erodes soils, particularly where natural vegetation cover
has been cleared from slopes. Drought aggravates the effects of overgrazing, increasing degradation of natural vegetation and soils. It also increases
risks of wind and water erosion, particularly where marginal land has been
cleared for cultivation or severe overgrazing has occurred. Finally,
drought intensifies other forms of environmental degradation, such as
deforestation. During drought years, owing to lack of cultivated fodder or
natural pasture, cutting of tree branches for fodder is common. This often
damages trees and hastens their decline. Such processes of environmental
degradation are well described by many of the authors in this volume.

Population growth has accelerated environmental degradation through
intensifying land-use pressure. As the human population has increased, so
have the numbers of livestock exploiting rangeland and forest areas. This
has amplified the risks of overgrazing and forest degradation. Expansion
of the cultivated area at the expense of rangeland and forests has been
another consequence of population growth. Newly cleared areas are
especially prone to environmental deterioration: they are usually areas
with low rainfall and/or unfavorable slopes — conditions that increase
vulnerability to land degradation. Clearing of wooded areas for building
materials and fuel are other consequences of North Africa's dramatic
population increase. Finally, the region's remaining wetlands, precious

islands of biodiversity, are under siege. Most of the chapters in this book examine problems that have emerged from tensions between population growth, increasing demand for resources, and environmental constraints. The following section focuses on population growth trends.

Demographic Trends

Population growth is one of the primary forces behind environmental degradation in Northwest Africa. As in most of the developing world, the magnitude of growth in Northwest Africa during the present century is without historical precedent. Prior to the 20th century, Northwest Africa's population remained in what demographers refer to as a "high stationary" phase. Population grew extremely slowly and irregularly. Although birth rates were high, they were almost totally offset by high death rates. Population gains during tranquil periods were periodically wiped out by famine, epidemics, and war. For example, famine and cholera reduced Morocco's population by roughly a fifth between 1878 and 1882 (Noin 1970). Life expectancy was low — averaging around 30 years (Escallier 1985). Until the present century, the region's total population remained below 12 million inhabitants.

During the first two decades of the 20th century, improved security and public-health measures began to reduce mortality. According to censuses undertaken by French colonial authorities in 1921, the region's total population was around 12.7 million (Table I.1). Following World War I, population steadily increased as a result of improved sanitation, better access to health facilities, more reliable food supplies, and reduced tribal warfare. Death rates began to fall, birth rates — already high — climbed even higher, and the region entered an expansive demographic phase. Population increased dramatically.

Epidemics and severe food shortages in the late 1930s and early 1940s caused a temporary population decline. However, this was followed by even more robust demographic growth. Public vaccination campaigns, availability of new antibiotics and sulfa drugs, and widespread use of DDT to eradicate malaria were key factors behind a renewed population explosion. This population explosion peaked during the 1960s, when population growth rates reached 3.4 percent in Algeria, 3.3 percent in Tunisia, and 3.2 percent in Morocco (Escallier 1985). Since around 1970, growth rates have gradually been declining.[5] However, they remain relatively high — roughly 2.1 percent in Morocco, 2.2 percent in Tunisia, and 2.4 percent in Algeria (World Bank 1994a).

Table I.1 records Northwest Africa's dramatic population growth. The combined population of the three countries more than doubled between

TABLE I.1 Cumulative Population Growth in Northwest Africa

Year	Morocco	Algeria	Tunisia	Total
1921	5,800,000	4,900,000	2,000,000	12,700,000
1937	7,300,000	7,300,000	2,700,000	17,300,000
1960	11,600,000	11,000,000	4,200,000	26,800,000
1980	19,400,000	18,700,000	6,400,000	44,500,000
1992	26,200,000	26,300,000	8,400,000	60,900,000
2000	30,000,000	33,000,000	10,000,000	73,000,000
2025	45,700,000	52,000,000	13,600,000	111,300,000
Projected population before stationary	59,000,000	81,000,000	18,000,000	158,000,000

Sources: FAO 1961, 1985; Escallier 1985, 1991; World Bank 1988, 1994b; WRI 1992.

1921 and 1960, growing from slightly less than 13 million to nearly 27 million. By 1992, this combined population had more than doubled again, reaching 61 million. Northwest Africa's population in the mid-1990s is *more than five times larger* than in the 1920s.

Although growth rates are now declining, there is substantial potential for further growth. According to World Bank demographers, populations in the region will not begin to stabilize until 2015 in Tunisia, 2020 in Morocco, and 2025 in Algeria (World Bank 1988). These are the years, respectively, in which the net reproduction rate (NRR) is expected to drop to one in each country. A NRR of one indicates that fertility is at a bare replacement level, with child-bearing women having only enough daughters to replace themselves. By the time this point is reached in Algeria — only 30 years from now — there will probably be slightly more than 111 million inhabitants in Northwest Africa. Such a population level is four times greater than that in 1960.

Given the powerful momentum in demographic growth dynamics, population will continue to grow dramatically in Northwest Africa, even after net reproduction rates reach a bare replacement level. According to World Bank projections, Northwest Africa's population will reach 158 million before stabilizing (Table I.1, final row). Broken down by country, there will ultimately be 59 million Moroccans, 81 million Algerians, and 18 million Tunisians.

The environmental implications of this unprecedented population expansion are obvious. Population pressure is clearly one of the key underlying causes of the deterioration of the North African environment. The capacities of the respective natural resource bases to support additional population, in a sustainable manner, are becoming increasingly strained.

However, population growth in Northwest Africa has not been equally distributed. Instead, it has become increasingly concentrated in urban areas. This has created an additional set of environmental problems. The following section provides a brief overview of urbanization and industrialization, highlighting their environmental consequences.

Urbanization and Industrialization

Over the course of the present century, population growth in Northwest Africa has become increasingly concentrated in the northern coastal lowlands. Within these lowlands, it has become increasingly concentrated in a few major urban areas, primarily centers of industrial activities. This has had major implications for the Northwest African environment. It has been the source of different forms of environmental deterioration, including air pollution, pollution of marine waters, groundwater pollution, and loss of productive agricultural land to urban land uses.

Urbanization in Northwest Africa is a relatively recent phenomenon. The 1936 censuses, for example, revealed that only around 21 percent of the region's population was urban: 15 percent in Morocco, 22 percent in Algeria, and 25 percent in Tunisia (Escallier 1985). Twenty years later, in 1956, the level of urbanization had barely increased and was estimated at 27 percent (Escallier 1985). Since the 1960s, however, urbanization has been one of the most remarkable socioeconomic trends in the region, completely transforming Northwest African society. By 1992, the urban population accounted for 47 percent of the total in Morocco, 54 percent in Algeria, and 57 percent in Tunisia (World Bank 1994b). This dramatic trend is expected to continue. In 2000, an estimated 76 percent of Algeria's population, 66 percent of Tunisia's population, and 55 percent of Morocco's population will be urban (Lacoste 1991).

The rate of urbanization has been substantially higher than the rate of population growth as a whole. In Morocco, for example, during the 1960-1990 period, population growth in urban areas averaged 4.3 percent a year, as opposed to only 1.5 percent in rural areas. In Algeria, during the same period, the urban growth rate was 4.7 percent, while the rural growth rate was only 1.6 percent. In Tunisia, the comparable figures were 3.6 percent growth for urban areas and 1.1 percent for rural areas (WRI 1992). In other words, urban populations grew three times as fast as rural populations.

The differences between urban and rural growth rates is accounted for almost exclusively by out-migration from rural areas — North Africa's "rural exodus." Rural exodus began in the region in the 1930s, accelerated in the 1940s, and has been a central dynamic of the region's population explosion since the 1950s. This phenomenon has affected all urban areas and settlements. However, the largest cities have attracted the largest percentage of rural emigrants. In Morocco, for example, since the 1940s, Casablanca alone has absorbed around 37 percent of the rural exodus. The highly urbanized coastal strip extending from Casablanca to Kenitra — including Mohammedia, Rabat, and Salé — has captured roughly 53 percent of the rural emigrants. In other words, these five rapidly expanding coastal cities have absorbed more rural outmigration than all other urban places in Morocco combined (Escallier 1985). Similar levels of urbanization from rural exodus have occurred in the major coastal cities of the other two Northwest African countries.

The cities that have received the most rural emigrants and experienced the greatest population growth have been the major centers of industrialization and economic activity. The prospect of jobs has been a powerful lure. In addition, poverty and lack of opportunity in the countryside have been compelling forces behind rural outmigration. Unfortunately, because of the relative absence of new opportunities in the cities, the majority of rural emigrants have ended up in unplanned squatter settlements ("bidonvilles") or have crowded into poorer, older neighborhoods.

It is difficult to estimate total populations living in unplanned settlements in Northwest Africa — first, because of lack of statistics, and second, because many of these settlements have gradually become incorporated into the urban fabric. However, at least 300,000 residents have become established in bidonvilles on the periphery of Tunis during the past 15 years (Henchi, this volume). The population living in Casablanca's unplanned settlements can be conservatively estimated to be at least 500,000 — though the Moroccan government has made a major attempt during the past decade to integrate these settlements. For Northwest Africa as a whole, unplanned settlements account for at least 10 percent of the total urban population. Although some unplanned settlements have gradually acquired services, many lack safe drinking water and most lack running water and sewage systems. This lack of sanitary facilities has resulted not only in heightened public-health risks but in extensive freshwater and marine pollution.

Levels of crowding in poorer, older urban neighborhoods are intense. In Algeria, for example, the typical urban household consists of 7 to 8 persons living in one or two rooms (Baduel 1991). In Tunisia, 50 to 60 percent of urban households consist of only one or two rooms. The shortage of urban housing in Algeria in the late 1980s was estimated at more than 2 million units. In Morocco, the urban housing deficit is nearly as high (Baduel 1991). Intense overcrowding in Northwest Africa's urban areas has overwhelmed existing sanitation facilities. This too has contributed to pollution of freshwater supplies and offshore marine areas.

Industrialization has been a significant force behind urbanization in Northwest Africa. Governments in all three countries have emphasized industrial development since independence (in 1956 in Morocco and Tunisia and 1962 in Algeria). All three countries have developed extensive basic industrial sectors encompassing food-processing, manufacturing of household and consumer items, and production of cement and other building materials. All three have given extraction and processing of mineral and energy resources a central role within their economic development strategies. Algeria has particularly focused on hydrocarbons, while Morocco and Tunisia have developed their extensive phosphate resources. Tunisia, and to a lesser degree, Morocco, have courted foreign investment in export-oriented industries, such as textile mills or assembly plants, that rely on low-wage levels. Algeria, with its strong post-colonial drive toward self-sufficiency, is the only country of the three to have extensively developed more sophisticated and capital-intensive industries, including manufacturing of steel, petrochemicals, tractors and other major capital goods, and higher-tech consumer items such as television sets.

Despite different policies, industrial development in all three countries shares two essential features: first, its highly concentrated nature in a few coastal locations; and second, poorly developed safeguards for the environment. In Morocco, most industry is concentrated in the Casablanca-Mohammedia region. In Algeria, despite government attempts to decentralize and establish growth poles inland, most industry remains concentrated in a handful of major urban areas and industrial zones along the coast. In Tunisia, half of all industry is concentrated around Tunis, and virtually all of the rest is centered in a few other coastal cities, particularly Gabes and Sfax. These heavy concentrations of industry along the coast multiply the risks of industrial pollution.

The potential for industrial pollution has been increased by weak and poorly enforced regulations in all three countries. Little has been done to prevent air pollution from industry or to treat industrial waste. Solid industrial waste tends to be carelessly stored on site or dumped into nearby ravines. Either way, it can readily pollute groundwater or be swept by runoff into streams and out to sea. Liquid waste is usually simply discharged directly into the environment. Industrial pollution in Northwest Africa has been poorly studied. However, the chapters by Henchi and Berriane in this volume and occasional reports in the North African media provide disturbing glimpses at the magnitude of industrial pollution in the region.

Conclusions

This introduction has briefly reviewed major underlying causes of environmental deterioration in Northwest Africa. These include environmental constraints, rapid population growth, uncontrolled urbanization, and poorly regulated industrialization. Such root causes are similar throughout the developing world. This volume demonstrates how they have become translated into environmental deterioration in a specific geographical and cultural setting.

In the chapters that follow, a multidisciplinary group of scientists and scholars examines the broad range of human activities causing deterioration of the North African environment. Specific environmental problems examined include deforestation, soil erosion, drought, desertification, air and water pollution, loss of wildlife habitat, and declining biodiversity. These environmental problems are interrelated manifestations of a growing environmental crisis in North Africa that has received relatively little attention from government policymakers and is poorly understood by North African peoples, the international development community, and scholars.

Contributors to this volume analyze the historical roots of current environmental problems, underlying socioeconomic and cultural factors, potential solutions, and differences in environmental policies among the North African countries. In particular, they explore the conflict between economic development and environmental sustainability. What emerges is a case study of a developing region attempting to reconcile traditional methods of land use with growing demand for resources, the exigencies of economic development, and the limitations of the natural resource base. It is a portrait of an environment at risk.

Notes

1. The terms "North Africa" and "Northwest Africa" are used in preference to "the Maghreb" in this book because this latter regional term is generally unfamiliar to non-specialists in the English-speaking world. Furthermore, "the Maghreb" usually is considered to include Libya (or at least its western half) and Mauritania. Admittedly, selective use of the term "North Africa" to refer to only a portion of northern Africa perpetuates a French colonialist perspective. During the colonial era, the French used the term *Afrique du Nord* almost exclusively to refer to their colonial possessions across the Mediterranean: Algeria, Morocco, and Tunisia. This selective regional bias continues in contemporary French scholarship, and North American scholars have tended to follow the French example. However, for reasons discussed in the text, there are strong arguments for considering Morocco, Algeria, and Tunisia as a coherent region for this case study on environmental problems.

2. The term "northern" here may be confusing because the arable coastal plains and plateaus in Morocco are largely along the Atlantic coast in the country's northwest (or west, from the perspective of most Moroccans), while those in Tunisia are in the northeast (east from the perspective of most Tunisians). "Northern" is used in this way to differentiate the *arable* coastal plains in Morocco and Tunisia, in the northern parts of their respective national territories, from the *desert* coastal plains in their more southerly parts where the Sahara extends to the sea.

3. In Algeria, the category "mountain highlands" includes the extensive, high-elevation, intermontane plateaus between the northern Tell Atlas mountain range and the more southerly Saharan Atlas range.

4. See the chapter by Swearingen in this volume. The risk of drought in North Africa appears to be increasing due to land-use changes and possibly global climate change.

5. Family planning programs were begun in Tunisia in 1964 and Morocco in 1967. However, the Algerian government did not initiate family planning until 1983 (Daoud 1991; Escallier 1991).

References

Baduel, P.-R. 1991. "L'écrasant problème du logement urbain, " in C. and Y. Lacoste, eds., *L'Etat du Maghreb*. Pp. 186-189. Tours: La Découverte.

Daoud, Z. 1991. "Démographie et migrations," in C. and Y. Lacoste, eds., *L'Etat du Maghreb*. Pp. 90-91. Tours: La Découverte.

Escallier, R. 1985. "Population et urbanisation," in J.-F. Troin, ed., *Le Maghreb: Hommes et Espaces*. Pp. 119-174. Paris: Armand Colin.

———. 1991. "Démographie et migrations," in C. and Y. Lacoste, eds., *L'Etat du Maghreb*. Pp. 79-97. Tours: La Découverte.

FAO. 1961. *FAO Production Yearbook 1961*. Rome: Food and Agriculture Organization of the United Nations.

———. 1985. *FAO Production Yearbook 1985*. Rome: Food and Agriculture Organization of the United Nations.

———. 1988. *FAO Production Yearbook 1988*. Rome: Food and Agriculture Organization of the United Nations.

Lacoste, Y. 1991. "Peuplements et organisation sociale," in C. and Y. Lacoste, eds., *L'Etat du Maghreb*. Pp. 29-34. Tours: La Découverte.

Maurer, G. 1985. "Mise en valeur et aménagement du milieu naturel," in J.-F. Troin, ed., *Le Maghreb: Hommes et Espaces*. Pp. 13-81. Paris: Armand Colin.

Mutin, G. 1985. "L'industrialisation: un phénomène général aux effets diversifiés," in J.-F. Troin, ed., *Le Maghreb: Hommes et Espaces*. Pp. 219-253. Paris: Armand Colin.

Noin, D. 1970. *La Population Rurale du Maroc*. 2 vols. Paris: PUF.

Yachir, Y. 1991. "Industrie: des choix différentes, des situations contrastées," in C. and Y. Lacoste, eds., *L'Etat du Maghreb*. Pp. 465-469. Tours: La Découverte.

World Bank. 1988. *World Development Report 1988*. New York: Oxford University Press.

———. 1994a. *Social Indicators of Development 1994*. Baltimore: Johns Hopkins University Press.

———. 1994b. *World Development Report 1994*. New York: Oxford University Press.

WRI. 1992. *World Resources 1992-93*. World Resources Institute in collaboration with the United Nations Environment Programme and the United Nations Development Programme. New York: Oxford University Press.

PART ONE

Historical Perspectives on Environmental Deterioration

1

Is Drought Increasing in Northwest Africa? A Historical Analysis

Will D. Swearingen

Northwest Africa is subject to a variety of natural hazards, including drought, earthquakes, floods, and locust invasions.[1] Of these, drought is the most frequent and economically significant. While drought has been a major threat in Northwest Africa throughout recorded history (Bois 1944, 1957), it has seemingly become more frequent since 1980. This has aroused fears that drought is increasing due to global climate change. Unfortunately, such fears are supported by scientific theory. Climate change models suggest that drought will gradually increase in Northwest Africa as a result of global warming.

According to one estimate, precipitation in this region may decrease by up to 10 percent (WRI 1990). Has this process already begun? If so, the implications for future economic viability and food security may be profound. This chapter argues that the drought hazard in Northwest Africa is indeed increasing.

Nevertheless, climate change is not the primary explanation. While such change may now be in progress, it is not the most significant factor. Rather, Northwest Africa's drought hazard has been gradually increasing since at least the 1920s in response to a variety of other factors, mostly socioeconomic or political. These include rapid population growth, the effects of European colonization, changing agricultural practices, changes in technology, and government policies.

To understand how these factors affect drought it is necessary first to define "drought" and understand how this phenomenon is conditioned by the socioeconomic context in which it occurs.

Defining Drought

Drought is difficult to define. Compared to other natural hazards drought is decidedly "fuzzy." Its origins are diverse and complex. It is characterized by slow onset and a diffuse nature, and it can occur virtually anywhere on earth. A major review of drought published during the mid-1980s discovered more than 150 published definitions. The authors concluded that "the search for a universally acceptable definition of drought appears to be a fruitless endeavor" (Wilhite and Glantz 1985: 113). Nonetheless, they found that most definitions fit into one of four categories.

Meteorological definitions are the most common. These usually compare precipitation levels with a long-term average and refer to a specified degree of dryness for a given duration — for example, "less than 50 mm of rain during a three-month period." Because "normal" precipitation levels vary greatly around the world, many meteorological definitions are too site-specific for general use. Nevertheless, some of the best-known meteorological definitions are more universal. For example, the Palmer Drought Severity Index compares differences between a given site's actual precipitation and precipitation shortfalls created by evapotranspiration (ET).

Hydrologic definitions are concerned with the effects of abnormally dry periods on surface or subsurface water supplies. Often they use historical reference marks to assess reductions in streamflow for a specific river or watershed. Some hydrologic definitions incorporate measurements of snowpack into their calculations. Hydrologic definitions are often relied on when the primary concern is water supplies for irrigation or urban-industrial needs.

Agricultural definitions focus on shortages of water for crop needs, particularly in rainfed (non-irrigated) agricultural systems. Commonly, they consider the water needs of crops at various stages of development and compare these to available soil moisture. For example, the Crop Moisture Index, used by the U.S. Department of Agriculture, defines drought in terms of the difference between potential and actual weekly evapotranspiration.

Finally, *socioeconomic definitions* highlight the effects of water shortages on human activity. Such definitions constitute a tiny minority of the corpus of drought definitions. Most definitions of drought focus strictly on drought's physical characteristics. Existing socioeconomic definitions are largely conceptual or highly general rather than operational. They typically view drought simply as an imbalance between the available water supply and a society or user group's water needs. As Wilhite and Glantz note, "few (if any) definitions adequately address the impacts of drought" (1985: 116).

All four categories address the same basic phenomenon — a shortfall of precipitation that results in water shortages. Each represents a different but useful perspective on drought. Nevertheless, there often is little congruence among these varied perspectives.

For example, in a given year Morocco's vast Gharb Plain may be experiencing meteorological drought (that is, unusually low precipitation), but not hydrologic or agricultural drought. This is possible because higher-than-normal precipitation might have occurred the previous year, with the result that both streamflow and soil moisture remain above normal. Conversely, hydrologic drought (that is, low streamflow) can occur without meteorological or agricultural drought, if low precipitation levels in prior years profoundly depleted the water table in the Atlas Mountains, source of the Gharb streams. Finally, agricultural drought can threaten farmers even when precipitation levels indicate that meteorological drought is not occurring. As a case in point, if rainfall during a critical part of the winter or spring growing season occurs only as occasional brief cloudbursts, it will largely be lost to runoff. A poor harvest can result, even though precipitation levels appear adequate to meet crop needs.

These examples demonstrate that drought is a complex, multifaceted phenomenon that is difficult to capture through the lens of a single discipline. Natural scientists — who constitute most of the drought-research community — have tended to neglect drought's societal impacts. And drought has been largely ignored by social scientists. As a result, the societal impacts of drought remain poorly understood. This is unfortunate: the rationale for studying drought is that it adversely affects human activities. Ultimately, drought is not significant unless it has significant socioeconomic impacts. Conversely, as will be shown in the following section, "drought" is conditioned by the socioeconomic context in which it occurs. If this context changes through time, vulnerability to drought changes accordingly. Changes in population, technology, land use, and other factors can either amplify or reduce the drought hazard in a given area — independent of physical processes.

The Environmental and Social Context of Drought

Northwest Africa, astride the Sahara Desert, is naturally vulnerable to drought. This region is on the margins of storm systems arriving from the northern Atlantic. As a result both the timing and total amounts of rainfall are irregular. Flooding from cloudbursts is an occasional hazard. Nevertheless, too little rain is more common. Precipitation levels are generally insufficient for prosperous rainfed agriculture in most of the region. Reduced rainfall is caused, among other factors, by the cold Canary Current off the region's western shores, which induces atmospheric stability and decreases potential for rainfall. High-pressure ridges periodically develop offshore during the autumn-spring rainy season, barring access to moisture-bearing storms. If these high-pressure ridges persist for extended periods, drought results.

Drought occurs frequently in Northwest Africa. Morocco's drought history is representative: since 1912 Morocco has experienced around 27 years of agricultural drought. The average interval between droughts during the past 80 years is only about 3 years. Unfortunately, there is no detectable periodicity. Each of the three principal Northwest African countries (Morocco, Algeria, and Tunisia) experiences roughly the same frequency of drought, although drought in one country commonly is not correlated with drought in the other two. For example, in 1988 Morocco enjoyed the largest cereal harvest in its history to that point, while Tunisia suffered drought-related crop failure — its worst harvest in more than 40 years (FAO).[2]

Drought has major socioeconomic significance in Northwest Africa because rainfed cereal cultivation is predominant. Since pre-Roman times this region has specialized in cereal crops, mainly wheat and barley.[3] During much of this period, and until the 1930s, Northwest Africa was a major exporter of grain to Europe. Today cereal crops still account for approximately 85 percent of the region's total cropland and are produced primarily by rainfed or non-irrigated means. Wheat and barley are the dietary mainstays. Nutritional surveys reveal that cereals account for roughly 60 percent of the daily caloric intake and 65 percent of the protein supply.[4] For the rural populations and urban poor, these percentages are even higher.

Drought in this region sharply reduces both cereal hectarage and yields, causing total production to plummet. This poses an immediate threat to food security. During a typical drought year cereal imports rise dramatically, substantially increasing foreign debt. Food prices also rise, food shortages develop, and malnutrition becomes more prevalent; herds perish or are slaughtered for lack of forage, peasants abandon their land and flock to the cities, and soil erosion and desertification increase. The affected country's economy also suffers a recession. For example, largely because of drought in 1986 Tunisia's Gross Domestic Product registered a *minus* 1 percent growth rate — a substantial decline from the previous year's 4.6 percent rate of growth (EIU 1987).

Good rainfed cereal harvests in Northwest Africa require adequate rainfall during *both* the planting season, normally October-December, and the subsequent growing season, which extends until harvest sometime between April and June in Morocco and even later in eastern regions of Northwest Africa. Poor harvests or crop failure related to drought can result from rainfall shortages during either season. Given the potential for extreme interannual variability in precipitation levels, 400 millimeters (mm) annual average precipitation is normally considered the threshold for viable rainfed cereal production in Northwest Africa (Lery 1982). Nevertheless, the timing of rainfall is just as critical as the total. For example, if northern Tunisia's entire precipitation during October and November falls during a single intense cloudburst, most will disappear as runoff and be unavailable for crop use. Thus, regardless of the total amount of rain, severe drought conditions will probably develop. By contrast, as little as 250 mm of rainfall can produce good harvests, if it occurs at critical moments during the agricultural year (Bowden 1979).

Probably at least a third of the total tonnage of cereals in Northwest Africa is still produced exclusively by traditional means, including animal traction and the lightweight swing or scratch plow. This traditional technology is more environmentally sensitive than modern agricultural machinery and helps prevent soil erosion. Nevertheless, it has two critical and interrelated shortcomings.

First, plowing with the traditional plow is a very slow process. In all, a farmer and his draft animal must trudge approximately 60 kilometers (km) to put a single hectare (ha) into production (Cleaver 1982). Commonly, fields must be traversed twice: once to break up the soil and a second time to plow under the broadcast seed. *Second*, peasants cannot normally begin plowing until approximately 150 mm of rain have fallen, softening the earth. This is because during the dry summer season the ground becomes baked too hard for the light scratch plow to penetrate.

Having to wait for rain presents major problems. The window of opportunity for planting is relatively limited, given the short growing season before the arrival of hot, arid summer conditions. Planting must generally be finished by the end of December or early January. Thus, if the autumn rainy season is delayed or short-lived, the amount of cropland that can be put into production is reduced.

The resulting contraction in hectarage can be quite substantial. For example, during the 1980s annual hectarage figures for cereal cultivation fluctuated by well over a million ha in each country.[5] To place this in context, the fluctuation was the size of roughly a fourth of Morocco's average annual cereal hectarage during this decade, and more than half of Algeria's. In Tunisia the fluctuation was even more extreme: it actually *exceeded* the average figure by some 6 percent. These enormous fluctuations obviously have a direct correlation with fluctuations in precipitation. Nevertheless, they are at least partly due to the technological limitations of the traditional plow *vis-à-vis* Northwest Africa's physical environment.[6]

Given the limitations of the traditional plow, the timing of rainfall is critical. Low production levels associated with drought can result not only from diminished crop yields, but also from a reduction in the number of hectares planted during the October-December period. Indeed, even when rainfall during the rest of the year is satisfactory, poor harvests can result if the autumn rains are late or poor. For example, Tunisia's disastrous drought-ravaged harvest in 1988 was due substantially to lack of rainfall during the autumn planting season, which radically reduced the number of hectares planted.[7]

Having to wait for rain before plowing *not only* reduces crop hectarage: it also significantly lowers crop *yields*. The reason is that with use of the traditional system a large percentage of total precipitation has already evaporated before the seeds even get in the ground. The magnitude of this factor is suggested by field tests in Morocco. These tests have demonstrated that planting (with tractor and steel plow) *before* the arrival of the rainy season can improve crop yields by roughly 30 percent — without any other changes in production methods (Cleaver 1982).

Northwest African peasants and government agronomists are well aware of the constraints of traditional technology. All three Northwest African governments have used financial incentives to promote agricultural mechanization, particularly since the late 1970s. As a result, the tractor and modern plow have substantially replaced animal traction and the traditional plow. More prosperous landowners, benefiting from government subsidies, have almost universally mechanized their operations. Often they gain extra profit from plowing the fields of neighbors who cannot afford to mechanize. In addition, plowing services are widely provided by an emergent group of rural entrepreneurs who have purchased farm machinery for this purpose. Smaller or poorer landowners who cannot afford to purchase tractors and modern plows usually find it cheaper to hire plowing service than hand labor. This, too, has contributed to the expansion of mechanization.

Nevertheless, a sizable percentage of the landowners in each country can afford neither agricultural machinery nor plowing services. Furthermore, many landholdings in Northwest Africa are too small, fragmented, or remote for plowing services to be feasible.[8] Or, they are located on slopes too steep for mechanized operations. Thus, animal traction and the traditional plow will continue to be extensively used. This will help prevent soil erosion, but it will also help preserve the region's vulnerability to drought.

In short, Northwest African governments have promoted mechanization as a way to drought-proof their rainfed cereal production sectors. Expansion of mechanization has helped overcome the problem of reduced cereal cultivation from sparse or late rains during the planting season. In this way, the drought hazard has been mitigated. Unfortunately, mechanization has initiated a reverse trend that is substantially increasing the drought hazard in Northwest Africa. As the next section discusses, it is the latest in a series of historical trends that, overall, have progressively increased the region's vulnerability to drought.

Increasing Vulnerability to Drought

Since the earliest historical times, drought has been a major hazard in Northwest Africa. An exhaustive historical survey of drought and other natural calamities in Morocco, for example, revealed that there were 49 major drought-related famines during the period from the late ninth century A.D. to the early 1900s (Bois 1957). In Tunisia, from 100 A.D. to the late nineteenth century there were at least 26 such drought-related famines (Bois 1944). While the drought hazard has probably existed in Northwest Africa since the advent of cultivation, during this century it has shown an increase.

Colonization in Northwest Africa initiated a series of processes that have steadily deepened the region's vulnerability to drought. Algeria became a French colony in 1830, Tunisia a French protectorate in 1881, and Morocco a French and Spanish protectorate in 1912.[9] The colonial period lasted until 1956 in Tunisia and Morocco, and 1962 in Algeria. In all three countries colonization introduced major changes. The net effect of these changes — and the subsidiary changes that they spawned — was a gradual increase in the drought hazard. Unfortunately, since independence this hazard has continued to increase.

Prior to the colonial period, agriculture in most of Northwest Africa consisted of an extensive system of dryland cereal cultivation and animal husbandry. Most land was owned communally. Landholdings were usually dispersed to provide for equity and help counter the risk of crop failure. Each peasant commonly farmed 5-10 dispersed plots. Surplus grain from bountiful harvests was stockpiled to cover crop failures during drought years.[10] Fallowing (periodically letting cropland lie idle instead of cultivating it) was widely practiced. Fallowing replenished soil moisture and helped restore soil fertility. Low population pressure gave a relatively underutilized appearance to the arable expanses of primary interest to the French colonists.

French colonial planners viewed Northwest Africa as a major exception within France's colonial realm. With its proximity to Europe, and the Mediterranean climate of its coastal plains and plateaus, this region was perceived as fit for large-scale French colonization. In all three countries colonization dislodged peasants from much of the best land. Europeans acquired roughly 30 percent of Algeria's arable land, or 2.7 million ha; nearly 20 percent of Tunisia's land, or 800,000 ha; and 13 percent of Morocco's land, or 1 million ha.

Exacerbating the effect of European colonization was land concentration by native large landowners. During the colonial period, indigenous landowners allied with the French were able to amass sizable landholdings in all three countries. In Algeria, some 25,000 native Algerians acquired a total of nearly 2.8 million ha, slightly more than 30 percent of the country's arable land (Pfeifer 1985). In Morocco, 7,500 Moroccan landowners acquired 1.6 million ha, or 21 percent of the arable total (Swearingen 1987a, 1987b). And in Tunisia, 7,200 Tunisians acquired 630,000 ha — 15 percent (Sethom 1985).

Land concentration during the colonial period had two important consequences: *First*, as land was expropriated, most peasants became concentrated on a diminished amount of land. Much usurpation was conducted by private European land speculators and settlers as well as by indigenous landowners. However, French colonial authorities exercised an official policy of *cantonnement* to create landholdings for state-sponsored colonization. They calculated how much of a given tribe's territory was needed to support the tribe, then "cantoned" tribal members on that land and appropriated the rest for colonization. Their calculations rarely allowed for the growth of the tribal group.

One major effect of land expropriation was that it reduced the ability of peasants to allow part of their land to lie fallow. With reduced landholdings, many peasants had to cultivate all of their land to produce sufficient food for their household needs. Reduction of fallow significantly increased the potential for drought. The primary purpose of fallowing in semi-arid regions such as Northwest Africa is to allow soil moisture to accumulate (WMO 1975). Approximately 20-25 percent of the precipitation falling during the fallow period (roughly 18 months between harvest and planting) is retained in the soil. Thus, fallowing substantially boosts the available water supply for subsequent crop use. In low-rainfall areas, this soil moisture component is often the critical difference between a successful harvest and drought. With the reduction of fallowing, this buffer was lost, and vulnerability to drought increased. In addition, excessive land-use pressure caused soil fertility to decline. Declining yields, combined with reduced hectarage, made it increasingly difficult for peasants to stockpile grain as a hedge against drought.

Second, large masses of peasants were dislodged to marginal land that was not sufficiently attractive for colonization. The marginal areas were commonly characterized by poor soils, unfavorable slope, and/or deficient rainfall. Previously, most of this land had been used only for livestock grazing. Because of its low-rainfall levels, it was more vulnerable to drought. Unfortunately, once cleared and plowed, it also became prone to erosion and desertification.

While land concentration was taking place during the colonial period, other significant changes were occurring. Health measures introduced by the French caused native death rates to plunge. Northwest Africa's population expanded dramatically, with probably a sixfold increase during colonial times. This population explosion — combined with expropriation of between a third and a half of the arable land by Europeans and indigenous large landowners—intensified pressure on remaining agricultural resources. Fallow was further reduced, peasant landholdings became increasingly fragmented, soil fertility continued to decline, and an increasing amount of marginal land was cleared and cultivated.

Already by the 1930s squatter settlements or *bidonvilles* were developing around the major Northwest African cities, inhabited by peasants who could no longer be sustained on their land (Montagne 1952). The rural exodus became a human flood during drought years, when crop failures forced many peasants to sell or abandon their land. During the catastrophic drought-related famine of 1945, for example, there was a wholesale reduction of small landholdings. The prevailing price for a hectare during this period was a mere 50 kilograms (kg) of grain (Istiqlal 1954). This was equal to only about a fifteenth of the average crop yield/hectare during a normal year.

Colonial agricultural policy, *per se*, also played a major role in deepening Northwest Africa's vulnerability to drought. Between 1915 and 1928, colonial authorities in all three countries had a mandate from the *métropole* to increase cereal production for France. The architects of this mandate were convinced that France's "Afrique du Nord" had been a bountiful breadbasket for Rome during classical times, and that France could restore this land to its former productivity (Swearingen 1985, 1987a). Various subsidies and bonuses were offered to encourage cereal cultivation, especially cultivation by mechanized means. High market prices were also offered, particularly for wheat. Agricultural mechanization and high crop prices enabled marginal areas to be profitably cultivated during higher-than-normal rainfall periods. Although Europeans and native large landowners were the primary beneficiaries of the subsidies and bonuses, lucrative crop prices also enticed peasant farmers into the cash economy and encouraged them to expand cereal production significantly.

The colonial cereal policy produced the desired results. In Morocco, for example, the area planted in cereals grew from 1.9 million ha in 1918 to nearly 3 million ha in 1929 (Hoffherr 1932). This was an increase of roughly 60 percent. Cereal production in neighboring Algeria and Tunisia also expanded dramatically. However, there were hidden adverse effects. Part of the new cereal hectarage came from the reduction of fallow, increasing the potential for drought. Much of the remainder came from the extension of cultivation to marginal low-rainfall areas. The proportion of cropland in drought-prone areas steadily increased.

Contributing to Northwest Africa's vulnerability to drought was the fact that the colonial policy favored wheat production over barley. Previously, barley had been the predominant cereal crop. However, wheat now became predominant, and consumer tastes changed to prefer this cereal. With the varieties at the time, the critical rainfall limits for barley were some 30 percent less than those for wheat.[11] In addition, barley ripens and can be harvested significantly earlier than wheat; therefore, it is less vulnerable to the untimely onset of hot, arid summer conditions (Dresch 1956). In short, by substituting wheat for barley, the colonial cereal policy increased the potential for drought.

Agricultural Policies Since Independence: The Food Security Crisis

Since independence each of the Northwest African countries has pursued a different development strategy. Algeria, emerging from a traumatic colonial experience and devastating war of liberation, has attempted to achieve economic independence through a comprehensive program of industrialization and hydrocarbon development. Morocco, by contrast, has developed its tourist sector and has also emphasized export agriculture, investing heavily in irrigated production of citrus fruits and market vegetables. Tunisia has adopted perhaps the most balanced development strategy: it has invested in both export agriculture and tourism, and has also encouraged export-led industrialization by multinational firms.

All three countries recovered ownership of colonial landholdings and have engaged in limited land reform. However, much of the former colonial land passed into the hands of more prosperous native landowners. Furthermore, most of the large landholdings acquired by native landowners during the colonial period were never subject to land reform.

For at least two decades following independence, the Northwest African countries seriously neglected domestic food production. By the 1980s all three countries were experiencing a severe food security crisis. The key symptoms of this crisis were declining *per capita* cereal production; alarming, ever-growing levels of cereal imports; heavy foreign indebtedness related to these imports[12]; and massive food subsidy programs.

By the early 1980s Algeria was importing approximately two-thirds of its cereal supply, Tunisia was importing nearly half, and Morocco was importing more than a third (FAO). In each country a large percentage of the population was experiencing hunger and malnutrition.[13] The political implications of this crisis became clear by 1981, when Morocco experienced a bloody food-related riot. Similar food-related riots erupted in Tunisia in 1983-1984, again in Morocco in 1984, and in Algeria in 1988.

Since the early-to-mid 1980s all three countries have been undertaking major agricultural reforms (Swearingen 1990, 1992a). The overriding objective is to increase dryland cereal production. Reforms include privatization of the state agricultural sectors to improve efficiency, and promotion of modern seed varieties and fertilizers. Of the reforms that have helped increase drought, however, the most significant involve changes in crop prices; promotion of agricultural mechanization; and a "new lands" scheme in Algeria.

Since independence, Northwest African governments have maintained tight control over producer prices of basic food crops. Prices for these crops, cereals in particular, were held artificially low until the 1980s. Indeed, for much of this period, crop prices were as low as a fourth to a half of what they would have been without government intervention (Cleaver 1982). The rationale was that low crop prices would enable these governments to provide cheap food to their urban populations, helping keep wages low, thereby assisting industrialization and other urban development initiatives. An ulterior motive behind the cheap food strategy was to help prevent social unrest among the growing ranks of the urban poor. Unfortunately, low crop prices acted as a major disincentive to farmers, creating a vicious spiral of declining production.

Beginning in the late 1970s, fixed producer prices for cereals and other basic food crops were gradually raised. In Algeria and Tunisia, these prices approached world market levels by the mid-1980s. These price increases may have been a significant factor behind increased cereal production in the two countries. Assisted by generally favorable weather, average annual cereal cultivation in Algeria during the 1988-1992 period was 22 percent higher than that during the 1980-1984 period (FAO). In Tunisia, there was a 27 percent increase in average annual production during these same two periods (FAO). Unfortunately, these increases were entirely offset by population increases. As a result, there was little or no net gain.

In Morocco, changes in pricing policy were far more dramatic. Here, the government boosted producer prices of barley and wheat to approximately *twice* world market levels. The stimulus effect was remarkable. Assisted by good weather, Moroccan production of cereals grew from an annual average of 3.8 million tons during the 1980-1984 period to 6.6 million tons during both the 1985-1990 and 1988-1992 periods. In part this growth has come from improved yields. However, it has also resulted in an expansion of cereal hectarage. Average annual cereal hectarage during the 1980-1984 period was slightly more than 4.4 million ha. However, by the 1988-1992 period, it had expanded to 5.4 million ha — an increase of nearly one-fourth (FAO).

This increase has resulted both from the reduction of fallow and the extension of cereal cultivation to marginal rangeland. By the early 1940s cereal cultivation had reached the 4.4 million ha figure that still prevailed during the 1980s. In short, virtually all viable cropland was already in production 50 years ago.

However, encouraged by extremely high crop prices beginning in the mid-1980s, Moroccan farmers have dramatically reduced the hectarage left in fallow. Because continuously cropped areas are not allowed to accumulate soil moisture — as they do when fallowed — the reduction of fallowing has effectively deducted an input of water from the cropping system and substantially increased the vulnerability to drought. Besides reducing fallow since the 1980s, Moroccan farmers have substantially expanded the area of cereal crops in marginal, low-rainfall regions. These marginal new lands are not only prone to desertification and wind erosion; they are also highly vulnerable to drought.

Government efforts to promote mechanization have facilitated the expansion of cereal cultivation to drought-prone rangeland. The tractor and disc plow have converted large stretches of rangeland to cereal hectarage in all three countries. In southern Tunisia, for example, roads created by oil exploration crews have enabled mechanized farmers to penetrate regions that previously were accessible only to pastoral nomads. Similar penetration of previously remote grazing lands has also occurred in the other two countries. Some of these new lands normally receive as little as 200 mm of annual rainfall (Dresch 1986). Their poor soils can sustain cultivation for a few years, so long as higher-than-normal rainfall prevails. However, the return of normal low rainfall levels ultimately forces their abandonment. Desertification quickly advances in the abandoned areas. Farmers are destroying the grazing potential of these lands through clearing the natural vegetation, unsustainably "mining" their fragile soils, and leaving them exposed to wind and water erosion.

In Algeria, cultivation of marginal lands has actually become official policy. In 1983, Algeria's government passed legislation that established an ambitious homesteading program. The purpose of this program is to encourage Algerian citizens "to maximize the agricultural potential of the country" through development of public domain land that has not previously been cultivated (*Grand Maghreb* 1985).

Prospective homesteaders have been required to pay the nominal sum of 1 dinar (approximately $0.12 in 1990). In exchange they are given an allotment of land within one of the numerous perimeters established by provincial authorities. The only stipulation is that they fully develop this land for agricultural purposes within a five-year period. At the end of five years they are granted unrestricted title and are free to sell or use their land as they choose.

The government views the homesteading program as a way to expand the agricultural resource base, increase the food supply, combat peasant exodus to the cities, and counterbalance excessive urban development along the country's northern coast. The goal is to put approximately 800,000 ha of new land into production (*Marchés Tropicaux* 1987; *Révolution Africaine* 1988). About half of this land will be in the Saharan zone where subsurface water is available for irrigation. However, the other half, some

400,000 ha, involves dryland allotments in the country's high plateau region. Virtually all new "cropland" in this region is low-rainfall steppeland suitable only for stockraising. The homesteading program, then, is significantly increasing the proportion of Algeria's cropland in drought-prone areas.

Unfortunately, the results of this homesteading program have not been encouraging. Large areas claimed under the homesteading program have already been abandoned. Stripped of their natural vegetation, these areas have since been attacked by wind and water erosion and are becoming barren wastelands.

The homesteading program is, however, only part of Algeria's current "new lands" scheme. In 1984, the Algerian government initiated a comprehensive agricultural plan that includes the goal of putting 2 *million* ha of new land into production. Two-fifths of this new land is to come from the homesteading program. The other three-fifths, or 1.2 million ha, is expected to come from reduction of fallow. This major reduction of fallow, for reasons previously discussed, is substantially increasing the risk of drought in Algeria.

Conclusions

Drought is an endemic natural hazard in Northwest Africa. Even with proper land-use management, this region would be vulnerable to drought. Nevertheless, as this chapter has shown, the region's drought hazard has actually been increasing due to a series of processes initiated during the colonial period.

To summarize, the drought hazard has been increasing primarily in response to the following two processes: First, expansion of cereal cultivation to drought-prone rangeland; and second, reduction of fallow. During the colonial period, these processes were fostered by large-scale land expropriation; by the dislodging of peasants to marginal lands; by a cereal policy offering high crop prices and other incentives; by agricultural mechanization, which facilitated the mining of marginal areas during periods of higher-than-normal rainfall; and by population pressure associated with rapid population growth. Other significant factors during this period include the gradual loss of peasant ability to stockpile grain as insurance against drought, and the progressive substitution of wheat for drought-resistant barley.

Since independence, populations in Northwest Africa have continued to increase at rapid rates. High population growth rates, along with neglect of cereal production, have precipitated a food security crisis. To counter this crisis, all three countries are taking steps to boost cereal production.

Unfortunately, the policies adopted are further promoting cultivation of drought-prone rangeland and reduction of fallow. In Morocco, crop prices established at *twice* world market levels have particularly encouraged these processes. In Algeria, such processes are actually goals of official policy. Within Northwest Africa as a whole, a precariously high level of cereal hectarage is now perennially vulnerable to drought. In Morocco, for example, at least 50 percent of the cereal cultivation is now located in "low rainfall" areas.[14]

All three Northwest African countries are striving for self-sufficiency in cereal production. Unfortunately, lack of viable new cropland, population growth, and periodic drought will help make this goal an elusive dream. During 1980-1993 the three Northwest African countries each experienced 6-7 years of drought.[15] This frequency of drought is strong evidence of a significant increase in the drought hazard in the region.

Although global warming processes may now be a factor, the drought hazard has *not* been increasing primarily as a result of declining precipitation. Rather, this heightened hazard is due primarily to changes in society. Northwest Africa's climate has remained essentially the same during the past century. However, population levels and land-use patterns have changed radically. Farmers have progressively intensified their land use, both "vertically" (through reduction of fallow) and "horizontally" (through extension to low-rainfall areas). These changes have provided short-term gains in agricultural production. Unfortunately, they have also gradually eroded away traditional buffers protecting society from drought and represent long-term threats to the North African environment.

Notes

1. Research for this chapter was supported by grants from the National Science Foundation's Human Dimensions of Global Change Initiative and the Program in Science and Technology Cooperation (PSTC) of the Office of Research, U.S. Agency for International Development. Much of this chapter is adapted, with the publisher's permission, from my chapter, "Northwest Africa," in M. H. Glantz, ed., *Drought Follows the Plow,* Cambridge University Press, 1994, pp. 117-133.

2. Morocco's total cereal production in 1988 was nearly 8 million metric tons, well over twice its average (3.8 million tons) during 1980-1984. By contrast, Tunisia's cereal production in 1988 was only 324,000 metric tons, slightly more than a fourth of its 1980-1984 average of almost 1.2 million tons.

3. Maize, oats, sorghum, millet, rye, and rice are also cultivated.

4. Sugar and vegetable oil account for roughly 50 percent of the remaining (noncereal) caloric intake (CREA 1985).

5. In Algeria, 3.2 million ha of cereals were harvested in 1980, versus 1.6 million in 1990. In Morocco, the fluctuation was between 6.3 million ha in 1990 and 4.3

million in 1982; in Tunisia, between 1.9 million ha in 1985 and 0.5 million ha in 1988 (FAO).

6. Other explanations for these fluctuations include the following: First, farmers with access to mechanized plowing simply decided not to plant because of reduced rainfall and the likelihood of a poor harvest; and second, in certain areas, drought caused such a poor crop that these areas were not harvested and consequently were not included in government agricultural surveys as part of the cultivated hectarage.

7. In 1988 only 513,000 ha of cereals were harvested, versus a 1980-1988 annual average of 1,340,000 ha (FAO).

8. Probably somewhere between 80 and 90 percent of landholdings in the region are smaller than 10 ha. Unfortunately, up-to-date statistics on holding sizes in Northwest Africa are virtually nonexistent. A conservative guess regarding land-holding sizes in the early 1990s is that more than 95 percent of the agricultural families in Morocco each own fewer than 10 ha of land. In Algeria, the comparable figure would be 85 percent, and in Tunisia it would be 75 percent. Ten hectares is generally too small a holding to support a peasant family unless the landholding is irrigated, and most are not.

9. Spain acquired the mountainous northern Rif region of Morocco flanking the Mediterranean, as well as the Saharan region in the far south along the Atlantic (now the disputed Western Sahara). However, because Spanish-colonial policies had relatively little impact on agriculture in these regions, this chapter focuses on French-held Morocco during the colonial period.

10. Stockpiling of grain occurred extensively at the local level and was carried out by various collectives and even by individual peasant families (Montagne 1930). Some stockpiling also occurred at the national level during pre-colonial times. For example, many of the Alawi sultans in Morocco maintained large granaries as a hedge against drought and famine (Meyers 1981).

11. The critical rainfall limits for barley were some 230-300 mm, versus 360-400 mm for wheat. This difference still largely exists; barley generally remains much more drought-resistant. Today this crop occupies 40-45 percent of the cereal hectarage in Algeria and Morocco and around 35 percent in Tunisia, yet usually accounts for a significantly smaller percentage of the total production (indicating that it is usually grown in more marginal areas.) Well over half of the region's barley supply is now used as feed grain for livestock. Unfortunately, barley has come to be regarded as an inferior food grain by many Northwest Africans.

12. *Per capita* cereal production — cereal production per person — decreased by 46 percent in Algeria between the 1958-1962 and 1980-1984 periods; in Morocco it decreased by 33 percent and in Tunisia by 4 percent (FAO). In Algeria, the average *annual* agricultural import burden by the early 1980s was approximately $2.2 billion. In Morocco it was $900 million; in Tunisia, $500 million. See Economist Intelligence Unit, *Country Report*, various editions (different editions for each country).

13. In the late 1970s, according to World Bank estimates, approximately 38 percent of Morocco's population was living in "absolute poverty," meaning that it was likely to be experiencing health-threatening hunger and malnutrition. For Algeria and Tunisia, during this same period the comparable estimate was 17 percent in each country (World Bank 1989).

14. The Moroccan government classifies cereal areas receiving less than 400 mm per year as "low rainfall" areas. In the government's survey of agricultural areas during the 1983-1984 season, it found that 51.1 percent of the country's cereal crops were being grown in low-rainfall areas, broken down as follows: durum or hard wheat, 35.3 percent; bread or soft wheat, 35 percent; barley, 63 percent; and maize (corn), 62.9 percent (AID 1986).

15. The total number of drought years each country experienced is open to interpretation for two major reasons. First, it depends on the critical threshold established for recognition of "drought." Second, in a given year certain regions of a country can suffer from drought while other regions have more or less normal rainfall. Thus, declarations of drought are somewhat arbitrary.

References

AID. 1986. *Morocco: Country Development Strategy Statement (FYs 1987-1991). Annex C: The Agricultural Sector in Morocco: A Description.* Unpublished report, February. Washington, D.C.: United States Agency for International Development.

Bois, C. 1944. "Années de disette, années d'abondance: sécheresses et pluies en Tunisie de 648 à 1881." *Revue Pour l'Etude des Calamités* 21:3-26.

———. 1957. "Années de disette, années d'abondance: sécheresses et pluies au Maroc." *Revue Pour l'Etude des Calamités* 26-35:33-71.

Bowden, L. 1979. "Development of Present Dryland Farming Systems," in A. E. Hall, G. H. Cannell, and H. W. Lawton, eds., *Agriculture in Semi-arid Environments.* Berlin: Springer-Verlag.

Cleaver, K. 1982. *The Agricultural Development Experience of Algeria, Morocco and Tunisia: A Comparison of Strategies for Growth.* Staff working paper 552. Washington, D.C.: World Bank.

CREA. 1985. *Les Modèles de Consommation et les Politiques Alimentaires dans les Pays du Maghreb.* Proceedings of a conference at the Centre de Recherche en Economie Appliquée, Algiers, Algeria, 17-19 December 1984. Algiers: Centre de Recherche en Economie Appliquée.

Dresch, J. 1956. *L'Agriculture en Afrique du Nord.* Paris: Centre de Documentation Universitaire.

———. 1986. "Remarques sur l'homme et la dégradation des écosystèmes naturels au Maghreb." *La Pensée* 252:89-95.

EIU. 1987. *Country Report: Tunisia and Malta.* London: Economist Intelligence Unit.

FAO. Various years. *Production Yearbook.* Rome: Food and Agriculture Organization.

———. 1987. *World Crop and Livestock Statistics, 1948-1985.* Rome: Food and Agriculture Organization.

———. 1991. *FAO Quarterly Bulletin of Statistics* 4.

Grand Maghreb. 1985. "Loi foncière d'août 1983: la vraie révolution agraire?" *Grand Maghreb* 38:112-113.

Hoffherr, R. 1932. *L'Economie Marocaine*. Paris: Recueil Sirey.

Istiqlal. 1954. *Morocco under the Protectorate: Forty Years of French Administration*. New York: Istiqlal Party.

Lery, F. 1982. *L'Agriculture au Maghreb*. Paris: G.-P. Maisonneuve et Larose.

Marchés Tropicaux. 1987. 43:1434-1437.

Meyers, A. 1981. "Famine Relief and Imperial Policy in Early Modern Morocco: The Political Functions of Public Health." *American Journal of Public Health* 71:1266-1273.

Montagne, R. 1930. *Villages et Kasbahs Berbères*. Paris: Alcan.

———. 1952. "Naissance et développement du prolétariat marocain," in C. Célier, ed., *Industrialisation de l'Afrique du Nord*. Pp. 199-222. Paris: CNRS.

Morocco. 1960. *Annuaire Statistique du Maroc*. Rabat: Service Central des Statistiques.

———. 1988. *Consommation et Dépenses des Ménages 1984-85. Premiers Résultats. Vol. 1, Rapport de Synthèse*. Rabat: Direction de la Statistique.

———. 1989. *Annuaire Statistique du Maroc*. Rabat: Direction de la Statistique.

Pfeifer, K. 1985. *Agrarian Reform under State Capitalism in Algeria*. Boulder, Colo.: Westview Press.

Révolution Africaine. 1988. 1244: 15-19.

Sahli, Z., and A. Abdenour. 1988. "Tendances de la consommation alimentaire." *Révolution Africaine* 5 August:43-48.

Sethom, H. 1985. "L'action des pouvoirs publics sur les paysages agraires et l'économie rurale dans la Tunisie indépendante," in P. R. Baduel et al., eds., *Etats, Territoires et Terroirs au Maghreb*. Paris: Centre National de la Recherche Scientifique.

Swearingen, W. 1985. "In Pursuit of the Granary of Rome: France's Wheat Policy in Morocco, 1915-1931." *International Journal of Middle East Studies* 17:347-363.

———. 1987a. *Moroccan Mirages: Agrarian Dreams and Deceptions, 1912-1986*. Princeton: Princeton University Press.

———. 1987b. "Morocco's Agricultural Crisis," in I. W. Zartman, ed., *The Political Economy of Morocco*. Pp. 159-172. New York: Praeger.

———. 1990. "Algeria's Food Security Crisis." *Middle East Report* 20(5): 21-25.

———. 1992a. "Government Agricultural Policies and the Growing Food Security Crisis," in J. P. Entelis and P. Naylor, eds., *Algeria: State and Society in Transition*. Pp. 117-149. Boulder, Colo.: Westview Press.

———. 1992b. "Drought Hazard in Morocco." *Geographical Review* 82:401-412.

———. 1994. "Northwest Africa," in M. H. Glantz, ed., *Drought Follows the Plow*. Pp. 117-133. Cambridge, England: Cambridge University Press.

Tunisia. 1981. *Enquête sur le Budget et la Consommation des Ménages 1980, Volume 3, Partie Alimentaire et Nutritionnelle*. Tunis: Institut National de la Statistique.

———. 1986. *Enquête sur le Budget et la Consommation des Ménages, 1985. Volume A, Présentation des Résultats de l'Enquête Budgetaire*. Tunis: Institut National de la Statistique.

Wilhite, D., and M. Glantz. 1985. "Understanding the Drought Phenomenon: The Role of Definitions." *Water International* 10:111-120.

WMO. 1975. *Drought and Agriculture*. Technical Note No. 138. Geneva: World Meteorological Organization.

World Bank. 1989. *Social Indicators of Development 1989*. Baltimore: Johns Hopkins University Press.

WRI. 1990. *World Resources 1990-1991*. New York: Oxford University Press for the World Resources Institute, the United Nations Environment Programme, and the United Nations Development Programme.

2

Development Trends and Environmental Deterioration in the Agropastoral Systems of the Central Middle Atlas, Morocco

Douglas L. Johnson

Livestock rearing has been a traditional means for rural Moroccans to derive a living from a habitat that is influenced, even in its most productive zones, by seasonal dryness and episodic, interannual drought. The Middle Atlas Mountains in central Morocco south of Fes and Meknes (Figure 2.1) provide a particularly appropriate environment in which to see how traditional pastoralists have used seasonally dry montane habitats in the past and how they are coping with contemporary pressures for change. Pressures and changes in the area are very intense, rapid, and spatially concentrated.

Pastoral systems in the central Middle Atlas concentrate on raising sheep. Sheepherders in this region were formerly nomadic, moving their herds between lowland winter and highland summer pastures to take advantage of altitudinal distribution of seasonally available grass and water. Although animal herding was always combined with cultivation, tilling the land was generally subordinated to livestock rearing. Beginning with the establishment of the French Protectorate, Moroccan herders were forced to alter traditional livelihood practices.[1] Subsequent population growth within the pastoral community — and in Morocco at large — created pressure for herd expansion. As Moroccans began to migrate from rural areas to cities, they created larger markets for meat and dairy products. Animal herders responded to these pressures and opportunities in a variety of ways.[2]

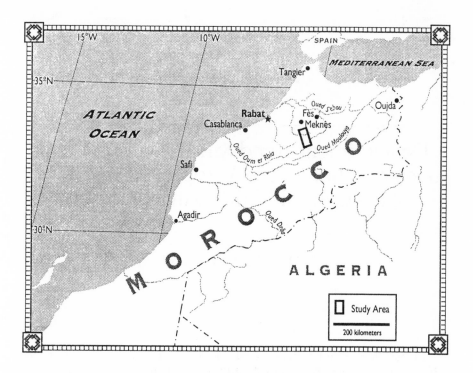

FIGURE 2.1 Morocco and the Study Area

Today Morocco's montane sheepherders are being transformed into managers of stall-fed animal fattening units. Both government-sponsored development projects and spontaneous private development efforts are part of this transformation process. The changes taking place have grave implications for the sustainability of the new institutions that are emerging, as overgrazing is widespread and forest regeneration is threatened by grazing pressure in many areas. Efforts have been made to counter land degradation by restricting access to forest grazing zones or by reforestation in areas that historically have been exclusively devoted to grazing. Such efforts, however, have had counterintuitive results; any subtraction of land resources from pastoralism results in intensified grazing of the remaining rangeland, with increased risk of overgrazing and land degradation. Despite the many changes that have taken place, considerable common-property grazing resources remain, and these areas continue to be managed by traditional tribal institutions in consultation with government range experts. At issue is the sustainability of both the remaining traditional institutions and the new intensive resource management systems that are emerging.

This chapter delineates the major changes affecting traditional pastoralists in the central Middle Atlas Mountains. It first considers some of the difficulties of identifying environmental changes and of determining whether such changes are good or bad. Then it describes the traditional pastoral regime of the area and its environmental setting. The intention is to provide a baseline against which contemporary changes can be understood. The bulk of the chapter explores the manifold pressures on the pastoral sector and seeks to identify responses adopted by herders to pressures for change. Particular attention is paid to the role that local common-property resource management systems continue to play in the region and the impact that intensification within the pastoral sector has on the physical environment. Throughout an effort is made to distinguish between pressures that lead to creative, sustainable responses on the one hand and destructive, degrading developments on the other.

Understanding Environmental Change

The identification of the status and trend of environmental conditions is never an easy process. Few objective measures exist upon which scholars agree, and assessments of environments are always conditioned by subjective experience.[3] Basic values inform one's judgment of whether converting forest into farmland, developing pasture at the expense of wildlife habitat, or replacing pastures with farmland and forests will result in desirable environmental change. Moreover, few of the environmental changes that occur represent an alteration from pristine conditions. Rather, environmental change takes place in habitats that have already undergone substantial modification. Often those changes occurred or were initiated centuries or even millennia in the past. In most cases contemporary resource-use systems have adjusted to the altered conditions so completely that few traces remain of the previous resource-use systems. Many changes that occur in environmental status and condition may be a result of natural processes over which people have little if any control, or they may be the product of combined societal and natural processes. Cause and effect are often difficult to link and change may occur more rapidly than it can effectively be addressed.

The assessment of environmental conditions is made even more difficult because of disagreement as to whether environments are fragile entities that are readily destabilized or robust structures that resist change. Thus, while our knowledge of ecological systems is improving, in most instances we have too little knowledge of the specifics of local ecotypes to be able to predict with reasonable certainty when the stability and resilience boundaries of those systems are in danger of being exceeded. In short, identifying environments that are at risk under the pressure of human use is a difficult task fraught with uncertainty.

Much of this uncertainty stems from the fact that not all change that occurs constitutes degradation. Many changes reflect a process of creative destruction in which biological productivity may be lowered and an ecotype altered or replaced by a human-manipulated system that is sustainable for a reasonable, foreseeable future. Changes of this type are acceptable from a human perspective, if the entity that results is capable of remaining viable for several generations. From this perspective, it is difficult to regard as degradation changes in the environment that provide life support for increased human populations, so long as those altered environmental states can themselves be maintained. Maintenance in this context does not mean a stable, unchanging balance but rather a pace of change that can be dealt with as the modified system undergoes further alteration.

Much less desirable are acts of destructive creation in which sustainability is not attained. This occurs when the effort to support human populations produces a mining of primary productivity, replaces an existing ecotype with an unstable system, and creates adverse environmental changes that cannot be restored by reasonable efforts at acceptable costs in a manageable time frame (approximately 50 years). Nature will restore all damaged environments eventually, but the geological time scale required for natural restorative processes without the assistance of human intervention makes reliance on natural processes alone unreasonable. Few environments in the central Middle Atlas Mountains of Morocco provide evidence for destructive creation. Almost all environments and land use systems in the region exhibit signs of extremely heavy use. But evidence for catastrophic failure, despite some signs of impending crisis, is rare. One of the more pressured habitats is the pastoral sector in the region — the formerly nomadic, now almost completely sedentarized, pastoral communities of the central Middle Atlas in the vicinity of Azrou, particularly the Ait Arfa tribal sections of the Tigrigra, Guigou, and Moulouya river valleys (Figure 2.2).

The Middle Atlas Environment and Traditional Pastoralism

The Middle Atlas Mountains are a southwest-to-northeast trending massif whose location along the southern fringes of the westerlies produces an abundance of moisture in the winter and spring. Largely calcareous, these mountains have also experienced episodes of volcanic eruption and intrusion (Beaudet 1969a). The combination of karstic erosion and volcanic eruption has created a complex topographic surface and a mixture of largely stony soil types. Precipitation follows the typical Mediterranean

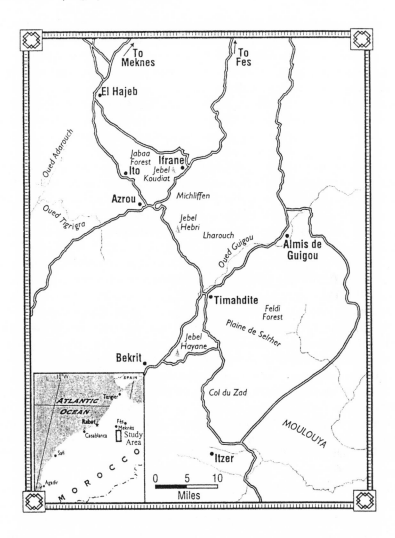

FIGURE 2.2 The Study Area (Central Morocco)

rhythm of winter-spring rain and summer-fall drought and increases with elevation.

Even the best-watered districts experience a substantial dry period during the summer. High annual precipitation totals on the northwest-facing mountain slopes, together with generally cool temperature, create good conditions for plant growth; substantial stands of evergreen oak (*Quercus ilex*) and Atlantic cedar (*Cedrus atlantica*) are found in these locations.

Peaks as high as 2,500 meters (m) create ideal conditions for orographic precipitation as well as a cold winter season that can last 3-5 months in locales above 1,600 m. This cold winter not only eliminates the prospect of cool-season crop production; it also poses a serious hazard to animal husbandry in the region. Without adequate stabling, it is difficult to keep animals on the high mountain plateaux during the winter, a complication that was one of the bases of the traditional agropastoral regime. At the same time, these cooler conditions are ideal for deciduous fruit production; horticulture is rapidly expanding in the region.

The high mountains that produce abundant moisture also create rainshadow effects that place severe limitations on the use of local environments. The contrast between the 1,500 mm of annual precipitation at Ifrane on the northwest side of the mountain range and the 250 mm characteristic of the Upper Moulouya Valley near Itzer on the eastern flank is striking. Locally dry habitats on southeast-facing slopes, such as those around Timahdite, the center of the Ait Arfa de Guigou high in the Middle Atlas south of Azrou, produce a steppe vegetation dominated by *Artemisia herba-alba* and *A. atlantica*. In contrast to these dry steppic conditions are the moister grassland habitats found in the bottoms of the basins and depressions that are widespread throughout the mountains. Wet, poorly drained soils, combined with the temperature inversions produced by air drainage, promote the development of herbaceous cover dominated by *Adenocarpus* and *Genista*, among others. These often extensive carpets of vegetation, with their associated seasonal pools of standing water, are the grazing centers of the region's sheep and goat concentrations during the late spring and early summer. These perennial vegetation resources are combined with an array of grasses and forbs to produce a rich mosaic of fodder resources for the pastoralists of the Middle Atlas (Lecompte 1986).

Traditional Agropastoralism

The traditional system for exploiting the mosaic of resources found at different elevations in the Middle Atlas included controlling a strip of territory that contained the full range of resources in the area (Beaudet 1969b). These resources invariably involved a mixture of agricultural and pastoral opportunities. While an individual lineage segment might claim exclusive access to only a small portion of the total strip, the group possessed rights to utilize other parts of the strip at different times of the year. The result was a complex arrangement of territorial claims and rights that were stratified by altitude.

Kinship units were linked together through an ascending series of genealogical ties and were loosely grouped into confederations that dominated large blocks of territory and served to defend territory threatened by outsiders. It was through membership in the lower-order kinship units that individuals were able to claim access to commonly held resources. Moreover, restrictions on the use of resources were maintained through these kinship groupings and their controlling institutions of tribal councils and individuals responsible for decisions about environmental protection (Venema 1992).

The overwhelming emphasis in most groups was upon the herding of sheep and goats. These animals were particularly suitable to the grazing conditions characteristic of the Middle Atlas because they were better able to cope with the stony surfaces and steep slopes of the region than other herd animals. Cattle were infrequently kept, except among the wealthy and more sedentary individuals in the population, in large part because their high water requirements made them a liability for most herders. Depending on wealth and local habitat conditions, donkeys, horses, mules, and camels were kept for transportation and plowing.

However, goats for subsistence needs and sheep, kept for sale or barter, dominated the production system. Concentration upon sheep and goats as the primary herding animals reflects both a pragmatic and cultural preference that contemporary economic development and the food preferences of the urban population have reinforced.

Cultivation also played an important role in the livelihood systems of the Middle Atlas. Indeed, it was the long-term viability of a combination of cropping and animal husbandry that characterized the pastoral regimes not only of the Middle Atlas but also of much of pastoral Morocco (Bencherifa 1988). Crops were planted in the agriculturally most favored portion of the tribal territory, but their care was not the most important part of the seasonal activity schedule. Securing adequate pasture and water for the animals dominated the concerns of pastoralists.

For this reason a mobile pattern of resource use was the predominant livelihood system in the Middle Atlas. Because pasture and water could not be guaranteed at all elevations throughout the year, confederation territories were aligned in northwest-southeast strips perpendicular to the crest line of the mountain range. This allowed herding groups to move between ecological units within lineage territories and to use access rights that were scattered throughout the ecological transect to which the group claimed access. Similar patterns of vertical nomadic pastoralism are widely encountered in North Africa and the Middle East (Johnson 1969).

The characteristic movement pattern involved wintering with the flocks in the lowland valleys in the Atlantic foothills of the Middle Atlas. After snow had melted from the highland passes, herds were moved to the upland plateaux and valleys where surface water and abundant pasture could be exploited (Célérier 1917; Bencherifa and Johnson 1991).

Crops were planted at an appropriate site that the tribal segment claimed where soil and water conditions promised to return an adequate yield. The bulk of the family, possibly leaving behind a guardian for the crops, would move with the animals to summer pastures, often at still higher elevations. When the crops were ready to be harvested, the family returned, the herds were pastured on post-harvest stubble and adjacent fallow land, and nearby steppe grazing was exploited for as long as possible. After temperatures had declined and the risk of snowfall had increased, herds were shifted to lower elevations until the threat of severe conditions had ended and it was again possible to move herds back to the higher elevations.

It is important to realize that this mobile system operated effectively at low population densities. It represented a spatially extensive rotational grazing system. No continuous pressure was placed on any one part of the environment for a lengthy period. The existing mosaic of upland forest and wet and dry steppic pasture, when combined with the lusher nonagricultural winter pasture in the lowlands, provided more than adequate forage for pastoral herds. Cultivation by the region's agropastoral communities was essential for dietary sufficiency but was not competitive for rangeland. Animal sales in the urban areas of the coastal lowlands were sufficient to provide the cash needed for items not readily produced within the pastoral community.

Environmental Changes

Before 1920 it does not appear likely that any significant regional destabilizing environmental change occurred in the area. Although it is certain that traditional urban demands in Fes and Meknes for timber and fuelwood had an effect on these cities' immediate hinterland, extensive deforestation deeper into the Middle Atlas undoubtedly was restricted by transportation difficulties. While agropastoral populations obviously extracted a toll on particularly advantageously located wood resources, and while some conversion of woodland to grassland occurred, these impacts were primarily of local significance. From the standpoint of the survival needs of the indigenous population, limited expansion of cropland and the growth of grassland at the expense of forest increased the diversity of useful resources accessible to resource users. These newly developed resources were likely to have remained stable for long periods after they had been brought into production; thus, there is every reason to regard them as positive changes that did not place the environment at risk.

There is evidence in sediment cores taken from lakes in the Middle Atlas to suggest that fluctuations in the species composition of forest vegetation of the region have taken place in the past (Lamb, Eicher, and Switsur 1989; Lamb, Damblon, and Maxted 1991). Deciduous oak replaced grassland after 8500 B.P., for example, and Atlantic cedar appeared in the area about 4000 B.P., apparently as a result of climatic changes that brought moister conditions.

Beginning about 1500 B.P. there is evidence for a decline in deciduous oaks and pines in favor of evergreen oak and cedar. Lamb, Damblon, and Maxted (1991), who examined two northerly and two southerly lake sites for these changes in the Middle Atlas, have suggested that anthropogenically induced pressures may be responsible for these most recent changes that they observed in the pollen record. The analyses revealed both altered pollen frequencies by species and greater occurrence of charcoal than would be expected from naturally occurring forest fires. Their explanation for the selective increase of evergreen oak is its ability to sprout from its base and root stock after having been chopped or burnt. Neither pine nor deciduous oak has this ability. A slow increase in the cultivation component of the local agropastoral economy may have been implicated in this transition. Cedar, though it lacks the ability to sprout, seems to have possessed an adaptive advantage in these more disturbed conditions. Its long lifespan meant that it could outlast periods of increased pressure and set seed from mature specimens whenever there was a decrease in grazing and land clearance activities.

The sites examined by Lamb and his colleagues hardly suggest a widespread deforestation of the Middle Atlas environment. The lake sites they examined are summer-season grazing and cultivation sites where agropastoral activities are likely to have been concentrated. Alteration of these most favorable locations under conditions of concentrated pressure is plausible, but extrapolation of these conditions to the entire mountain massif before the present century would appear to be untenable. The current mosaic of semi-arid *Artemisia* rangeland in orographically dry sites; wet steppe grassland in karstic basins and depressions resulting from impeded soil drainage and temperature inversions; and oak and cedar forest on steeper, stony slopes has an ancient origin (Lecompte 1986). What the region's agropastoralists have done historically is modify somewhat the distribution of that mosaic by expanding the extent of grassland at the expense of trees. In so doing, agropastoralists have promoted their own comparative advantage in a coevolving system.

The Middle Atlas Environment and Contemporary Agropastoralism

Most observers agree that the pastoral environments of the Middle Atlas today are experiencing considerable pressure (Assal 1978; Bencherifa and Johnson 1990, 1991; Bouderbala, Chiche, and El Aich 1992; MARA 1980; Venema 1992). Conservative estimates of range carrying capacity in the Timahdite area southeast of Azrou suggest that this highland range can tolerate no more than one sheep per hectare (ha) (MARA 1980). Yet during most of the year stocking ratios 3-4 times that figure are the norm

(Bencherifa and Johnson 1991). These ratios appear to prevail throughout the pastoral zones of the Middle Atlas.

Thus a discrepancy exists between what the range management expert regards as desirable and what the local herder perceives to be acceptable (or necessary). The local herder regards the range condition as one of heavy but acceptable use, while the resource manager sees overstocking and degradation. Range management plans invariably call for a reduction in the stocking ratio. Equally inevitably, these plans meet with resistance from local herders, particularly those with large herds who have the most to lose by destocking. It is simplistic to attribute this difference in perception of how best to use rangeland resources solely to a "tragedy of the commons" as described by Hardin (1968: 1243). The pressures currently affecting the pastoral areas of the Middle Atlas can be comprehended only by understanding the array of historical factors that have altered the traditional pattern of resource use described in the previous section.

The Effects of Land Alienation

Land alienation following the establishment of the French Protectorate over Morocco in 1912 was the major factor intensifying grazing pressure on the environments of the Middle Atlas. Colonial authorities regarded the extensive, mobile land-use practices characteristic of the traditional pastoral environments of Morocco as a poor use of potential productivity. They sought to raise productivity by promoting more intensive patterns of resource use. To this end, the colonial administration encouraged agricultural development by European settlers. The aim was to establish a modern, large-scale, wheat-producing, French-dominated agriculture in the most favorable Moroccan habitats (Swearingen 1987).

In Ait Arfa territory this meant the development of a substantial settlement nucleus in the Tigrigra Valley near Azrou, where prime winter grazing land was converted to more intensive agricultural uses. In similar fashion a large modern grazing enterprise was located in the Adarouch Valley to the northwest of Azrou. Modern ranching schemes, such as the Adarouch enterprise, were even more serious competitors with traditional pastoralists than wheat ranches or orchards because livestock were maintained on the scheme year round, thus completely denying grazing resources to nomadic users. On cereal farms it was at least possible for migratory herders to graze their animals briefly on the post-harvest crop residues and therefore maintain some of their traditional rights to seasonal fodder resources. The size of the territory alienated to alternative uses was never enormous, when the total amount of available land was considered. But the resources alienated were invariably critical resources in the traditional pastoral context. Without these rich grazing lands in the northwestern lowland valleys, adequate winter grazing for mobile flocks was difficult to find. Consequently, herds had to be concentrated on smaller areas with lower grazing potential for longer periods during the year. Yet these same herds had to support at least the same number of people. The inevitable consequence was initiation of land degradation pressures. This pattern of land alienation was encountered in other environmental zones.

Traditionally pastoralists were able to move freely through forests between the major grazing areas and were entitled to the fodder and fuel resources present in those wooded habitats. Under traditional pastoral conditions, the intensity of these uses posed little threat to the viability of forest resources. Nevertheless, as movement patterns were disrupted by the alienation of grazing land to other uses and as the French "pacification" process placed restrictions on the freedom of pastoral movement, localized pressure began to appear. As a result of concern about the preservation of an important part of the national resource endowment, efforts were made to restrict and control access to the forest. Goats were (in theory) denied access to the forest and the cutting of trees was prohibited. Although hardly uniformly applied, these restrictions represented important constraints on the availability of land for pastoral pursuits. The natural tendency to preserve forest resources for future use, however, drifts into tree fetishism when areas long denuded of tree cover or never having supported trees are extracted from rangeland and devoted to afforestation.

In many parts of the Middle Atlas there exists a struggle between the Forest Service and present pastoral users as traditional rights to grazing are lost to forest extension. This reflects a dramatic difference in perspective between national interest in forest land that will produce an output in decades and local concern for immediate livelihood support. However valuable more forest land might be, loss of contemporary grazing resources to afforestation projects continues a nearly century-long tradition of resource loss. These subtractions from pastoral space inevitably increase the pressure on those portions of the rangeland resource base that remain in pastoral use. Since 1912, nearly 50 percent of Ait Arfa du Guigou land has been lost to state control (Bencherifa and Johnson 1991), a tremendous restriction in the resource base available to sustain pastoral activities.

The Decline of Traditional Common-Property Resource Use

Much of the forest and grazing land in the Middle Atlas in pre-Protectorate Morocco was held in varying forms of common land tenure. Despite the privatization of large parcels of land during the Protectorate and since independence in 1956, much land continues to be held in common, generally under state administration (Bouderbala, Chiche, and El Aich 1992). There has always existed a contrast between state claims over land not specifically registered to private tenure, and the functional reality of communal control over these resources by groups organized by kinship and tribe.

This problem is not unique to Morocco but is common throughout North Africa (Bedrani 1983, 1991) and elsewhere. Central governments have seldom accepted the reality of such common-tenure claims, viewing them as impediments to progress and development; yet before the twentieth century central administrations were usually powerless to enforce their authority. Common-property resources were generally managed effectively by local tribal councils and leaders who were able to impose community sanctions on miscreants who violated resource-use rules.

A widespread common-property institution in Morocco is the *agdal*, a collective pasture with agreed-upon rules governing opening and closing dates (Gilles, Hammoudi, and Mahdi 1986). When well managed, an *agdal* is a very effective device for controlling common-property grazing resources. The major difficulty today in maintaining these institutions is the degree to which the Protectorate period undermined traditional institutions.

This happened both deliberately, in order to undercut opposition to the Protectorate administration, and indirectly as powerful local individuals used their influence with the central authorities in order to promote their own self-interest. Artz, Norton, and O'Rourke (1986) describe the difficulties experienced by a subfraction of the Ait Arfa du Guigou in maintaining its *agdal* in the face of the refusal of some of its members and individuals from neighboring groups to abide by the *agdal*'s limits on animal numbers and grazing periods. Like many such cooperative associations, the refusal of some to abide by the community's rules, and the ineffectiveness of the community in enforcing its sanctions, led to the collapse of the grazing association.

Some communal pastures still continue to be managed in the traditional pattern, albeit often with substantial input from government agricultural experts. These areas continue to place limits on who can graze on the common range, with outsiders usually scrupulously excluded, and exercise closure restrictions when needed. The Ait Mhammed's (one of the four subtribes of the Ait Arfa du Guigou) common summer grazing area of Feldi, southeast of Timahdite, for example, was closed to grazing during late spring and summer of 1988 because forage was insufficient to sustain the group's flocks.

Such districts continue to be heavily used, however, and they offer an indigenous management model with a reasonable prospect for successful employment in the future. Generally, however, as respect for common-property resources declined it was typical for individuals to assert private ownership over some portion of the communal space. This could most readily be accomplished by plowing and planting land. Often the sites chosen for agricultural development were places in which the individual family had been accustomed to graze. Every scrap of land converted to cultivation, however marginal and ephemeral, represented a decrease in the amount of rangeland available to sustain sheep and goats.

In the scramble to claim something from the common resource base, some groups — for example, those on the plateau between El Hajeb and Azrou — responded to colonial administration pressure and encouragement and established permanent dispersed homesteads. In other groups the more elite portions of the community benefited disproportionately from permanent access to common grazing land because they were able to invest resources into the development of animal shelters and water supplies. Among the Ait Arfa du Guigou some 266 stables were built on communal pastureland in the uplands (Venema 1992) 30 years ago, at a time when government policy encouraged the practice. Possession of a stable was essential to the health and safety of the herd if it was to be kept in the highlands during the winter months. Only the relatively rich herders had the capital resources to build such shelters, and these herders increasingly came to dominate the use of communal grazing. Until recently the Lahrouch communal pastures — a semi-arid steppe zone just north of Timahdite — were without substantial water resources; possession of either a truck to bring in water or the funds to pay for water were essential for the district's year-round exploitation. Among the Ait Mhammed, arguably the least prosperous of Ait Arfa du Guigou fractions, only 28 percent of the group's families continue to herd sheep on the Lahrouch collective pastures (Bencherifa and Johnson 1991). Poorer members of the fraction have largely been squeezed out of the pastoral business by lack of requisite resources. The reason these pastures can be used for most of the year — and thus are subjected to a level of grazing pressure never experienced in the past — is the combination of new technology and preferential access on the part of the surviving elite of successful herd managers.

The Effects of Land-Use Intensification

Efforts to increase pastoral production are a major source of pressure on the Middle Atlas rangeland. The general growth in Ait Arfa population, which more than tripled during the last 50 years (Bencherifa and Johnson 1991), is simply a reflection of the more general growth in population that characterizes modern Morocco (Findlay and Thompson 1985).

Such growth, coupled with the movement of large numbers of Moroccans to cities, has created an increased market for animal products. This demand has been met in most areas by at least a doubling in herd size, with particular emphasis on sheep. More animals are kept in the substantially smaller spaces that remain available to pastoralists. This is accomplished by investing much more capital in the animal rearing process than at any time in the past. Most of this investment is concentrated on the direct care and maintenance of the animals themselves rather than on the range resources. The individual investments of stables and water transport already mentioned are only part of the investment process that is transforming pastoral operations. Use of medicine and veterinarian services is widespread, and is commonly encountered even among less well-to-do herders, particularly when and where low-cost government programs are available. Government subsidies for herding cooperatives, feed purchases, parasite removal, water development, breed improvement, and animal acquisition all encourage the presence of greater numbers of animals on the range.

Under these circumstances, the amount of rangeland available is approaching or exceeding its maximum carrying capacity. The limited migratory movements that most herders can still make are insufficient to relieve pressure on existing rangeland. Intensification processes within the commercial agricultural sector — most recently with field crops giving way to tree crops — create field settings into which farmers are reluctant to allow animals. Exclusion of animals from orchards continues the process of eliminating post-harvest stubble fodder that was initiated when cereal farming replaced the best natural winter grazing. Moreover, the remaining post cereal harvest straw resources are now too valuable to "waste" on casual foraging arrangements. Instead, the straw is collected and sold to wealthy herders in need of supplemental fodder for their animals.

These changes increasingly place the less prosperous herder in a steadily deteriorating competitive position. Especially among poorer herders, it is common to see animals grazing as much as possible on unclaimed grazing areas along public roads or to encounter women who are collecting fodder in these and similar settings for transport back to their settlement site. The purchase of straw from agricultural zones has become increasingly necessary in order to sustain herds during those periods of the year when natural pasture is insufficient, although only the well-to-do can hope to engage in this practice on a regular basis. Surprisingly, there is as yet little evidence for widespread cultivation of fodder crops within the agricultural sector in the Guigou Valley, many of whose farms are owned by herders in the adjacent communal pastoral terrain (Bencherifa and Johnson 1991).

Rather, intensification processes work differently. Profits generated by cash crops, in particular the increasingly popular cultivation of potatoes, are readily invested in animals, which are placed on the rangeland whenever possible. Because the traditional agropastoral system always involved direct engagement in cultivation, this type of activity carries no social stigma. On the contrary, it is seen as a desirable way to generate needed income that can be invested in the most lucrative, most rapidly growing investment: sheep. Selling animals to raise cash needed for the purchase of fodder or reducing stocking ratios when range conditions are poor are options that are not readily engaged in by most herders. Every effort is made to sustain or increase herd size until a propitious moment for sell-off arrives. Such offtake for commercial purposes is a regular event that reaches its peak around the Islamic holidays, particularly at the end of the month of Ramadan.

Experiments conducted more than a decade ago on the more arid rangelands of eastern Morocco indicate that substantial weight gains can be made by sheep if a combination of altered animal management techniques and rangeland reseeding are employed (Graves et al. 1978). Some of these introduced practices might prove successful in the better-watered highland pastures, but it is questionable whether Moroccan herders are willing to accept the full package of management and value changes that are needed to make such practices viable. A less drastic approach would be to try to increase the integration between cropland and pastoral components of the Ait Arfa du Guigou production system. An irrigated agricultural scheme covering 5,000 ha has been developed in the Ait Arfa tribal lands along the Guigou and is an important contributor to local subsistence.

This scheme replaced pastureland with cropland in a pattern that mirrors the frequent competition between cultivation and animal husbandry elsewhere in Morocco. Despite the fact that most of the major herders on the Lahrouch communal pastures own substantial farms in the adjacent irrigation perimeter, little emphasis is placed on cultivating fodder crops. The preference seems to be either to continue cultivating the traditional mix of cereal crops, for which both domestic consumption and urban markets provide a major demand; or to cultivate a valuable cash crop such as potatoes, the revenue from which can be invested in the animal sector of the local economy.

Better integration between the local, spatially adjacent cropping and pastoral activities offers an important potential step toward reducing pressure on the Middle Atlas rangelands. That this pressure is heavy is shown by the results of an inadvertent experiment presently being carried out on the Plateau of Ito adjacent to the Forest of Jabaa between El Hajeb and Azrou. Two thousand hectares of communal grazing land were closed to grazing in the spring of 1988. Access to the land was restricted by a fence and the land was planted with a mixture of trees, including native oaks and cedar. The intention is to reclaim for forest production an area that has long been utilized for grazing by Ait Arfa du Tigrigra agropastoralists. In 15-20 years, when the trees have reached sufficient height to be protected from grazing and browsing pressure, the intention is to reopen the area to controlled grazing.

Aesthetic improvements for tourism and general environmental amelioration were additional benefits envisaged for this stark and rocky space. Four years later grass grows high within the protected afforested perimeter and young seedlings cautiously and sporadically poke their tops above the highest grasses. The richness of the herbaceous vegetation, which has regenerated from local seed sources, is a testimony to the primary production potential of the Middle Atlas rangeland. Equally compelling is the much more heavily impacted vegetation outside the afforestation project fence. Yet the lush protected vegetation does no one much good in the short run. And the heavily used vegetal resource outside the project fence is adversely impacted by the loss of the grazing resource now locked up tantalizingly beyond the herder's reach. Like so many other stories in the Middle Atlas, this project merits long-term evaluation.

Additional Indicators of Land Pressure

Additional environmental pressure points exist in the Middle Atlas. These include the forested areas with which the region is well endowed. For if one aspect of environmental status in the region is the history of the alienation of land from grazing for forestry, the other side of the equation is the heavy pressure brought to bear on forests by the region's agropastoralists. Venema (1992: 5) estimates that 80 percent of the forest is potentially open to grazing. Laws prohibiting goat grazing and wood cutting notwithstanding, the forest resources of the Middle Atlas are heavily used by pastoralists. Goats — only one percent of the total herd among the Ait Arfa du Guigou — and sheep are commonly herded together. Separating the species makes little sense from a practical standpoint because the greater intelligence and initiative of the goat makes it a useful leader in the flock. As a matter of common practice, goats are always present when a herd is grazing in or moving through a forested area.

Despite the myth that goats are particularly harmful to trees, their small numbers in the Azrou-Timahdite region means that sheep are the main culprits in removing grass and seedlings from the forest floor. Moreover, under the pressure of necessity, herders do not hesitate to cut branches from deciduous trees, particularly ash, for fodder. The signs of pressure on forests are widespread. They include browse lines on mature woody specimens, an absence of seedling regeneration in many areas, limited grassy groundcover even in open spaces within the forest, and nearly ubiquitous multistemmed oak specimens, which result from sprouting from the base of trees disturbed by fire or axe. Such signs attest to the major impact that cutting, browsing, and grazing have on the forest.

Contrary to expectations in an environment that is as heavily used as the Middle Atlas, evidence of soil erosion, rilling, and gully development are not widespread. These land degradation processes most commonly can be found in specific sites adjacent to development projects. The northern edge of the Adarouch ranch is a particularly distinctive example of this phenomenon. Here small-scale private grazing operations on former communal pasture place such concentrated pressure on slopes adjacent to the rich valley bottom that rilling and gullying can be observed.[4]

Also, growth in population centers at all levels in the settlement system is taking place in the Middle Atlas. These centers present their own set of environmental issues, including the "land degradation" that inevitably results when productive agricultural land is converted to urban infrastructure. At the same time, any nucleation of population brings with it a corresponding concentration of animals, both within and adjacent to the urban area. These animals inevitably place a great deal of pressure on the groundcover of slopes near the settlement site. This occurs because localized herds, after exhausting fodder potential of the available fallow land within the nearby agricultural sector, find much of their fodder on the nonagricultural slopes nearby. Despite intense grazing, however, few of these slopes show signs of substantial destabilization.

A final indication of the degree to which land pressure exists in the Middle Atlas highlands is the extraordinary effort undertaken throughout the region to create productive land or exploit marginal environments. Enormous amounts of labor are invested to clear stones from fields and bring into use land that in less constrained contexts would not be considered worth the effort. This extends to the cultivation of steep slopes and the micromanagement of high-altitude plots. These rainfed high-slope fields reflect a sensitive local understanding of the soil and the moisture capabilities of the individual land facets.

These fields also indicate the degree to which the crops and animals are an integral part of one management system. Limited resource opportunities make the risk of cultivating such plots worthwhile. For if moisture is inadequate supply, grain planted will mature and can be harvested to meet basic nutritional needs. Should precipitation fail, the crop can always be grazed off by animals, thus salvaging something from the investment.

As a further bonus, cultivation in these marginal settings establishes a claim to resources that may be recognized ultimately by the government despite the fact that such land is most often currently held under communal tenure. The need to cultivate marginal fields in these constrained settings is to some degree a measure of the stress present in highland agropastoral systems. It is also a remarkable statement about the ingenuity and optimism of the human species in the face of difficulties.

Conclusions

The increasingly pressured and heavily used agropastoral environments of the Middle Atlas reflect an 80-year pattern of change that was initiated during the French Protectorate and that has continued since independence. The limited resources presently at the disposal of herders and farmers are all that were left after a lengthy process of land alienation. It is not surprising that these habitats have begun to experience problems sustaining their own population growth and contributing to national market demands. Much of the heavy use that characterizes the current pastoral environment is the result of the disruption in traditional resource systems and in the way that the costs of development in the Middle Atlas have been imposed on the region's remaining sheepherders.

While the economically more marginal herders have been forced out of production, those who have managed to continue have made major adjustments in their production system in order to remain viable. The shift toward an increasingly stall-fed animal management system with limited or no seasonal mobility is clearly observable. Better integration between the herding and the crop-production segments of the local agropastoral economy would improve this process and thus help to reduce environmental degradation.

The remarkable feature of the Middle Atlas environment is the resilience that its major ecological systems exhibit under the heavy use to which they are subjected. Finding ways to lighten that pressure without diminishing productivity for human needs is essential to the continued health of the region's cultural ecological systems.

Notes

1. Land alienated for colonial farms, cattle ranches, and forest reserves constricted the territory available to herders. Colonial authorities forced pastoralists to remain more continuously in a limited portion of their traditional range.

2. Primarily they intensified the animal production system by keeping larger numbers of animals in smaller areas; by capitalizing their operations more heavily; by shifting feed sources from natural grasses to larger amounts of supplemental fodder; and by investing in more inputs (medicine, breed improvement, participation in government subsidized cooperative programs, parasite removal, water development, and so on).

3. Even reaching agreement on whether changes in environmental conditions are good or bad is difficult. Equally complicated is deciding whether natural or human systems are the primary focus of concern in environmental status assessment.

4. Remarkably, this slope disturbance does not seem to have progressed substantially over a 4-year period, an observation that may have more to do with the low erodibility of some Moroccan soils (Merzouk and Blake 1991) than the wisdom of local herd management practices.

References

Artz, Neal E., B. E. Norton, and James T. O'Rourke. 1986. "Management of Common Grazing Lands: Tamahdite, Morocco," in National Research Council (NRC), *Proceedings of the Conference on Common Property Resource Management.* Pp. 259-280. Washington, D.C.: National Academy Press.

Assal, A. 1978. "Analysis of Sheep Production in the Tribe of Ait Arfa du Guigou (Rural Commune of Timahdite)." Janet Stein, trans. Mimeograph.

Beaudet, G. 1969a. *Le Plateau Central Marocain et ses Bordures: Etude Géomorphologique.* Rabat: Inframar.

———. 1969b. "Les Beni Mguild du Nord. Etude Géographique de l'Evolution Récente d'une Confédération Semi-nomade." *Revue de Géographie du Maroc* 16: 3-80.

Bedrani, Slimane. 1983. "Going Slow with Pastoral Cooperatives." *Ceres* 16 (4):16-21.

———. 1991. "Legislation for Livestock on Public Lands in Algeria." *Nature and Resources* 27 (4):24-30.

Bencherifa, Abdellatif. 1988. "Agropastorale Organisationsformen im atlantischen Marokko." *Die Erde* 119:1-13.

Bencherifa, Abdellatif, and Douglas L. Johnson. 1990. "Adaptation and Intensification in the Pastoral Systems of Morocco," in J. G. Galaty and D. L. Johnson, eds., *The World of Pastoralism: Herding Systems in Comparative Perspective.* Pp. 394-416. New York: Guilford.

———. 1991. "Changing Resource Management Strategies and their Environmental Impacts in the Middle Atlas Mountains of Morocco." *Mountain Research and Development* 11 (3):183-194.

Bouderbala, N., J. Chiche, and A. El Aich. 1992. "La Terre Collective au Maroc," in A. Bourbouze and R. Rubino, eds., *Terres Collectives en Méditerranée: Histoire, Legislation, Usages et Modes d'Utilisation par les Animaux.* Pp. 27-59. Rome: Réseau FAO Ovins et Caprins/Réseau Parcours Euro-africain.

Célérier, J. 1917. "La Transhumance dans le Moyen Atlas." *Hespéris* 17:53-68.

Findlay, Anne M., and Ian B. Thompson. 1985. "Morocco Tops the 20 Million Mark." *Geography* 70:252-254.

Gilles, Jere L., Abdellah Hammoudi, and Mohamed Mahdi. 1986. "Oukaimedene, Morocco: A High Mountain Agdal," in National Research Council (NRC), *Proceedings of the Conference on Common Property Resource Management.* Pp. 281-304. Washington, D.C.: National Academy Press.

Graves, Walter L., Philip Roark, F. Rudolph Vigil, and Hamidou Bouyayachen. 1978. "Increasing Animal Production in Morocco (North Africa) through Rangeland Renovation and Animal Management," in Donald N. Hyder, ed., *Proceedings of the First International Rangeland Congress.* Pp. 130-132. Denver: Society for Range Management.

Hardin, Garrett. 1968. "The Tragedy of the Commons." *Science* 162:1243-1248.

Johnson, Douglas L. 1969. *The Nature of Nomadism: A Comparative Study of*

Migrations in Southwestern Asia and Northern Africa. Research Paper No. 118. Chicago: University of Chicago, Department of Geography.

Lamb, H. F., U. Eicher, and V. R. Switsur. 1989. "An 18,000-year Record of Vegetation, Lake-level and Climatic Change from Tigalmamine, Middle Atlas, Morocco." *Journal of Biogeography* 16:65-74.

Lamb, H. F., F. Damblon, and R. W. Maxted. 1991. "Human Impact on the Vegetation of the Middle Atlas, Morocco, During the Last 5,000 Years." *Journal of Biogeography* 18:519-532.

Lecompte, M. 1986. *Biogéographie de la Montagne Marocaine: le Moyen Atlas Central.* Mémoires et Documents, Centre National de Recherche Scientifique.

MARA (Ministère de l'Agriculture et de la Réform Agraire, Direction Provinciale de l'Agriculture de Meknes). 1980. Projet Moyen Atlas: Dossier de Base. Vol. I.

Merzouk, A., and G. R. Blake. 1991. "Indices for the Estimation of Interrill Erodibility of Moroccan Soils." *Catena* 18:537-550.

Swearingen, Will D. 1987. *Moroccan Mirages: Agrarian Dreams and Deceptions, 1912-1986.* Princeton: Princeton University Press.

Venema, Bernhard. 1992. "Ecological Crisis and Local Power Constellations: The Case of the Middle Atlas," in *La Recherche Scientifique au Service du Développement: Actes de la troisième Rencontre Universitaire maroco-néerlandaise.* Pp. 1-12. Rabat: Publications de la Faculté des Lettres et des Sciences Humaines, Série Colloques et Seminaires No. 18.

3

Sustained Past and Risky Present: The Tafilalt Oasis of Southeastern Morocco

James A. Miller

The Tafilalt is a broad, arid basin on the edge of the Sahara Desert in southeastern Morocco. Oasis cultivation of dates, wheat, and barley has dominated the lives of its people for millenia, with nomads herding sheep and goats in the vast surrounding dry lands.[1] The Tafilalt is given life primarily by the Atlas mountain streams converging in it, the most important of which are the Ziz and the Gheris. Beyond the Tafilalt the streambeds are empty and the desert stretches unbroken for well over a thousand miles until it reaches the black African farming communities of the Sahel.

For more than 1,200 years of recorded history the Tafilalt has been a nexus of civilization and environmental change. Its ancient city-state Sijilmassa, which flourished from caravan trade and the minting and distribution of African gold, directed the Tafilalt's early environmental development. In the late nineteenth century the Alaouite dynasty attempted a broad renewal of the Tafilalt through irrigation development.[2] Life in the Tafilalt today is provided focus by the modern Oued Ziz Dam, the town of Rissani, and development policies pursued by the Moroccan government in the northern Sahara.[3]

The organization of the Tafilalt throughout history has reflected a variety of human responses to the environmental possibilities afforded by nature. The varying milieux obtained by the successive development of the Tafilalt represent illuminating case studies of the relationship between political authority, technology, and environment. This chapter examines the underlying ecological organization of the Tafilalt oasis and focuses on two distinct periods of environmental development, that of *Ancient Sijilmassa* and the

Tafilalt Present. It argues that the *Sijilmassa* manipulation of the region, designed to cope with both drought and flood, provided long-term, steady-state solutions to the problems of survival in the region — while development during the *Tafilalt Present* offers merely short-term, nonsustainable solutions that threaten the very vitality of the oasis.

Location and Environment of the Tafilalt

The Tafilalt is the single largest oasis in Morocco.[4] It is approximately 15 km wide at its maximum extent and about 20 km (160 km²) in length.[5] To the east the Tafilalt is enclosed by the stony desert of the Guir Hammada; to the south by the Erg Chebbi, the largest sand sea in southeastern Morocco. To the west it is bounded by rugged eastern extensions of the Anti-Atlas mountains. South of the Tafilalt, small oases such as Merzouga and Taouz punctuate the aridity and unpopulated nature of this Saharan region. Just south of Taouz, the Ziz and the Gheris converge near the Algerian border to form the Oued Daoura, a relic stream from the Pleistocene.[6] Although the Daoura Valley is uninhabited and barren, it traces a pathway across the desert that in traditional times was the gateway for the Tafilalt's transsaharan trade. The water resources of the Tafilalt — the Ziz, Gheris, and the Todghra — originate in the relatively dry highlands of the eastern High Atlas to the north. The eastern High Atlas, characterized by high peaks overlooking long, regular limestone folds cut by faults, accounts for approximately two-thirds of the entire High Atlas chain. It is distinctly drier than the rest of the Atlas owing to its continental location.

Much of a typical year's precipitation in the eastern High Atlas is received as snow from November to April, providing a water reserve for the rest of the year. Water quickly penetrates the limestone rock of the eastern High Atlas; within the mountains and beyond their confines, springs are numerous. The Oued Ziz reflects the high altitude, near-desert conditions of the eastern High Atlas. Precipitation throughout the watershed is highly variable and usually low. Though the Ziz dries up completely one year out of three, it is likely to flood when spring temperatures result in rapid snow melt. Floods accompanying Saharan thunderstorms in September-October are also a nearly annual hazard. Traditionally, before the damming of the Ziz at Errachidia, flood waters periodically covered portions of the Tafilalt. Though these floods disrupted human life, the water table, lifeblood of the date palm, was replenished. Numerous relic streams and channels in the Tafilalt served as fingerlike extensions of major streams in times of flood.

The harshness of the Tafilalt climate is a result of aridity, high temperature, and *chergui*, which are low-pressure dust storms. Precipitation diminishes rapidly southward from the eastern High Atlas, from 140 millimeters (mm)/year at Errachidia to 59 mm/year at Rissani 140 km south.[7] There is no doubt that the Tafilalt is among the hottest regions in Morocco, and evapotranspiration is very high.[8] *Chergui* add to the region's harshness; they are common in summer and may occur at any point during the year, lasting from two days to a week. A severe *chergui* can damage date palms by breaking fruit and ripping fronds. Nevertheless, a microclimate prevails in the oasis; irrigation water and shade provided by the date palm render the environment at the ground less arid, relatively more humid, and lower in temperature.

Environmental Constraints and Ecological Contradictions

Life in the Tafilalt oasis poses a set of environmental constraints and contradictions. The essential constraints of the pre-Saharan environment — extremely low precipitation and very high temperatures — are counterbalanced by the flow of rivers from the mountains into the region, which not only bring their surface waters but afford the area springs and an accessible water table. The array of water sources available in nature has been developed by human populations over time through a web of irrigation technologies. Thus, human settlement has emerged in an environment that is generally inhospitable.

While life in any riverine environment poses a risk of flood, desert life is always jeopardized by lack of water. Here, the twin challenges of flood and drought combine. The "ordinary" constraints of Saharan oasis life in the Tafilalt are mitigated by the presence of the seasonal rivers, Gheris and Ziz. Water, often in abundant quantity, is available through nature and improved by irrigation, but risk of flood is added.

Flood waters are essential to the maintenance of a healthy oasis ecosystem. Floods replenish the water table, feed springs, and create the shoals of the wadi bottoms (*gueltas*), important sources of water during dry periods. The flood waters generally cleanse the oasis environment and provide near- and medium-term water resources. Without flood, the oasis languishes; with flood, human life is endangered: such has been the traditional ebb and flow of life in the Tafilalt.

Both historical and archaeological records of the Tafilalt indicate that the fabric of society has been repeatedly challenged by the waters that sustain it. Over the ages, Filalis — the Tafilalt natives — have adapted to floods as they could. The history of the Tafilalt can be read as the episodic conquest of a desert river. As the wadis of the Tafilalt have been harnessed for human use, irrigation systems have laced the oasis, utilizing different technologies and methods of control at different points in history.

The Period of Ancient Sijilmassa

Organizer of the Tafilalt

The earliest history of Sijilmassa, founded in 757 A.D. as the second Islamic city in North Africa after Kairouan, reflects the transition of Berber nomads from a herding to a settled and urban economy in which religious doctrine played a formative ideological role. Sijilmassa organized the Tafilalt as it built its power on the gold trade with subsaharan Africa.[9] Sijilmassa's commercial dominance over the southern Moroccan oases and the transsaharan trade is remarkable from the city's earliest days. Sijilmassa's early leaders were intent on creating a great and beautiful city based on commercial wealth.

Accounts by medieval Arab geographers and travellers confirm that Sijilmassa was indeed magnificent.[10] As Sijilmassa grew, the city took on a majestic form suggested by Al Bakri: "high houses, great buildings and lots of gardens."[11] The city's extensive walls, first built in the 790s and enclosing buildings, gardens, and date palms, were described by Al-'Umari as 70 to 80 km in extent.[12] The image of a model Islamic town emerges: city walls and gates, ruler's palace, public baths, fine houses, a bustling market (*suq*), a variety of crafts, extensive gardens, and presumably, well-tended date palms.[13]

Although gold became Sijilmassa's reason for existence, we know nothing of how the gold trade came about.[14] At Sijilmassa, gold was transformed into coin and re-exported to the rest of North Africa.[15] The "Golden Trade of the Moors" made Sijilmassa an independent and prosperous kingdom as local (Atlas) sources of mineral wealth, particularly silver, added to the city's strengths.

Following a period of occupation by the Shi'ite Fatimids of Tunis in the mid-900s, local Zenata Berbers known as the Maghrawa took control of Sijilmassa in the 970s and expanded the boundaries of the city-state's political power from the Draa on the west to Sefrou in the north.[16] Until the period of independent Sijilmassa ended with the rise of the Almoravids in the 1000s, the city held exclusive or near-exclusive control over the trade routes with subsaharan Africa.

Under the Almoravids (1054-1145), Almohads (1139/45-1255), and Merinids (1255/57-1400) Sijilmassa was repeatedly conquered for its wealth and diminished in stature as it was absorbed into broader economic and political frameworks. In the last decades of Merinid rule, the political situation deteriorated into squabbling between regional governors and Merinid sultans. Firmly enmeshed in the economy and politics of the hapless Merinid Empire, Sijilmassa virtually disappeared overnight in 1393.

Sijilmassa's Demise

Leo Africanus visited the Tafilalt in 1514-1515, and it is from him that the most reliable account of the destruction of Sijilmassa in 1393 is drawn.[17] Although a variety of histories recount different versions of the destruction of Sijilmassa, its end was prompted by a number of factors.

The Merinid regime became politically unstable, and Sijilmassa no longer had a monopoly on the gold trade yet was being exploited for tax revenue. Trading partners in the south shifted as Ancient Ghana declined and new African polities rose in the 1100s and 1200s in Timbuktu and Gao and farther east (Songhai) in the late 1300s. The Portuguese arrived along the West African coast in the 1300s, enlarging their share of the African trade.

Disruptions were also wrought by the nomadic Arabs, who were pushed westward out of Egypt by the Fatimids and poorly absorbed into Maghribi society. Finally, the effects of harsh drought and the plague known as the Black Death in the late 1300s wreaked havoc upon the region. Although no one factor can be considered entirely responsible for the demise of Sijilmassa, in concert they tolled its death knell.[18]

It is important to note, nevertheless, that none of the factors was a function of the mismanagement of the local environment. In fact, it seems clear from the historical record that the oasis environment emerged unscathed from the destruction of Sijilmassa.

Everyday Life in Sijilmassa: An Analysis

Archaeological findings indicate that Sijilmassa extended along the banks of the Ziz for some 13 km, was up to a kilometer-and-a-half wide, and contained 20,000-30,000 people.[19] Historical descriptions reveal that Sijilmassa was a single long, narrow city containing most or all of the Tafilalt population. Al-Bakri describes Sijilmassa as "surrounded by numerous suburbs."[20]

That Sijilmassa was a single city, not a set of dispersed *qsour* like the Tafilalt today — and that it sustained itself within the Tafilalt oasis — can be explained by the long history of water development, the compact shape of the oasis, and the mercantile nature of Sijilmassa.[21] That Sijilmassa was aligned along the waters of the Ziz demonstrates that the Ziz was fundamental to Sijilmassa's growth. Sijilmassa, although a sophisticated urban place, grew in response to the agricultural mastery of the oasis. The contours of the oasis lay directly outside the city walls and were entirely within walking range of the population living within the walls.

A picture emerges of a bustling caravan center in the Tafilalt 1,000 years ago. Yet most of its population on most days was involved in agriculture:

the tending of dates; the irrigation of the land by *seguias* diverting water from the Ziz and assisted here and there by *noria* (water wheels) and *arhrour* (traction wells); the plowing of the fields for barley and vegetables.

Who was this population?

Those who tended the dates and plowed the fields were not those who directed and shared the wealth of the gold trade. The society of the Tafilalt was a mixed, stratified society of rank, in which Arabic-speaking religious notables held prestigious spiritual roles. Arabs and Berbers conducted the trade and administered government; mixed-race people, *haratin* (echoing the original oasis mix of blacks and Berbers), did most of the manual labor and probably accounted for a majority of the population — much as they do today in many *qsour*. They were indentured to free Berbers and Arabs. African slaves in the Tafilalt foreshadowed the development of the African slave trade following the discovery of the New World.

Until the 1960s Jews, numerous in Sijilmassa, held a special place as traders and merchants in precious metals. They were probably the best gold and silversmiths of ancient Sijilmassa. Travellers wrote their accounts of the wonders of the place and viewed the labor and irrigation works of Sijilmassa as unremarkable: gold, not hydraulic engineering, was their interest.

The Ziz: Moved and Improved

The Tafilalt is a "little Mesopotamia," between the Ziz and the Gheris. That the Ziz and Gheris do not flow together is a recent geophenomenon. It appears that, at early points in the post-Pleistocene, the Ziz flowed westward to join the Gheris just downstream from Erfoud. Today, as a result of later alluviation, the two rivers go their separate ways after coming within a few km of each other at Erfoud. The Ziz was pushed east, into a separate channel. The Tafilalt oasis was thus framed on the east by the Ziz and on the west by the Gheris.[22]

The Tafilalt is a society conceived in irrigation. An age-old objective in the Tafilalt has been to redirect the Ziz westward, toward the Gheris, so that the combined effect of their waters (and water tables) might be used for the production of dates, barley, fruits, and vegetables. In 1992 fieldwork near Erfoud (at the northern entrance to the Tafilalt) investigated massive ancient earthworks aimed at diverting the Ziz out of its natural channel westward into a relict streambed. It is this artificial course of the Ziz that is known and called the Ziz throughout its length down the middle of the Tafilalt oasis.[23]

The diversion of the Ziz has a long history, dating back to Sijilmassian times.[24] It is difficult to weed through the many layers of irrigation systems existing in the Tafilalt; furthermore, many fossil streambeds have been used as irrigation channels and subsequently contoured by flood over the ages. It is my belief, however, that the diversion of the Ziz dates from a point perhaps some 200 years following the founding of Sijilmassa, and reflects the city's very success. It needed to grow.

Others have developed this theme earlier. Margat, for example, suggested that the diversion took place in either the 900s or 1000s. Margat proposed that large-scale management of the Ziz began with a dam and a diversionary canal, which was intended to carry a moderate, occasional amount of water into a relict stream, but "it enlarged rapidly due to floods and became an 'artificial oued' taking on the majority of the flow of the Ziz."[25] Enlarged and improved, it is what is seen at the western margins of the Sijilmassa site today and known as the Ziz through the oasis.

Oral history and everyday knowledge in the Tafilalt support these views. It is common knowledge that the Amerbouh is the "true bed of the Ziz" and that the Ziz rejoins its natural streambed just south of the oasis in times of flood. What is not recognized today, however, are the motivations that led to this engineering project.

The diversion of the Ziz had numerous benefits for the ancient city. The location of Sijilmassa in the center of the oasis allowed it to expand laterally along the newly diverted Oued Ziz. Sijilmassa's elongated shape, noted by travelers after the mid-900s, reflects its reliance upon the diverted Ziz. The city's shape also facilitated access to the entire oasis from residents living within the city walls. If we take today's north-south oasis length of 20 km as an approximation of the size of Sijilmassa's oasis, the entire oasis could have been effectively exploited by residents of the ancient city. Fields most distant from the farthest northern or southern suburbs of Sijilmassa would be no more than 3.5 km away — a reasonable walking distance. Furthermore, the compact nature of the oasis would allow effective management of land east and west of Sijilmassa. Again, following the modern analogy, the maximum width of the oasis, 15 km, provides a reasonable maximum distance for peasants to commute to their most distant fields: 6 to 7 km. The diversion of the Ziz undoubtedly encouraged further development of arable land.

The location of the diverted Oued Ziz is tilted to the western half of the oasis: toward the Oued Gheris. Although we have no way of knowing how planned the result was, running the waters of the Ziz a few kilometers parallel to the Gheris multiplies the resources of the conjoined water tables. The effect of combining the water tables of the two streams allowed Sijilmassa to reach its environmental maximum of population and agricultural surface. The simple, successful, and long-lasting nature of the diversion of the Ziz was validated by nearly a thousand years of use, until the construction of the modern dam at Errachidia. Further refinements to the Sijilmassian system were added by the Alaouites, who added some seventeen low masonry dams along the Gheris and the diverted Ziz. The addition of *rhettara* (chain wells) to the Tafilalt's network of irrigation appears to have been a post-Sijilmassa development.[26]

The Tafilalt Present

The modern period in the Tafilalt began in October and November 1965. Heavy rains in the eastern High Atlas swept down the mountain slopes into the Ziz; for several days in November, floodwaters up to 3 m deep covered much of the left bank of the diverted Ziz. Dams and *seguias* (irrigation channels) broke, *qsour* were washed away, and many lives were lost. The Government of Morocco announced that the Ziz would be dammed at Errachidia (then known as Ksar Es-Souk). The dam was built through a United States AID contract and completed in 1971. Water for irrigation from the dam began to flow in 1973. Now, more than 20 years later, the impact of the dam on the Tafilalt is becoming clear.

The dam is the most tangible element in a web of profound and rapid change in the Tafilalt. Social forces have altered the fabric of everyday life fully as much as modern hydraulic engineering. But as social and technological change has created the landscape of the modern Tafilalt, underlying ecological changes are operating behind the scenes. These bring into question the continued existence of the Tafilalt as an agricultural oasis.

Social Forces in the Tafilalt

Three societal factors in the Tafilalt are altering the face of the region. One of these, the liberation of the *haratin* caste, is a local, oasis phenomenon. The second, labor outmigration, is found in many marginal regions of Morocco. The third factor, population growth, is a driving force country-wide. Together these forces have created a human landscape in the Tafilalt far different from that of a generation ago.

The liberation of the *haratin*, a class held as chattel, has had important consequences for the agricultural economy of the Tafilalt. *Haratin* were expected to plow, weed, cultivate, harvest, and perform many other tasks. As they have freed themselves from their traditional taskmasters, many essential tasks have been slowly abandoned. Foremost among these is the maintenance of the *rhettara* system.

Rhettara need annual maintenance. Furthermore, if the water table goes lower, the entire chain of wells needs to be deepened and relevelled. *Rhettara* digging and maintenance is difficult and dangerous work. An entire class of *haratin*, known as *khattater*, were specialists in this task. Their existence as an occupation is now a memory, although some *khattater* are still living. As a result, much of the elaborate *rhettara* system of the Tafilalt has been abandoned over the last generation.

Another task the *haratin* typically performed was the pollination of the date palm. This arduous job, central to life in an oasis specializing in cultivation of the date palm, is beginning to fall by the wayside where the *haratin* were the dominant workforce. The number of date palms in the Tafilalt is in decline, quite independent of the effects of the date wilt virus (*bayyoud*).

As the ex-*haratin* have turned away from agricultural labor — perhaps out of lingering distaste for the exertions of the past, perhaps for lack of money with which to buy land — they have turned to occupations in the city of the Tafilalt, Rissani. In Rissani they are welders, mechanics, and butchers, jobs others disdain. Many have migrated out of the Tafilalt. There are large *haratin* communities in Casablanca and the other big cities of Morocco-over-the-mountains. With the *haratin's* slow, steady disengagement from their feudal past, the landscape of the Tafilalt has changed as well.

Exterior labor migration has attracted the male population of the Tafilalt. Although data on outmigration from the Tafilalt has not yet been collected, the effects of it are obvious in the more than 120 villages (*qsour*) of the oasis. Those with a family member overseas or with a good job in the Moroccan North have higher standards of living.

These are the families who have led the movement out of the *qsour* and into individual family houses on their own privately owned plots of land in the oasis. These are the families who have invested in a diesel motor pump to bring up water from the shallow water table (10 to 15 m) of the Tafilalt. If the family is in the northern reaches of the Tafilalt, they may be on new land made arable by virtue of the motor pump.

Significant expansion is taking place along the northern margins of the Tafilalt, into lands last farmed when Alaouite hydraulic technology was intact and where abundant sources of underground water exist. These families prosper despite the paucity of water provided from the dam. They are likely to invest their money from overseas in education for their children, providing economic pathways for themselves out of the Tafilalt in the next generation. A growing pattern of economic inequality results from the differential access to exterior resources.

Population growth in the Tafilalt has been considerably lower than the Moroccan national rates.[27] Rissani's population grew from 2,844 in 1960 to 3,565 in 1971 to 4,985 in 1982.[28] Rates of population increase in the Tafilalt appear to have begun to meet national averages of 2.5 percent and higher; recent national data suggest that the birth rate in Morocco is falling generally and fairly rapidly. In the Tafilalt, a finite environment, the effects of population growth are most visible in the growth of Rissani and the development of housing outside the confines of the *qsour*.

Effects of the Oued Ziz Dam

The Filali view of the Hassan ad-Dakkhil Dam on the Ziz at Errachidia is mixed. Research in summer 1992 discovered that people in the Tafilalt recognize that the damming of the Ziz has had an overall transformative effect on their lives, and can enumerate numerous benefits. Foremost among these is flood control. There has not been a single flood in the Tafilalt since the reservoir was filled. In 1992, people pointed to the high waters in the Gheris in the spring of 1990 to say, "If the Ziz had had that much water in it, Rissani would have been swept away!"

Filalis also recognize that the "government canals" (as canals from Hassan ad-Dakkhil Dam are called) provide a measured, reliable amount of water at critical periods during the year. Some parts of the Tafilalt, particularly the central area around Rissani (known as Oued Ifli) now have no water resources except for those coming from the dam. The degree of enthusiasm for the dam depends on how much water people have available from other sources: *rhettara* linked to their *qsar*, public pumped underground water (there are several systems), or private diesel motor pumps.

In recent years the water authorities have distributed water down the new "government" canals four times during each agricultural year for 20-23 days each time, alloting 10-12 hours of irrigation water per *qsar*. People recognize that this allotment is insufficient (generally reckoned to be half to two-thirds of their needs), but they are grateful for the water they get (it is unmetered and free). In more general terms, positive effects of the dam include a program of clean drinking water for the Tafilalt with water from the dam piped directly to each *qsar*.

The negative side of the balance sheet is more serious. It is interesting to note that the creation of a major dam on the Ziz with the primary mission of improving conditions in the Tafilalt has had a profound (and unintended) effect on Errachidia. There, the growth of a technical and administrative class associated with the dam plus the steady infusion of state funds into Errachidia for the dam and its maintenance have created a steady economic boom. Its population grew from 16,775 in 1971 to 27,040 in 1982 — an increase of nearly two-thirds.[29] It is no accident that Errachidia became a provincial capital in the mid-1970s following completion of the dam. All this is far from the original purpose of the dam. Growth of Errachidia is likewise sustained by water from the dam, water that would have earlier flowed down the Ziz. Urban water uses are beginning to crowd out water use for downstream agriculture.

Electricity expected to come from the dam has not materialized; there is not enough water power to irrigate and turn turbines. Thus, electrification of the Tafilalt is occurring only now, some 20 years after it was first promised, and the power comes from Bin el-Ouidane Dam (on the western side of the Atlas). But these are minor points compared with the environmental changes that the dam has imposed on the Tafilalt.

Conclusions

The Hassan ad-Dakkhil Dam presents typical problems of dams in hot, arid regions. Evapotranspiration rates at Errachidia are extremely high, reducing the economic utility of the dam. In addition, sedimentation rates in the reservoir are high owing to overgrazing, fuelwood collection, and extensive erosion in the watershed. Silt is rapidly filling in the reservoir, shortening the life of the dam, and is not reaching fields in the Tafilalt where it historically enriched the soil.

Equally critical are the wide annual swings in precipitation in the Ziz watershed, meaning that the amount of water in the reservoir has varied widely over the 20 years of its life. Water resources normally are insufficient to meet the Tafilalt's water needs, especially given the rapid urban expansion of Errachidia upstream.

Most important, the end of the natural flow of the Wadi Ziz has had distinctive negative consequences for the life of the Tafilalt oasis. The oasis is no longer fed by the occasional flood or heavy spring runoff in the Ziz. Like a sponge that has become dry, the Tafilalt has become less moist and less healthy since the inception of the dam.

Although the effects of the drying out of the Tafilalt are slow, they are incremental. Many people point to fewer date palms and say that the lack of underground water is responsible. Others have done the obvious, and invested in diesel motor pumps. They then build wells down to the water table and pump at will, further lowering the water table.[30]

The Tafilalt oasis is at a crossroads. There is no going back to an earlier time or undoing the technology that now exists. The events and trends of the last half of the twentieth century have removed the ecological equilibrium established for more than 1,000 years. Filalis stand at an open door.

Notes

1. A detailed picture of regional protohistory is outlined in Jacques-Meunie (1982: 54-55, 159-188). In general, evidence for agriculture in the Tafilalt exists back to at least 1000 B.C., and perhaps twice that long.

2. The Alaouite dynasty emerged from the Tafilalt to rule over Morocco in the 1630s. In the second half of the 1800s, Alaouite sultans Sidi Mohammed and Moulay Hassan implemented impressive irrigation technologies and generally improved the quality of life in their Saharan frontiers. Echoes of Alaouite engineering long lingered. The French conquest of the Tafilalt in 1933 was followed by the rediscovery of the utility of the Alaouite works and the effort of the Protectorate to restore them to life.

3. Significant investments have been made in the region, although it is located on the Moroccan periphery. These efforts have focused on building and managing a dam on the major water course of the Tafilalt, the Oued Ziz. A new basis of change, as sweeping as any in the past, has been established.

4. The single best reference for the physical geography of the Tafilalt is Margat (1962).

5. This figure is for the contiguous palm oasis directly surrounding Rissani. It does not include outlying plantations such as Oulad Zohra and does not include Erfoud.

6. The Ziz-Gheris is similar to the Oued Draa to the west and the Oued Daoura to the east in that their channels, worked by the tremendous quantities of water flowing south out of the Atlas in Pleistocene times, are clear far out into the Sahara. Water rarely travels in the Daoura (Algeria), but a constellation of oases marks its course and its underground water supplies. Likewise, water rarely flows beyond the inhabited portions of the Ziz-Gheris (that is, the Tafilalt) or the Draa at Mhamid. The flow of water to those points was, until modern times and the construction of dams along them, relatively reliable.

7. Rainfall figures are from Ruhard (1977: 363, Table 8.3); and from Margat (1962: 71-73).

8. Calculated by Joly, potential evapotranspiration for Rissani ranges from 212 mm in July to 12 mm in January and totals 1,159 mm per year. Margat (1962: 76).

9. Evidence for the analysis of the Tafilalt environment comes in part from historical sources as well as field reconnaissance and satellite and air photo data accompanying a continuous archaeological project at the ruins of Sijilmassa. The joint project of the Moroccan Department of Antiquities and Middle Tennessee State University (USA) held its second season of digging at Sijilmassa in May-July 1992. This project began in 1988 and is conducted locally by Dr. Lahcen Taouchikht, Director of the Center for Alaouite Studies at Rissani. Dr. Taouchikht; Prof. Ron Messier, head of the American unit of the Sijilmassa Project; and Dr. Dale Lightfoot, also a member of the Sijilmassa Project, have contributed ideas and substance to this chapter.

10. Foremost among these was Ibn Hawqal (Kitab Surat al-ard, "Description of the Earth") who visited in the 950s. Al Bakri, who never visited Sijilmassa, included it anyway in the Kitab al-Massalik wa-l-Mamalik ("Book of Itineraries and Kingdoms," 1068). Like others to follow, such as Al-Idrissi in the 1290s, Al Bakri relied heavily on Ibn Hawqal and a scattering of others who actually travelled to the Tafilalt. Together their descriptions of Sijilmassa paint a portrait of life in the caravan city some 200 years after its establishment.

11. Monteil (1968: 42). The Monteil translation of Al-Bakri has been used throughout.

12. Quoted in Taouchikht (1989: 50).

13. On the critical elements of the model North African Islamic town plan, see F. Stambouli and A. Zghal, "Urban life in Precolonial North Africa," 1976. The outlines of Sijilmassa as a model Islamic city is discussed in Taouchikht (1989: 106-127). Taouchikht enumerates Sijilmassa's waterworks for drinking water, planned streets and alleys, great central mosque, market at or near the center, specific quarters for different ethnic groups, walled fortifications, public buildings, and studios and other places for artisans and scholars.

14. Transsaharan trade existed long before the emergence of Sijilmassa. Roman accounts speak of the barter trade conducted for gold in Africa.

15. Messier (1974) gives an idea of the quantity and direction of the flow of gold outward from Sijilmassa during the Almoravid period (1054-1148 A.D.).

16. Ibn Hawqal, a Baghdadi merchant who was in the employ of the Fatimids and was in effect on a covert reconnaissance mission during his several-month stay in Sijilmassa in the 950s, estimated that the city produced one-half the revenue of the entire Fatimid state. (Ibn Hawqal, 1948: 97).

17. See Jacques-Meunie (1982: 296-297).

18. Jacques-Meunie suggests (1982: 296-297) that heightened water scarcity and the evolution of levees along the Ziz may have played a role in the disintegration of Sijilmassa. Levees, she suggests, were breached and disastrous flood(s) occurred. However, no indication of these phenomena exist in either history or archaeological findings thus far produced.

19. The tenth-century traveller Al-Mas'udi described Sijilmassa as having a great main artery a half-day's walk long (Taouchikht, 1989: 119). Oral sources in the Tafilalt today say that the ancient city was a half-day's walk long for a man and a full-day's walk long for a woman.

20. Monteil (1968: 42). Taouchikht (1989: 108) cites Al-Idrissi, Al-'Umari, and Al-Muqaddassi as promoting the view of Sijilmassa as a single, coherent city.

21. *Qsour* (pl); *qsar* (s): literally "castle" in Arabic, is used throughout North Africa to indicate the compact villages of the northern Sahara. *Qsour* range in population from a few tens of people to several thousands; they are often subdivided into ethnic quarters. The adobe *qsar* is often walled and embellished by architectural motifs decorating exterior surfaces. There are approximately 120 *qsour* in the Tafilalt today.

22. Margat (1962: 25). Increased deposition in the Soltanian period of the Quaternary heightened the general convex nature of the Tafilalt basin and pushed the Ziz eastward to be in what is now called the Oued Amerbouh, the oued which runs along the eastern side of the Tafilalt basin.

23. So it is that the Oued Ziz as seen today in the Tafilalt is merely a diversionary canal. From its diversion at Erfoud to the southern end of the Tafilalt, the Ziz flows through a relic channel or channels made by human means. The true bed of the Ziz lies along the eastern edge of the oasis in what has become known as the Oued Amerbouh. The dry streambeds of the Amerbouh and the Oued Ziz join just south of the foot of the Tafilalt oasis. On close inspection, the morphology of the channel of the Ziz through the oasis bears little resemblance to the natural stream channels of the Tafilalt, namely the Gheris and the Amerbouh.

24. Al Bakri's geographical description of Sijilmassa is interesting at this point: "The city of Sijilmassa is located at the confluence of two streams, both of which

arise at the springs of Ajlef. Not far from Sijilmassa, this sole river divides into two branches, one of which goes by the city on the east and the other on the west." (Monteil: 42). The springs of Ajlef are generally held to have been north of Erfoud along the Ziz. It may be that the two streams Al Bakri refers to are the Amerbouh (that is, the true Ziz), and the diverted Ziz (which fronts the western edge of the site of Sijilmassa as it was when al-Bakri saw it in 950). The springs he mentions ("Ajlef") are not known in the region today but could well have been just upstream from Erfoud at a place along the Ziz known as Timdhrine.

25. Margat (1962:91).

26. Margat (1962:191) believed that *rhettera* entered the Tafilalt in the 1500s — more than a century after the destruction of Sijilmassa.

27. Tafilalt population estimates and census counts are incorporated into the following table (Taouchikht, 1989:26-27):

1890	45,000	1960	47,133
1910	47,000	1971	55,994
1951	51,282	1982	67,065

28. *Population Légale de Maroc* (1983:81) and Taouchikht (1989:27).

29. *Population Légale de Maroc* (1983:45).

30. Recognizing that the water table of the Tafilalt needed strong replenishment following the prolonged drought of the 1980s, the authorities closed off all other diversions from the Ziz and allowed several artificial "floods" to go down the Ziz in the late 1980s. The single most important improvement that could now be made would be to protect Ziz irrigation from evaporation as it flows through the "government canals." Irrigation techniques other than sheet flow across the land could save immense amounts of water.

References

Boubekraoui, M., and C. Carvemac. 1986. "Le Tafilalt d'aujourd'hui: régression écologique et sociale d'une palmeraie sud marocaine." *Revue de Géographie du Sud-Ouest* 57:449-463.

Bouderbala, N. et al. 1984. *La Question Hydraulique. 1: Petite et Moyenne Hydraulique au Maroc.* Rabat: Presses de Graphitec.

———. 1965. *Kitabl Surat al-'Ard,* ed. Saad Zaghlul. Beirut.

Combe, M. 1977. "Le Haut Atlas calcaire," in Royaume du Maroc, Ministère du Commerce, Division de la Géologie, ed., *Ressources en Eau du Maroc. Tome 3: Domaines Atlasique et Sud-atlasique.* Rabat: Editions du Service Géologique du Maroc.

Ibn Batuta. 1971. *The Travels of Ibn Batuta.* New York: Lenox Hill.

Ibn Hawqal. 1948. *Kitab Surat al Ard,* tr. J. H. Kramers and G. Wiet. Paris: Editions Maisonneuve.

Jacques-Meunie, D. 1982. *Le Maroc Saharien des Origines a 1670.* 2 vols. Paris: Librairie Klincksieck.

Margat, Jean. 1962. *Mémoire Explicatif de la Carte Hydrogéologique au 1/50000 de la Plaine du Tafilalt.* Rabat: Editions du Service Géologique du Maroc (Notes et Mémoire du Service Geologique, No. 150 bis).

Mezzine, Larbi. 1987. *Le Tafilalt: Contribution a l'Histoire du Maroc aux XVIIe et XVIIIe Siècles.* Rabat: Publications de la Faculté des Lettres et des Sciences Humaines (Série Thèses 13).

Monteil, Vincent. 1968. "Al-Bakri (Cordoue 1068), routier de l'Afrique Blanche et noire du Nord-Ouest: Traduction nouvelle de seize chapitres." *Bulletin de l'I.F.A.N.* 300 (B-1):38-116.

Royaume du Maroc. 1983. Ministère du Plan, de la Formation des cadres et de la Formation Professionnelle. *Population Légale du Maroc.* Rabat: Direction de la Statistique.

Royaume du Maroc, Ministère du Commerce; Division de la Géologie. 1977. *Ressources en Eau du Maroc. Vol. 3: Domaines Atlasique et Sud-atlasique.* Rabat: Editions du Service Géologique du Maroc 231.

Stambouli, F., and A. Zghal. 1976. "Urban Life in Precolonial North Africa." The British Journal of Sociology 27(1):1-20.

Taouchikht, Lahcen. 1989. *Etude Ethno-Archéologique de la Céramique du Tafilalet (Sijilmassa): Etat de Question.* Ph.D. thesis (unpublished), University of Provence, Aix-Marseille I.

PART TWO

Desertification and Land Degradation

4

Desertification and Degradation of Algeria's Environmental Resources

Keith Sutton and Salah Zaimeche

The 1980s witnessed heightened international concern for the environment. Although this concern has encompassed the misuse of resources, the governments and citizens of developing nations often appear unaware of the damage being done to their ecosystems in the name of progress. Among these nations is Algeria, where oil wealth has masked failings of agricultural production while, in concert with industrialization, providing a veneer of economic development at the expense of the environment.

This chapter examines the tragic dimensions of environmental degradation in Algeria. It draws upon individual observations and reports during the 1980s and early 1990s of Algeria's media—primarily newspaper and television, which are employed to disseminate official information. Environmental problems examined include desertification, soil erosion, soil salinization, excessive cultivation and overgrazing of marginal lands, losses of agricultural land to urbanization and industrial pollution, deforestation, freshwater and marine pollution, growing water scarcities, and the increasing risk of drought.

Desertification

Desertification has been defined as the impoverishment of terrestrial ecosystems under the impact of man. The process of deterioration in these ecosystems can be measured by reduced productivity of desirable plants, undesirable alterations in the biomass and diversity of micro and macro fauna and flora, accelerated soil deterioration, and increased hazards for human occupancy (Dregne 1983:4-5). Extensive study of desertification was conducted during the 1970s, prompted by the 1969-1973 drought in the Sahel of West Africa. Results of this research were presented at the 1977 UN Conference on Desertification.

Hare and others (1977:332-346) suggested that desertification "is a human phenomenon that arises from society's search for secure livelihoods in dry environments." Warren preferred to emphasize "ecological change which takes place only on the desert's edges" (1984:335), but agreed that to equate desertification with the movement of the desert edge is too simplistic. Desertification is indicated, rather, by meteorological indices or evidence from degraded vegetation formations or soil systems with the caveat that *if anything is certain at the desert edge, it is uncertainty*. Although there is some doubt that droughts are responsible *per se* for desertification, it is generally agreed that droughts exaggerate the harmful effects of improper land management (Dregne 1983:4). As Dregne observed: "the deadly combination is land abuse during good periods and its continuation during periods of deficient rainfall" (1983:8).

Most of these writers consider human activity rather than climatic change to be responsible for desertification. "Recent desertification," Hare noted (1977:333), "cannot be ascribed to variation of the long-term macroclimate" but to human misuse of land resources such as overgrazing during a period of temporary drought.

The 1992 UN Conference on Environment and Development held in Rio de Janeiro considered desertification "land degradation in arid, semi-arid, and dry subhumid areas resulting from various factors including climatic variations and human activities" (UNEP 1992). The UN Conference departed from earlier ideas that desertification was irreversible. Other authorities contend, nevertheless, that no consensual definition of desertification has been reached, nor any conclusive explanation of its dynamics or of the best means for controlling its spread (Bakhit 1993). A growing number of scientists recommend discarding *desertification* and substituting the term *land degradation* (Warren and Agnew 1988).

Dregne (1983) mapped and tabulated the occurrence of desertification around the world, recognizing four classes of desertification: slight, moderate, severe, and very severe. Most of Algeria's Tell (northern coastal plains and mountain massifs) and High Plains regions may be categorized as suffering severe desertification. The Saharan Atlas Zone and the western High Plains suffer from moderate desertification; only the eastern Tell fringe appears unaffected by the problem. The Sahara, naturally, experiences slight desertification but is already hyperarid (Figure 4.1). To add to this, irrigated areas of Algeria frequently suffer problems of salinization and waterlogging. Altogether, Dregne estimates that about 90 percent of

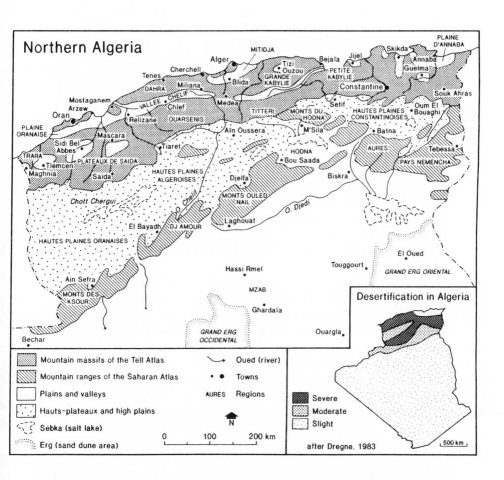

FIGURE 4.1 Locations and Desertification in Northern Algeria. *Source*: Zaimeche and Sutton 1990, reprinted with permission of John Wiley and Sons.

Algeria's rainfed cropland and pastoral rangeland is affected by desertification (Table 4.1).

The Destruction of Algeria's Land Resources

Experience has shown that often a combination of adverse factors, notably the inappropriate use of soils, has led to disastrous outcomes

TABLE 4.1 Estimates of Algerian Land Affected by Desertification (early 1980s)

	Total area (ha)	Area affected (ha)
Irrigated Land	292,000	65,000
Rainfed Cropland	4,500,000	4,000,000
Pastoral Rangeland	83,000,000	76,500,000

Source: Adapted from Dregne 1983: 183.

whereby affected land resources were lost forever. Examples include parts of the Fertile Crescent of the Middle East, and Sudan's Kordofan Plains. When fossil soils erode, as they so often do in Algeria, the resource loss is permanent, and it cannot be remedied under present soil-forming conditions.[1] Furthermore, soil is essential for its moisture-retention capacity; thus the soil erosion problem is compounded by edaphic drought as more of the rainfall runs off or percolates rather than remaining near the surface available for plant growth.

In Algeria arable land has been adversely affected by two major factors: the marginal semi-arid nature of the country and socioeconomic changes that have occurred in recent decades. As a consequence land degradation has reached alarming proportions. The useful northern Tell strip of Algeria is too narrow for modern demands. It nonetheless comprises most urban areas, most industrial and agricultural activities, and, above all, most of the population. Arable land accounts for only 6.96 million ha of the total area of 238 million ha and is chiefly concentrated in this northern Tell strip.[2] Very little land is left in reserve as the land resources of the Tell strip are depleted.

Algeria suffered from overexploitation and population pressure during French occupation (1830-1962). Colonization deprived Algerians of their best lands and pushed them into marginal areas. The overexploitation of these margins by a rapidly increasing population has caused them to deteriorate. Large areas have been completely degraded.

This degradation of land continued following independence and took many forms. It was estimated in the early 1980s that soil erosion claimed a yearly average of 36,000 ha (*Révolution Africaine* 19-25 February 1987). The Minister for the Environment stated that the total land area under threat of desertification stood at approximately 20 million ha (*El Moudjahid* 4 December 1980). Despite these dangers the country has been pursuing a policy aiming at self-sufficiency in food production. The outcome may well be even greater destruction to land resources. It was estimated in 1988 that 1.1 million ha of marginal lands are cropped each year (*Actualité Economique* August 1988).

In the *wilaya* (administrative region) of Tlemcen uncontrolled use of marginal lands has caused the desert to make an alarming "advance," with desert sands and more xerophytic vegetation recorded a mere 50 km from the town center of Tlemcen. In some parts of the *wilaya*, lands continue to be overexploited despite very low cereal yields (200-300 kg/ha). Some farmers, in an effort to evade official attempts to control overuse by restricting the area cultivated, tilled "one hectare in daytime and twenty at night" (*El Moudjahid* 15 May 1989: 13).

Similarly, the steppeland pastures have suffered from destructive overgrazing. Traditionally the slow movements of the herds allowed the grasslands to regenerate; now, with the widespread use of trucks to transport livestock, large areas of pasture have lost all vegetation cover. Estimates in 1989 suggested 720,000 ha of steppelands have been lost in recent years and more land is under threat. Uprooting vineyards, as in the Oran Region, has also contributed to land degradation by exposing the fragile soils to erosion. In 1993 Algerian television reported that large tracts of former steppeland had become competely barren.

Farther south, inappropriate agricultural activities in Saharan oases have served to increase soil salinization. Dubost (1986) has estimated that on average 8-10 metric tons of salt accumulate annually per hectare of agricultural land in Algeria's marginal Saharan lands.

Further loss of agricultural land has resulted from inappropriate industrial and urban developments that have destroyed thousands of hectares, often of the best lands. The SONACOME state engineering corporation, producing engines for cranes and construction vehicles at Ain S'Mara southwest of Constantine, was established on farmlands that formerly boasted the region's highest yields. The housing program of El Khroub, near Constantine, has been located on some of the best grain-producing land of the region. In Skikda the establishment of refinery and gas plants has likewise deprived the region of much good agricultural land. Similarly the Mitidja Plain has been invaded by housing, industrial, and infrastructural projects. Between 1962 and 1989 the *wilaya* of Blida, largely in the Mitidja, lost 10,000 ha of agricultural land to urban and industrial development (*Algérie Actualité* 21-27 December 1989). Politicians have frequently denounced such losses, and Ordinance 75/03 of August 27, 1975, was passed to forbid the use of agricultural land for other purposes. In the early 1980s there was even a campaign to demolish houses constructed illegally on agricultural land, notably in the Mitidja Plain.

Yet more agricultural land in the Mitidja is still fast disappearing. On a visit to the *wilaya* of Blida in April 1989 the Algerian prime minister drew attention to the uncontrolled urbanization of the Mitidja Plain, and again called for urgent action. Elsewhere in El Milia, in the *wilaya* of Jijel, an immense new steel complex is slated to be positioned on hundreds of hectares of the best available agricultural land. Some of the regions worst affected by urban or industrial growth are in western Algeria. Television reports in 1989 showed that in Ain Témouchent the ENAL detergent complex has completely destroyed a vast area of arable land (*TV Algiers* 6 June 1989). Not far from there dust, smoke, and waste from the Ghazaouet zinc electrolyte complex have destroyed all wildlife in the vicinity and have rendered formerly arable land unproductive and barren.

Because of these losses of land and the rapid increase in population, the ratio of agricultural land to people, already low, has further deteriorated, falling from 0.75 ha per person in 1963 to 0.40 ha per person in 1979 (*El Moudjahid* 12 October 1989). Extrapolating, this ratio would reach the alarming figure of only 0.14 ha/person by the year 2000. In the absence of reserves of potentially arable or readily reclaimable land, any extension of agriculture will invariably involve clearing the remaining forest areas or exploiting marginal land on the desert fringes.

Under present conditions Algeria has little chance of reversing this process of land degradation unless radical measures are taken. Television reports praise a few projects that, at high cost in terms of finance and effort, have managed to cultivate limited plots of desert land. Elsewhere, all over the country thousands of hectares of good arable land are fast disappearing. Several projects designed to "green the desert" have been launched amid great publicity and euphoria.

Often these have failed lamentably. One such project at Abadla, southwest of Béchar, attracted much publicity when launched in the early 1970s. It was proposed that the Abadla region supply vegetables and fruits, with 17,000 ha to be cultivated in the initial stages and with possible extensions later. Nevertheless, in time this "El Dorado" began to give way to desertification. The area reclaimed from the desert reached 5,400 ha, then began to shrink in the early 1980s to a mere 2,000 ha. The reservoirs constructed to irrigate these lands have practically dried up as climatic constraints have been ignored by the planners. The Djorf Torba Dam can now supply little more than Béchar's urban water supply, let alone all agriculture (Dubost 1986). The U.S. firm that initially managed the project left in 1975. Its replacement, an Algerian enterprise working with national service labor, proved wasteful and bureaucratic, and the whole project fell into decay in the early 1980s.

More recently another project was launched in southern Algeria to rehabilitate some 10,000 ha. Nevertheless, this scheme managed to reclaim a mere 1,700 ha, and that at very high cost (*Algérie Actualité* 26 January 1989-1 February 1989). Farther north a more ambitious project was launched at Benni Slimane in 1975. This was intended to improve more than 200,000 ha, spread over several *wilayate* (administrative regions) of central Algeria. Nevertheless, five years later and after considerable expense the project was abandoned as no longer feasible (*El Moudjahid* 4 May 1980). Similar failure affected the ambitious irrigation program that aimed at achieving the national goal of 500,000 ha of irrigated land by 1980. The two *Four Year Plans* of 1970-1973 and 1974-1977, despite considerable investment, attained only 34.0 percent and 24.0 percent of their respective targets as part of this wider irrigation program (RDAP/MPAT 1980). While agricultural land was being lost, and land reclamation schemes were failing, Algeria's vegetation cover, which helps protect the land, was also being badly affected.

Forests and Vegetation Cover

Algeria has a lower proportion of wooded surface area than its neighbors, Morocco and Tunisia, with less than 11 percent in scrubland and forests. These now cover less than 40 percent of the area originally forested. As forest vegetation cannot survive where annual rainfall is less than 300 mm, woodland is restricted to the more humid coastal uplands, especially the eastern parts, and to the summits of the Ouarsenis, Aurès, and Saharan Atlas. Even in such localities, forest vegetation often is not in balance with the summer aridity of the present climate and, once destroyed, does not regenerate but is replaced by secondary maquis or garrigue scrub that is better adapted to summer drought. In the hinterland of Algiers the last stage of degradation is formed by the dwarf palm known as *palmitto* (Wojterski 1990).

So the true forest stands of evergreen oak (*Quercus ilex*), cork oak (*Quercus suber*), and, at higher altitudes, cedar (*Cedrus atlantica*) are diminishing despite the activities of the 120 Chantiers Populaires de Reboisement, which in the 1960s planted about 64 million trees (about 450 square kilometers [km²] of woodland) with the aid of the UN World Food Program (Viratelle 1970). More generally there is an urgent need to reforest more than 2 million ha to protect soils and slopes, but this has been neglected. One indication of the extent of this neglect is that the *Annuaire Statistique de l'Algérie* regularly devotes only one page to forestry matters, and that is shared with data on alfalfa production. According to this source, the Fonds National Forestier, or state forests, amount to 4,003,650 ha, of which 3,670,000 ha are in northern Algeria (ONS 1991). These figures are gross overestimates and probably date from the French occupation period. The maximum is nearer 3,000,000 ha of mostly degraded forests.

Degradation of vegetation stems from Algeria's complete mishandling and misunderstanding of the question of desertification. The fight against desertification and campaigns for reforestation should have been given higher priority by Algerian planners. This has not been the case. Instead,

Algerian administrators have held the view that the desert makes a frontal advance and that a greenbelt or *barrage vert* alone could stop it.

In the early 1970s the Algerian government revived an earlier scheme to establish a green barrier of trees along a 1,500 km belt to the north of the Saharan Atlas. With a width of 10-20 km this *barrage vert* would eventually add 3 million ha of forest to Algeria's depleted forest area. The planned alignment of the barrier was from near Ain Sefra in the west, past El Bayadh, Aflou, Djelfa, Bou Saada, and the Hodna Mountains to Batna in the east. One official Front de Libération Nationale source suggests some progress with 3,500 ha a year planted, 1967-1978, and then 9,500 ha planted annually, 1979-1982 (Commission Nationale 1983). This represented a growing proportion of Algeria's total national reforestation, amounting to 19,000 ha annually, 1967-1978, and 54,000 ha annually, 1979-1982. The use of cheap National Service labor assisted this limited program, but the contribution of the army left something to be desired. The overuse of Aleppo pine was not always environmentally appropriate and instances of new plantations perishing have been noted.

From the outset there was much skepticism about the effectiveness of the proposed *barrage vert*. Stewart (1974) made an early evaluation. He noted that the microclimate within the linear plantation would be modified in a favorable way. But this amelioration would not extend beyond the barrier to modify the regional climate. The barrier would not stop desertification to the north of the linear forest. Any increased precipitation would be marginal and would probably fall south of the barrier, given the prevailing winds. Le Houérou (1977: 417) agreed with Stewart that "greenbelts can have no climatic consequences except in their immediate vicinity at distances shorter than half a kilometre." Wind speed is reduced only at a distance of 2 to 5 times the height of the trees to windward and 20 to 30 times leeward. The width of the shelterbelt has no impact on this. Warren (1984) considered the *barrage vert* a ludicrous scheme, arguing that overgrazing would occur on either side of the belt of trees unless social changes were introduced. Indeed, in its infancy the *barrage vert* would require strict protection from grazing. In any event, by the end of 1988 it was estimated that only 160,000 ha of the *barrage vert* had been planted (*Actualité Economique* October 1988). In comparison with the official goal of 3 million ha of forest and in view of the publicity the *barrage vert* has received, these results are miniscule.

Unfortunately, deforestation is not treated with any urgency nor has any committed, scientific, or rational response been undertaken. On the contrary, there often seems to be a total disregard of the many ways trees are destroyed. Clearance of woodland has been widespread around urban areas where the extension of the built-up areas and associated road networks has eaten into arable land, greenbelts, and woodland. The practice of burning trees from the inside by setting fire to the trunk — merely for fun — has reached alarming proportions. This vandalism has decimated large numbers of urban trees planted in French colonial times. In places such as Greater and Lesser Kabylia, fires are started by groups of arsonists and aggrieved graziers in concerted actions to stretch the fire services to the full.

Losses from fires have reached tragic levels. In summer 1983, the worst year so far, forests were ablaze throughout the country, and 102,592 ha were destroyed (*Révolution Africaine* 18 July 1986-24 July 1986). This scale of destruction was more critical than during the worst fires caused by napalm and explosive bombing in the War of Independence. If 1983 remains the worst, other years also had their destructive toll with 17,930 ha burnt in 1980 and 21,000 ha in 1988, up to August 30 (*El Moudjahid* 13 September 1988). By mid-November 1988 forests were still burning all over the country ("TV Reports" [Algiers] November 1988). Similarly, in 1990 serious forest fires raged all over the country, and tens of thousands of ha of cork oak and pine were lost. In July and August 1993 many serious fires were also recorded (*Le Monde* 10 August 1993). These affected large stretches of forest and five villages, and arsonists were arrested in connection with them.

If lack of awareness and selfishness play a major part in this destruction, the absence of strict legislation, as well as the action of some local authorities, also account for much of the damage. Many officials regard the implementation of strict legislation as unnecessary in view of the "lightness" of the offense. Others regard penalties to be imposed on offenders as relics of colonial legislation to be disregarded, avoided, and even rejected. The authorities, for their part, not only fail to see the dangers of deforestation or fail to take action but, even worse, they cause more destruction.

In early 1989, the *wilayate* of Jijel and Skikda were the scene of a massive clearing program to reclaim land for agriculture involving one of the last and most beautiful forests of holm oak trees. Similarly in March 1989, in the M'Sila region, the authorities saw the orchards as the only area for more urban development and so allowed the felling of hundreds of trees (*Horizons* 16 March 1989). The same disregard for woodland and orchards has occurred around most towns and cities, with the encroachment of Algiers to the east and south causing nearly total destruction of greenbelts and orchard trees. Shelter belt trees surrounding orchard groves reportedly have been logged as the price of wood has increased with growing scarcity. Lines of plane trees, cypress, poplars, and other species have disappeared from the landscape with relatively little official effort at their protection (*La Nation* 3-9 February 1992).[3]

While this process of destruction proceeds, campaigns for reforestation remain complete failures and do not make up for the losses. Between 1963 and 1982 about 560,000 ha were supposedly reforested, while forest losses were estimated at about 500,000 ha for the same period (*El Moudjahid* 21 March 1982). In fact reforestation programs often have taken the form of publicity campaigns, with hundreds of townsfolk reluctantly transported to the countryside, dressed in their best clothes, to plant trees in front of television cameras. Whatever was planted, the totals generally inflated by party officials, was done carelessly or haphazardly. Consequently rates of successful reforestation in some *wilayate* were as low as 5 percent (*El Moudjahid* 18 November 1980).

Water Stress and the Pollution of Algeria's Water Resources

Frequent drought since 1980 has focused attention on the vulnerability and finiteness of Algeria's water resources. An "*économie de l'eau*" ought to be established but the complacency of the "economy of oil" continues to prevail. Out of an estimated precipitation total of 65 billion cubic meters (m^3), 47 billion are lost through evaporation. This leaves 15 billion m^3 in surface runoff and 3 billion in underground aquifers after infiltration (Arrus 1985). Perennes (1986, 1990, 1991) suggests a higher figure of 19.12 billion m^3, of which 6.7 billion are in underground aquifers. Of this total, Perennes argues that only 8.5 billion m^3 are "regularisable," that is, guaranteed to be usable 9 years out of 10.

Thus the constraint of physical limits is fast approaching. Given the growing demand from an increasing population, Algeria will likely experience serious water scarcity by the year 2000 and, with other North African countries will, according to Falkenmark (1989),"have arrived at absolute water scarcity by 2025." Algeria could well run out of water before it exhausts its oil and gas resources.

As Allan (1992: 378) stresses, "the dangerous fallacy underlying agricultural and especially food production of the countries of the Middle East is that water is free." This fallacy is encouraged by underpricing of water at 1.65 dinars/m^3 compared with an average price in Europe of about 30 dinars (*El Watan* 26 March 1992). If the real costs of water in Algeria were properly considered water would be allocated to appropriate uses of greater benefit to the economy. These would bring an optimum return now and in the future according to sustainable economic principles.

In the 1960s Algeria's only polluted river was the Oued El Harrach, east of Algiers. By the early 1990s, because of the inappropriate location of many new industries, the level of water pollution had become disastrous. The discharging of industrial and domestic waste into rivers has reached such a scale that it is often impossible to enter any urban area without having to suffer obnoxious smells and offensive views of black, narrow waterways filled with rubbish and pollutants. A 1986 media report (*Révolution Africaine* 15-21 November 1986) gave a bleak account of the situation. Daily in Annaba the Seybouse river was receiving 50,000 m³ of effluent containing sulfuric acid from the city's phosphate complex while the nearby Wadi Saf Saf, near Skikda, has been seriously polluted both by dust from the marble complex and by oil, tar, and other waste from the refinery. In Azzaba, again near Skikda, all water resources have been dangerously affected by waste from the mercury complex, making local water usage very risky. In western Algeria, near Mostaganem, the SONIC paper complex has been polluting the area with caustic foam, so that swimming has had to be banned at all local beaches.

In the late 1980s the situation worsened. In the west, the Maghnia ceramics complex polluted nearby water resources, and the Wadi Rhiou, near Chleff, was reported to contain increasing amounts of waste salts and metals such as lead and copper. The river Chleff was reported to contain various pollutants coming from the five *wilayte* it passes through. Its waters are filled with numerous impurities and metals, among them zinc, chrome, and acetone (*El Moudjahid* 16 April 1989). Chrome comes from the washing of leather at the SONIPEC factory in Ain Defla, carbon dioxide from cement plants, and other toxic wastes from SOGEDIA in El Khemis. Measures to alleviate the pollution problem along the Wadi Chleff have been sidelined for lack of funds (*Le Matin* 14 January 1992).

In central Algeria, around Algiers, more than 100 industrial enterprises emit waste into the wadis Smar and El Harrach. The latter has become notorious as the most polluted river in the country. As a consequence samples of sea water and shellfish taken between Algiers and Bordj El Kiffan, farther east, are heavily contaminated (*Révolution Africaine* 17 March 1989).

The Algerian organization "Friends of the Sea" has sampled 55 industrial units throughout the country. Thirteen of these emit lethal pollutants, 26 are deemed dangerous to health, 13 are potentially dangerous, and only 3 are considered safe. Out of a total of 133 communes bordering the Mediterranean Sea, 44 include industrial complexes with no systems for treating waste before it is released into the sea (*Horizons* 29 December 1992). By 1989 a total of 24 major wadis and 16 estuaries had been reported to receive yearly, on average, 500,000 tons of hydrocarbon wastes, 65,000 tons of waste from poultry industries, 54,000 tons of residues from the wine industry, and 30,000 tons of impurities from the edible oil industry (*Actualité Economique* March 1989). Solutions such as water recycling and water purification lag well behind requirements. Water purification plants are being operated well beyond their capacities and often break down. Thus in late 1988, out of 20 water purification stations only 2 were working properly. These occurrences threaten public health on a massive scale. The problems of water-related disease are widely underreported; nevertheless, 400 cases of typhoid were reported throughout the country in 1988 (*Horizons* 4 April 1989).

Drought, Desertification, and Rehabilitation

There long has been wide agreement that periodic droughts have served to intensify manufactured or "cultural" dessication: "Drought has simply administered the *coup de grâce*" (Hare et al. 1977: 377). It can "push" an already damaged agricultural or pastoral ecosystem to a state of more permanent degradation. A decade of increasingly frequent drought years (the 1980s), together with 20-30 years of agricultural and pastoral misuse under conditions of increasing population pressure and growing competition for scarce water resources, have served to degrade the Algerian environment to a potentially disastrous degree.

The recent cycle of drought years in Algeria and elsewhere is increasingly being interpreted as indicative of climatic change associated with global warming. Over much of North Africa this warming trend may be as much as a 4°C increase in the annual mean temperature (Beaumont 1989). A similar estimate by Le Houérou (1992) predicts temperature in the Mediterranean region will rise by 3°C plus or minus 1.5°C by the year 2050. The 1990 summer heat wave in Algeria, where the death toll from two months of heat wave attained 38 by late July, may well have been a portent of future summers (*The Guardian* 28 July 1990).

Rainfall changes associated with global warming scenarios are more difficult to predict. The predictions of a 30 percent rise or fall in precipitation levels over the next 50-100 years are speculative at best. Nevertheless, there is cause for concern in that much of the Mediterranean region's precipitation is influenced by interactions between the jet stream and orography. Changes in jet stream flows are virtually certain; and a northward shift of the main upper westerly flow could reduce the length of the rainy season, particularly in the western and central parts of the region (Jeftic, Milliman, and Sestini 1992). Nonetheless, even if precipitation levels varied little, future higher temperatures would increase evapotranspiration rates and so increase aridity.

Le Houérou (1992) estimates that the resulting rise in evapotranspiration would be 180-200 mm a year, thus increasing the soil moisture deficit in semi-arid zones. Global climatic models differ with respect to future precipitation levels in subtropical regions and are inconclusive about those predictions (Hansen 1988).

Less disagreement exists about the greater likelihood of more extreme climatic events, including droughts and heat waves together with a shift polewards of vegetation zones by 50-75 km per decade (Thompson 1989).

Both of these trends will add to Algeria's already urgent problems of desertification, especially when exacerbated by present misuse of environmental resources.

In view of the growing consensus that global warming has already begun it is worth briefly considering 1980s trends in Algeria's precipitation levels. Brulé and Fontaine (1986) stress the variability of Algeria's precipitation and note that deficits of 25-30 percent in a year are frequent. Three or 4 years out of any 10 will be deficit years. In the interior of the Oranais region Bisson and Callot (1985) record the destructiveness to nomadism of 8 successive years of drought since 1978. Similarly Aimé and Remaoun (1988) demonstrate that there has been a phase of drought at Tlemcen since 1975 with precipitation totals frequently falling well below the mean of the previous 30 years.

A range of precipitation totals in Table 4.2 reveals frequent below-average rainfall totals in the 1980s at stations as widely separated as Annaba, Skikda, Sétif, and Oran. Even wetter locations such as Algiers and Miliana can show deficit years. Many authors have stressed the considerable variation in precipitation in stations scattered across the Maghreb, with variances of 80 percent or more (Douguedroit 1988; Aimé and Remaoun 1988).

This variability extends to the mean precipitation values themselves. In Table 4.3 the 1951-1980 means are often lower than the 1913-1938 means, especially for eastern stations at Constantine, Annaba, and Skikda. Nevertheless, intermediate means for 1941-1970 confirm this variability with "cycles of drought" rather than a trend. Indeed, for Algeria, valid means may well require longer time periods than the conventional 30 years. Le Houérou (1986) has pointed out that stations at Algiers, Constantine, and Biskra have weather records for more than 100 years and that earlier analyses of these could not detect any long-term trend in rainfall, nor any cyclic behavior. Clusters of years with above- and below-average rainfall are detectable but display no predictable pattern. Perhaps the 1980s values represent another such disaster.

Is Recovery from Desertification Possible?

Can desertification be stopped and reversed? Dregne (1983) felt it could be, although he warned that anti-desertification programs should be part of a broader rural development program. As the situation in Algeria is worsening it is evident that current coping mechanisms are inadequate and changes in land management techniques are necessary. Pilot testing of different methods is desirable.

Hare (1977) advocated better climate monitoring, cloud seeding to try to increase rainfall, and especially research into the environment's "carrying

TABLE 4.2 Algerian Rainfall Totals (mm), 1980s

	1980	*1981*	*1985*	*1986*	*1987*	*1988*
Algiers	766	442	704	746	485	579
Annaba	637	464	551	836	617	582
Batna	409	241	463	355	328	206
Constantine	544	494	462	561	474	512
Djelfa	408	296	363	393	299	336
Miliana	850	378	739	1013	732	618
Oran	498	242	258	397	322	264
Setif	408	236	409	432	320	425
Skikda	796	551	629	847	819	706

Sources: ONS, *Annuaire Statistique de l'Algérie 1981, 1985-86, 1990*; NOAA 1987, 1988.

TABLE 4.3 Changing Mean Precipitation Values in the Twentieth Century (mm)

	1913-1938[a]	*1941-1970*	*1951-1980*
Algiers	672	702	763
Annaba	787	720	578
Batnan	n.d.	340	n.d.
Constantine	594	504	533
Djelfa[b]	308	384	254
Miliana	950	797	824
Oran	428	394	423
Setif	469	442	n.d.
Skikda	830	702	696

[a]Some are for shorter time periods.
[b]Omits December's average rainfall.

Sources: ONS, *Annuaire Statistique de l'Algérie 1981*; NOAA 1988, 1989; Mahrour 1970.

capacity" to help find sustained agricultural or pastoral yield strategies. They recognized the role of certain traditional, well-adapted land uses, including more flexible and mobile nomadic land-use systems in keeping with the variable nature of the environment. Dregne (1983) also advocated less pressure on fragile environments; better water management; the use of mixed livestock herds (including even the much-maligned goat); and restriction of fuelwood cutting and the firing of pastureland.

Le Houérou (1977) was more skeptical, recognizing that sometimes vegetation has been too damaged to recover. Focusing on the exponential growth of the population since the beginning of the twentieth century, Le Houérou (1986) sees little but a continuation of negative consequences for the environment. Based on his research in Algeria he recognizes that desertification can be practically irreversible in certain circumstances — for example, when rainfall is below 100-150 mm a year or when soils are shallow and easily eroded.

In theory increased plant cover will reduce erosion and desertification. Contour-plowing, fertilization, and the breaking-up of hardpans can all speed up natural recovery, as can the planting of drought-resistant fodder and fast-growing trees, such as eucalyptus, for use as shelterbelts. Another strategy is the promotion of dune stabilization.

Dregne (1983) offered a program to combat desertification, which he felt should have at least four components:

1. A national commitment to initiate and carry it through, which should mobilize the societal will;
2. The concentration of rehabilitation efforts in the most favorable areas where they are likely to have the greatest and most immediate impact;
3. The development of related small-scale agricultural industries; and
4. The improvement of the nation's economic and educational base.

It is pertinent to reflect that such labor-intensive programs of rural renovation or "Defense and Restoration of the Soil" schemes have existed in Algeria since the 1960s as described by Monjauze (1960, 1961); Stewart (1985); and Tiano (1967). In retrospect, the rejection of these programs in favor of an economic development strategy based on the exploitation of hydrocarbons and promotion of heavy "industrializing industries" will make 1990s efforts to reverse desertification all the more difficult and costly. In the mid-1980s Dubost (1986) estimated that to reclaim 1 ha of desert land would cost 50-80,000 dinars (1 dinar = 0.18 US $ in 1986) and the renovation of old palm groves 500 dinars per palm tree. A modest project to reclaim 70,000 ha for cereal cropping and 16,000 ha for horticulture would cost Algeria the equivalent of 25 percent of the total agricultural investment between 1980 and 1984. Earlier neglect will now prove to have been an expensive mistake.

Conclusions

This paper has discussed the various manifestations of environmental degradation in Algeria. There is accumulating evidence that the series of largely drought years in the 1980s could well portend drier and hotter climatic conditions as future global warming occurs. Environmental problems have been seriously exacerbated by society's misuse of water, soil, and vegetation resources. Physical marginality has been ignored in a "technocratic push" for economic development within an overall urban-industrial strategy that is overreliant on oil and gas resources. As the drops in oil prices of the 1980s revealed the fragility of the "industrializing industries" strategy, so too were the fragility, finiteness, and degradation of the country's environmental resources becoming apparent. Arguably the increased media coverage in newspapers and on television reflected a growing awareness on the part of some in the Algerian government of these environmental problems.

The Secretary of State for the Environment at an international meeting on the preservation of the environment held in February 1993 reported that the ecosystem in Algeria's steppes was threatening to break down completely within a few years. She also admitted to serious pollution of Algeria's wadis and underground aquifers (*El Watan* 8 February 1993). Nevertheless, government policies still lack coherence and do not provide an effective response to these environmental challenges. More generally, inappropriate policies have been implemented and environmental priorities ignored. Degradation threatens to reach tragic, irrecoverable dimensions. Unless radical policies are implemented in the immediate future the country appears headed for environmental disaster. It is no surprise that Algeria ranks on a "black list" of nations suffering "considerable harm" from soil erosion and degradation (Simmons 1989: 339).

The solutions can and ought to be manifold. The Algerian government could initiate harsher legal penalties for environmentally destructive practices. Recycling of refuse and waste, plastics, oils, metals, paper, and glass would recover materials that at present are deposited in forests and waterways. Other actions should include establishment of water purification plants for both used waste water and seawater, construction of artificial reservoirs to store runoff, and mobilization of unemployed youth in reforestation and land reclamation schemes. To complement these policies there is also the urgent need to devise an altogether new approach to development, one giving priority to assessment of environmental costs.

One major step toward this new approach could be the opening of a major university focusing on the arid zone, not merely an institute as is now the case with the Centre National de Recherche sur les Zones Arides at the University of Algiers. Such a specialized center would bring together arid-land experts, students, and equipment, and would benefit from focused federal support. Among its aims would be to devise coherent, well-planned responses to environmental challenges facing the country. Such an academic base would ensure that any development action or program undertaken would be based on proper study of all appropriate ecological factors. Algeria's present (1993-1994) political strife is undoubtedly pushing environmental considerations into the background. The country's need for development and economic growth remains paramount. Nevertheless, to ignore the undeviating pattern of severe desertification with its impending dangers could in time incur repercussions substantially more serious than those caused by prevailing political and economic difficulties.

Notes

1. The vulnerability of Algeria's ecosystems has been stressed by Côte (1983).

2. Only 500,000 of Northern Algeria's 38-40 million hectares (ha) receive more than 600 millimeters (mm) of rain and have slopes below 3 percent (Côte)

3. Symptomatic of national attitudes towards trees is an extensive report (*Algérie Actualité* 29 June 1989-5 July 1989) on the fate of the El Hamma Botanic Gardens in Algiers. These gardens were established in 1832 by the French and became one of the world's most important. In 1867 they contained 8,214 species of plants, native and exotic. By 1962 that number had fallen to 6,000. Then deterioration accelerated rapidly, and by 1989 only 1,500-2,000 species were left. In 1993 a project involving French cooperation commenced to rehabilitate these gardens.

References

Aimé, S., and K. Remaoun. 1988. "Variabilité climatique et steppisation dans le bassin de la Tafna (Oranie occidentale)." *Méditerranée* 63:43-51.

Allan, J. A. 1992. "Substitutes for water are being found in the Middle East and North Africa." *GeoJournal* 28:375-385.

Arrus, R. 1985. *L'Eau en Algérie de l'Impérialisme au Développement. 1830-1962.* Algiers/Grenoble: Office des Publications, Universitaires/Presses, Univ. de Grenoble.

Bakhit, A. H. 1993. "Desertification: reconciling intellectual conceptualisation and intervention effort." *Geojournal* 31:33-40.

Beaumont, P. 1989. *Environmental Management and Development in Drylands.* London: Routledge.

Bisson, J., and Y. Callot. 1985. "Des monts des Ksour au Grand Erg occidental. Adaptation ou disparition de la vie nomade," in P. R. Baduel, ed., *Désert et Montagne au Maghreb. Hommage à Jean Dresch.* Pp. 357-358. Aix-en-Provence: Edisud.

Brulé, J. C., and J. Fontaine. 1986. *L'Algérie: Volontarisme Etatique et Aménagement du territoire*. Tours: URBAMA.

Commission Nationale de Préparation du Vme. Congrès du Parti. 1983. *Evaluation des Plans de Développement*. Front de Libération Nationale.

Côte, M. 1983. *L'Espace Algérien: Les Prémices d'un Aménagement*. Algiers: Office de Publications Universitaire.

Douguedroit, A. 1988. "The recent variability of precipitation in north-western Africa," in S. Gregory, ed., *Recent Climatic Change. A Regional Approach*. Pp. 130-137. London: Bellhaven Press.

Dregne, H. E. 1983. *Desertification of Arid Lands*. Chur and London: Harwood Academic Publishers.

Dubost, D. 1986. "Nouvelles perspectives agricoles du Sahara algérien," in P. R. Baduel, ed., *Désert et Montagne au Maghreb. Hommage à Jean Dresch*. Pp. 339-358. Aix-en-Provence: Edisud.

Falkenmark, M. 1989. "The massive water scarcity now threatening Africa. Why isn't it being addressed?" *Ambio* 18:112-118.

Hare, F. K., R. W. Kates, and A. Warren. 1977. "The making of deserts: climate, ecology and society." *Economic Geography* 53:332-346.

Hansen, J. et al. 1988. "Global climatic changes as forecast by the Goddard Institute for Space Studies 3-dimensional model." *Journal of Geophysical Research* 93: 9341-9346.

Jeftic, L., J. D. Milliman, and G. Sestini, eds. 1992. *Climatic Change and the Mediterranean*. London: Edward Arnold.

Le Houérou, H. 1977. "Biological recovery versus desertization." *Economic Geography* 53:413-420.

———. 1986. "The desert and arid zis of Northern Africa," in M. Evenari, I. Noy-Meir, and D. W. Goodall, eds., *Ecosystems of the World 12B. Hot Deserts and Arid Shrublands. B*. Pp. 101-147. Amsterdam: Elsevier.

———. 1992. "Vegetation and land use in the Mediterranean basin by the year 2050: a prospective study," in L. Jeftic, J. D. Milliman, and G. Sestini, eds., *Climatic Change and the Mediterranean*. Pp. 175-232. London: Edward Arnold.

Mahrour, M. 1970. *Recherches Cartographiques pour un Atlas Pratique de l'Algérie*. Thèse de Troisième Cycle, Université d'Alger.

Monjauze, A. 1960. "Buts et principes de la DRS en pays aride et semi-aride." *Agriculture Algérienne* (Algiers) 1.

———. 1961. "Rénovation rurale en Afrique du Nord." *Développement Africaine* (Paris), Special Issue.

NOAA (National Oceanic and Atmospheric Administration). 1987, 1988, 1989. *Monthly Climatic Data for the World*. Asheville, N.C.: National Climatic Data Center.

Perennes, J. J. 1986. "La politique hydro-agricole de l'Algérie." *Maghreb-Machrek* 111:57-76.

———. 1990. "Les politiques de l'eau au Maghreb: d'une hydraulique minière à une gestion sociale de la rareté." *Revue de Géographie de Lyon* 65:11-20.

———. 1991. "Evolution de la notion de rareté de l'eau au Maghreb: regards d'un économiste," in URBAMA, *L'Eau et la Ville dans les Pays du Bassin Méditerranéen et de la Mer Noire*. Pp. 29-41. Tours: Fasc. de Recherches No. 22.

ONS (Office National des Statistiques). 1991. *Annuaire Statistique de l'Algérie (No. 14) 1990*. Algiers: ONS.

RDAP/MPAT. 1980. *Synthèse du Bilan Economique et Social de la Décennie 1967-78*. Algiers: République Democratique Algérienne Populaire, Ministère du Plan et de l'Aménagement du Territoire.

Simmons, I. G. 1989. *Changing the Face of the Earth*. Oxford: Basil Blackwell.

Stewart, P. J. 1974. "Un nouveau climagramme pour l'Algérie et son application au Barrage Vert." *Bulletin de la Sociéte d'Histoire Naturelle de l'Afrique du Nord* 65: 239-252.

———. 1985. "Halt erosion or migrate: the Algerian peasant at the crossroads." IDS Discussion Paper No. 69.

Thompson, R. D. 1989. "Short-term climatic change: evidence, causes, environmental consequences and strategies for action." *Progress in Physical Geography* 13:315-347.

Tiano, A. 1967. *Le Maghreb Entre les Mythes*. Paris: PUF.

UNEP (United Nations Environmental Programme). 1992. *Status of Desertification and Implementation of the United Nations Plan of Action to Combat Desertification*. Nairobi: UNEP.

Viratelle, G. 1970. *L'Algérie Algérienne*. Paris: Editions Economie et Humanisme.

Warren, A., 1984. "The problems of desertification," in J. L. Cloudsley-Thompson, ed., *Sahara Desert*. Oxford: Pergamon.

Warren, A., and C. Agnew. 1988. "An Assessment of Desertification and Land Degradation in Arid and Semi-Arid Areas." Paper No. 2. International Institute for Environment and Development.

Wojterski, T. W. 1990. "Degradation stages of the oak forests in the area of Algiers." *Vegetatio* 87: 135-143.

Zaimeche, S. E., and K. Sutton. 1990. "The degradation of the Algerian environment through economic and social 'development' in the 1980's." *Land Degradation and Rehabilitation* 2:317-324.

Newspapers and Magazines Cited

Actualité Economique, Algiers (monthly)
Algérie Actualité, Algiers (weekly)
El Moudjahid, Algiers (daily)
El Watan, Algiers (daily)
Horizons, Algiers (weekly)
La Nation, Algiers (weekly)
Le Matin, Algiers (daily)
Révolution Africaine, Algiers (weekly)

5

Land Degradation in Tunisia: Causes and Sustainable Solutions

Sadok Bouzid

Over the past few decades central and southern Tunisia have undergone unprecedented environmental degradation and desertification. The climatic severity and uncertainty characterizing these regions have been exacerbated by recent socioeconomic shifts, particularly the transformation of land use systems.[1] Mechanized agriculture is fast expanding at the expense of the best pastoral zones. Livestock are placing increased pressure on diminishing rangeland. Woody vegetation is rapidly disappearing for fuel, fencing, and other purposes. Profound socioeconomic shifts are transforming a traditionally nomadic population into a sedentary population.

Such developments increase the fragility of Tunisia's ecosystems, further weaken their abilities to regenerate and produce, and precipitate different processes of degradation leading to the rapid advance of desertification.[2] Sand has now spread over vast agricultural areas, engulfing oases, villages, roads, and other infrastructures. And salinization has occurred in soils in irrigated areas increasingly exposed to brackish waters, rendering these soils barren.

To meet these challenges Tunisia has for several decades undertaken a variety of programs. These include dune fixation, reforestation, rangeland improvement, storage of runoff waters, and measures to prevent salinization. A national strategy for combating desertification has been developed under the authority of the Ministry of Agriculture through its *Direction de la Forêt* and the *Institut des Régions Arides* in Médenine. This strategy encompasses the inventory of renewable natural resources, professional personnel training, desertification monitoring, public information campaigns, and development projects. Unfortunately, these programs are encountering difficulties relating to basic concepts, techniques used, and follow-up. This chapter provides a comprehensive examination of environmental degradation and desertification in Tunisia.

Aeolian Erosion and Sand Expansion

The Present Situation

The winds of southern Tunisia follow a seasonal rhythm. In winter the dominant winds blow from inland to the sea. In the summer this regime is reversed. These winds are generally dry. The sky is usually clear but frequently laden with dust and fine sand particles. Aeolian erosion occurs in southern Tunisia in three successive phases. First, soil particles are lifted from the surface by the aerodynamic action of the wind, according to Bagnold's formula (the volume of the displaced soil is proportional to the cube of the wind velocity). Second, during the transfer phase, the distance that soil is carried depends on the size and density of its particles. This transfer phase can involve several thousands of kilometers (km). Third, the sedimentation phase results from the loss of power of the aeolian flux and is influenced by the size and density of particles. The earliest deposits are composed of layers of sand, which ultimately can form dunes that invade settled areas. Sand expansion is the ultimate expression of desertification.

More than two-thirds of the national territory is vulnerable to aeolian erosion. Contrary to what we are inclined to believe, maximum intensity is located not in the extreme south but in the area encompassing the provinces (governorates) of Mehdia, Kairouan, Sidi Bouzid, and Gabes, and centered on the governorate of Sfax. In this region the annual amount of aeolian soil erosion is estimated at 50-200 tons (t)/hectare (ha)/year. Aeolian erosion in other regions, including the stretch from Kairouan to the extreme south, is estimated at 10-50 t/ha/year (Akrimi and Abaab 1991).

Presently the phenomenon of sand expansion in Tunisia is impressive in both extent and speed of progression. Agricultural areas, settlements, oases, access routes, and water points are all increasingly threatened. Certain oases, such as Ksar Ghissia, have been virtually engulfed. The railway linking Gafsa to Gabes is sealed off at the level of Menzel Habib following virtually every sand storm, and many water points are threatened by sand invasion. Sand dunes now cover more than 2 million ha in central and southern Tunisia.

Stopping Sand Expansion

In Tunisia, two types of dunes are found: seacoast dunes resulting from marine and fluviatile deposits, and continental dunes that are the outcome of the degradation of steppe or desert soils or the reshaping of wadi alluvium. The traditional technique used since 1886 to stabilize continental dunes is the following: Sand is stopped by erecting an obstacle perpendicular to the wind, provoking its slowing down and thus the fall of sand grains. For this purpose, fences are made of palm leaves or, for lack of these, of undulated sheets of cement. These are regularly raised until the equilibrium profile is reached. In addition, dune stabilization is carried out through establishing vegetation between the dune and the area to be protected (an oasis, a village, a water point).

Only since 1962, when national planning for economic and social development was initiated, did control of sand expansion begin to receive special attention. An inland area of 70,000 ha is now being protected thanks to the construction of more than 3,000 km of fences and the planting of sylvopastoral species over roughly 5,500 ha. Afforestation has also taken place on more than 22,000 ha of maritime dunes. The most used species are *Tamarix, Calligonum, Acacia raddiana, Acacia liguiata, Parkinsonia, Casuariana glauca, Retama raetam, Lycium arabicum, Nitraria retusa,* and *Aristida pungens.* These protection works involved more than 100 oases as well as many villages, water points, and highways. The investments to finance these actions amounted to more than 10 million dinars for the period 1977-1986 (Jalel 1991).

The plan of action against sand expansion in Tunisia should form part of a global strategy of integrated rural development. The struggle against sand invasion from the Sahara will not yield the expected impact if measures against other causes of sand expansion are not carried out in tandem. These causes include eradication of woody species for fuelwood and fencing, overly intensive mechanized cereal cultivation, and overgrazing. On all sides the desert seems to be attacking zones of degraded vegetation. In effect, arid lands form a heterogeneous collection of microenvironments. Their vulnerability to desertification is determined by the local characteristics of topography, soil, and microclimate. Barren patches join together and the desert spreads, in the manner of a skin disease rather than an advancing tide (CNUD 1977).

Surface Water Erosion and Conservation of Water and Soils

Rural Tunisia has undergone dramatic changes during the past 75 years. In 1920, only 1.2 million ha were under cultivation; today the cultivated area exceeds 5 million ha. Also in 1920, the Tunisian population consisted of only 2 million inhabitants; since then, it has increased almost fourfold to nearly 8 million (Missaoui 1991). Demographic growth, vast land clearing, and the resulting reduction in rangeland and overgrazing have greatly increased Tunisian vulnerability to water erosion. This vulnerability is exploited by sporadic intense rainfall, particularly during the autumn rainy season when the land is parched and there is little vegetation cover.

During intense rainfall episodes, soil is readily stripped away. The eroded materials are subsequently deposited in depressions and plains, which are then subject to aeolian erosion (Akrimi 1986). Water erosion results in the deterioration and disappearance of the soil's arable layer. Its intensity is a function of topography, the nature and the density of the vegetal cover, and the character of precipitations. Annual loss of soil from hydroerosion in Tunisia is estimated at 49 million cubic meters (m^3), the equivalent of 10,000 ha of useful agricultural area (FAO 1980). An additional 1,000 ha are stripped away by periodic floods (ANPE 1991).

Fighting hydroerosion and harnessing stream waters for irrigation has been a major preoccupation of Tunisia's inhabitants throughout history. For many years the inhabitants of southern Tunisia have planted olive trees and cereals behind small stone dams called *jessours*, which are constructed across the beds of intermittent or ephemeral wadis. Soil deposits accumulated by the *jessours* comprise the fertile zone.

During 1968-1976, as a result of a project supported by the United Nations, 37,546 *jessours* were erected in the governorates of Gabes and Médenine. As a result of these *jessours*, 12,529 ha were recuperated. This type of land improvement, along with other small-scale hydraulic works to capture water for irrigation, allows both for a productive use of runoff water from rainstorms and an efficient fight against hydroerosion.

Moreover, in order to ensure protection against flooding wadis, to slacken their flow, and to increase the number of fields, people have built numerous ditches (*mgouds*) in wadi banks to divert water to their fields. At the beginning of the present century, virtually every family in certain regions owned its own *mgoud*. The situation was probably the same in more ancient times (Hamza 1991).

Degradation of the Vegetal Cover

Present Vegetation

Tunisia's present vegetation originated during the Miocene, an era very rich in flora. During this era Tunisia was situated in a convergence zone of tropical and subtropical vegetation, temperate zone or pontic vegetation, and a first group of plants that were typically Mediterranean.

Drastic impoverishment of the flora followed during the Quaternary, leading to the prevalence of Mediterranean elements that constitute the present vegetation of North Africa. Losses of species were extensive during dry and/or cold periods and involved tropical, subtropical, and pontic elements. Until a recent era, Tunisia was linked to southern Europe by the Tuniso-Sicilo-Calabrian land bridge. This land bridge allowed invasions of plant species from the north, contributing to North Africa's biodiversity. However, during the Quaternary, this land bridge was submerged and the Strait of Sicily was formed, isolating North Africa from Europe.

North Africa's isolation between the Mediterranean and the Sahara hampered the reinvasion of those sensitive flora during more humid periods. The possibilities for active floristic exchanges were largely limited to the Maghreb and Sahara, two regions marked by aridity that provide non-xerophytic flora with little shelter for conservation. There is much evidence that the process of floristic impoverishment is still continuing in Tunisia.

Aridity of the later climatic periods is responsible for the recent disappearance of cedar and fir trees. Moreover, aridity imperils the remnants that have sought shelter on highland summits (zeen oak, Montpellier maple) or that have been confined to the beds of perennially flowing wadis.

It should be stressed that the birth and evolution of flora and fauna are the result of a lengthy past during which climatic conditions similar to those at present predominated. This favored multiple convergence of plant species. Humans, who for 2,000 years have cleared ("sterilized") millions of hectares, have participated in this process of impoverishment of floristic biodiversity more than in the reverse process of enrichment through introduction of exotic species such as eucalyptus, casuarina, and Australian acacia.

Degradation of the Present Vegetation Cover

Tunisia is the first country in North Africa, and one of the first countries in the world, to have established a complete inventory of its natural vegetation (Emberger et al. 1957). Researchers agree that a retrogressive evolution is occurring, affecting biovolume, biomass production, and vegetation recovery, and including the degradation of vegetal structures and deterioration of the hydrological balance. This retrogressive evolution began during the time when the Sahara was covered with forests of cedar, cypress, and Aleppo pine trees, and when wild beasts lived in southern Tunisia: the last specimens of lions, Saharan crocodiles, and ostriches became extinct only about 130 years ago (Le Houérou 1959).

Relics of Phoenician juniper, Aleppo pine, and gum trees (*Acacia raddiana*) and conservation of natural vegetation around sacred maraboutic shrines all provide a relatively accurate picture of Tunisia's natural vegetation. It is clear that Tunisia's natural vegetation cover has thus witnessed an important regression in terms of range and variety.

The climax forests that covered 3 million ha at the beginning of the Christian era covered only 350,000 ha by the time of Tunisia's independence in 1956. The alfa (*Stipa tenacissima L.*) steppes resulting from the extreme deterioration of the climax forests have undergone an important degradation themselves. The disappearance of climax vegetation and the ensuing deterioration of natural ecosystems have engendered general degradation of the country's biological, faunal, and floral wealth. The national floral patrimony comprises at present 2,200 plant species, 307 rare plants, and 99 very rare plants. As for fauna, biological diversity is represented by 75 mammal species, 350 bird species, and more than 500 reptile and fish species. Nevertheless, all the large mammals, save for the wild boar, are considered threatened in Tunisia, and 12 bird species are near extinction (ANPE 1991).

National Parks and Gene Banks

To preserve Tunisia's remaining biodiversity five national parks have been established. These are the parks of Bou Heudma (1957); Chambi (1975); Zembra (1980); Boukornine (1987); and the famous park of Ichkeul (1980). Three other areas are considered natural reserves and also enjoy special protection: Sidi Toui (south of Ben Gardane); Ras Jbil (south of Douz); and El Feija. These parks, representing the main ecosystems of Tunisia, are the focus of intensive ecological management and conservation and improvement measures. It is noteworthy that in Chambi National Park the number of species has apparently more than doubled since the establishment of the park. This evidence of resiliency is based on comparison of results from floristic surveys carried out before the park was created (1955) and later on (1986).

Moreover, the National Park of Bou Heudma was created in an area where Libyan refugees, who had fled their country and settled, had seriously damaged the forest.[3] Furthermore, during World War II the city of Sfax was supplied with wood for heating from that area. In 1957 only a few trees remained from the forest. The same year, 700 ha were put under National Park protection, and populations living there were required to move away. Today the forest has been completely reconstituted. Examples such as Bou Heudma or Chambi are rare. They demonstrate that with substantial effort and financial resources the natural vegetation can be reestablished, despite former degradation. Unfortunately, restoration is no longer possible in many areas of Tunisia; among them are desertized steppes, steppized forests, and soils transformed into salty *sabkhas*.

Several studies have been carried out to identify plant and animal species that are rare or endangered. Measures regulating exploitation of the country's genetic resources have gone into effect, and gene banks are being established in various research and development institutions (*Institut des Régions Arides, Direction des Forêts, INRAT, INRST,* and others*).

The Problem of Overgrazing

The average density of livestock in southern Tunisia, which receives less than 200 millimeters (mm) of rainfall per year, is 1 sheep to 6.5 ha. In central Tunisia (200-350 mm) this average density may reach 1 ovine head per 1-2 ha (Le Houérou and Froment 1966). These densities are at least three times higher than densities considered suitable in ecologically comparable zones in Australia, South Africa, and the southern United States. Overgrazing can be defined as grazing that exceeds the annual production of the vegetation. The overgrazing intensity is, therefore, proportional to the difference between the quantity of withdrawn vegetal biomass and its annual increase.

The Action of Livestock

It must be stressed from the outset that livestock are less responsible for the destruction of the natural vegetation than is the pastoral system itself. Indeed, experience has shown that pastoralism can at times be beneficial for vegetation. Consider the case of a reserve at Sidi Toui (south of Ben Gardane); here, perennial vegetation protected inside the reserve perished progressively, whereas that located outside it remained in much better condition.[4]

Normally, however, animals select the most palatable plants and ignore toxic and odorous plants, as well as thorny plants such as *Astragalus armatus*, eaten only by camels. Thus, overgrazing leads to the replacement of useful species with inedible species over time.[5] Another problem when stocking rates are too high is compaction of the soil. Treading of soil by livestock provokes its compression and modification of its physiochemical characteristics, ending in the formation of a hard layer at the surface. This results in a decrease of permeability, therefore of soil moisture, and a correlative increase in runoff and erosion.

Overgrazing is particularly spectacular around settlements and water points. These sites are aureoled with concentric circles, where a more or less intense degradation extends outward for 5-6 kilometers (km), the maximum distance that livestock travel away from water in the summer.

The Causes of Overgrazing

Three factors lead to overgrazing:

1. *Overstocking.* When several good rainfall years occur in succession, the numbers of livestock increase considerably. However, when climatic conditions subsequently deteriorate, there are too many livestock, but livestock owners are reluctant to part with the surplus, hoping that conditions will improve. Vegetation is therefore grazed mercilessly down to the roots and dies out progressively. If droughts last, livestock are decimated.
2. *Lack of rotation.* The system of stockraising commonly consists of uninterrupted pasturing that does not allow for renewal of the rangeland vegetation. When the young shoots are cropped as they emerge, reserves cannot form, and the main stem weakens and dies.
3. *Extension of cultivation to rangeland.* The best pasturelands have disappeared, resulting in increased pressure of animals on marginal lands and acceleration of degradation.

Improvement of the Production of Natural Pasturelands

If degradation of the vegetative cover has not reached a stage that is too advanced, there are several actions, proposed by various authors, that can be employed to improve rangeland vegetation:

1. Creating fodder reserves, principally woody shrubs with edible leaves;
2. Creating reserves where grazing is prohibited; and
3. Establishing stocking rates according to the nature of the pasture and its capacity for production.

According to Floret et al. (1978), improvement of stockraising should be based on the constitution of fodder reserves, limitation of cultivation, and controlled stocking rates. Ionesco (1975) proposes a methodology based on use of fodder as well as rational exploitation of pasturelands. Le Houérou and Pontanier (1987) think it possible to intensify production of pasturelands through fodder plantations of *Atriplex nummularia, Acacia salicina, Opuntia fiscus-indica,* and similar species. Several other authors (Neffati and Akrimi 1991; Akrimi 1990; and others) advocate direct reseeding of pasturelands, because in the majority of arid areas, degradation of the vegetation cover has reached such an extent that natural regeneration cannot be expected to occur.[7]

Other Factors

Opportunistic Cultivation of Marginal Lands

After each rainy season, populations of Tunisia's arid zones and steppes are mobilized to plant wheat and barley. Cereal crops have been extended far beyond the isohyet of 100 mm, where chances for harvest are very dim. This expansion of cereal cultivation is a direct consequence of Tunisia's demographic growth (2-2.5 percent/year). This lottery-like cultivation of very marginal areas was formerly limited to subsistence crops in low-lying areas that are subject to brief inundations (Martel 1965).

Extensive plowing of low-rainfall areas produces deplorable results. After a couple of years, fields are abandoned, leaving barren lands that are invaded by annual weeds, without any pastoral interest and, moreover, unable to hold the soil, which becomes prone to wind erosion. In southern Tunisia, examples abound of sand dunes forming in certain areas and sterile limestone crust being exposed in other areas — all from wind erosion acting on rangeland that should never have been cultivated.[8]

Eradication of Woody Species

The need for fuelwood has prompted the inhabitants of arid zones to pull up woody vegetation by the roots. Sometimes even plants of small size, such as *Artemisia*, are not spared. This eradication has spread in concentric aureoles around centers of sedentarization. Both sedentarized and nomadic people have engaged in extensive clearing of woody vegetation for fuel. The minimum daily consumption of woody vegetation per rural household is around 5 kg (Le Houérou 1969). Therefore, annual consumption would be about 1,500-2,000 kg of fuelwood per household. Theoretically, this consumption would correspond to the degradation of 1-2 ha of steppe per annum per household. A population of 100,000 people could lay bare 20,000-40,000 ha annually.

On the edge of the mountain masses of the Tunisian spine, rosemary distillers have also contributed, together with charcoal burners, to the destruction of woody vegetation. Stockraisers also set fire to the forest to clear land and create pastures. There is a false, unfortunately tenacious, belief that fires make the soil richer in organic minerals. The eradication of woody species combined with overpasturing and erosion has led to the desertification of several tens of thousands of hectares annually along the Saharan borders of North Africa.

The Impact of Demographic Pressure and Change in the Way of Life

It is well established that from the Roman era to the Middle Ages (twelfth century), central and southern Tunisia were characterized by relatively rational management of the soil and vegetation, especially through terraces and the construction of dams and cisterns for runoff waters. Agriculture was both varied and complementary.

From the Middle Ages through independence in 1956, these same regions were subjected to the action of nomads unconcerned with maintaining old works and eager to draw maximum profit from the environment, driving it to ecological instability. Colonization, followed by allocation of the most productive lands to colonizers, forced the autochthonous peasant population into the hillocky lands and less fertile mountains.

Mechanization of plowing has had deleterious effects and has accelerated degradation. Moreover, the banning of slavery and development of mechanized transportation have greatly contributed to the impoverishment of southern Tunisia's population, who used to take advantage of the Saharan traffic (gold, slaves) as well as the yearly two-way passage of Maghrebian pilgrims. Deprived of those resources, the population turned to rural activities (stockraising and cultivation of new lands). In those regions, the demographic growth rate rose from 0.5-2.3 percent in half a century (Attia 1966). This increase can be explained by several factors, including the end of tribal wars since the second half of the nineteenth century; progress in healthcare that considerably reduced morbidity (especially child mortality); and cessation of epidemics and famine. This vertiginous growth of the population has had as a corollary a concomitant increase in cultivated areas. It can be estimated that, along with population, cultivated areas have increased fourfold in size since the beginning of the century (Le Houérou 1969). Despite this, the cultivated area per individual has remained the same but average yields have considerably diminished as cultivated lands have become increasingly marginal and unsuited for cultivation. Thus, direct action of man (landclearing, etc.), heavy demographic and animal pressure, and climatic precariousness have proved disastrous, provoking increasingly rapid degradation.[9]

Conclusions

Awareness of the causes of land degradation and the seriousness of the risks it engenders necessitates the formation of a national strategy to counteract this degradation. Such a strategy should be based on the concept of sustainable development. Such a strategy must look beyond a purely financial, short- and medium-term orientation to guarantee the stability of Tunisia's natural resources, which are the bases of economic and social growth.

The development approach that has been followed since the country's independence has emphasized the modern sector, where research accompanying technological transfer has been active. Unfortunately, the traditional sector has been marginalized by the entire process. This approach has shown its limits; the success of the modern sector has been achieved at the expense of the traditional.

Marginalization of the traditional sector has resulted in the deterioration of a large part of the territory. Excessively populated by a peasantry with no social alternatives, the traditional sector has been overloaded with livestock and overexploited by subsistence cultivation. Loss of vegetation cover has resulted in the erosion of soils, followed by unemployment and rural exodus. Attempts to stop this process have proved inadequate, even risky.

A new research and development approach has become necessary to reassess potentials and devise more appropriate methods to improve production and safeguard natural resources. Disillusionment resulting from development efforts stems from the fact that the adopted strategies have not seriously taken into account the human factor in the fight against land degradation. Indeed, this factor is the key to the success of such actions. We strongly urge that concerned populations participate, not simply as observers but as partners from the beginning of the planning stage through execution. The problems of rural development must be tackled by favoring motivation and training of rural populations.

Notes

1. In Tunisia, arid and Saharan areas cover almost 120,000 km^2, which amounts to about three-fourths of the national territory. Rainfall in the arid areas ranges from 100 to 350 mm/year; that in the Saharan areas is less than 100 mm/year. The rainfall shortage, due to high potential evapotranspiration, is aggravated by a double irregularity: interannual and interseasonal. The often stormy character of rains, in addition to the physical damages caused to soils (especially through amputation of their arable layer through erosion), allows for only a partial exploitation of those rains. What is left over is lost to runoff.

2. Recent studies have pointed out the absence of important climatic changes since the end of the nineteenth century. Therefore, desertification is not now due to climate changes but to human and animal pressure exerted on a fragile and

vulnerable milieu (Akrimi and Abaab 1991), which manifests through: (i) inadequate use of the soil (extension of fruit-tree arboriculture and cerealculture to zones of a pastoral vocation); (ii) use of inappropriate technology, for example, use of the polydisk plow in sandy soils that are very sensitive to aeolian erosion; (iii) increase of livestock numbers and reduction of pastureland, hence excessive overgrazing resulting in the deterioration of soil as well as a decrease in the number of useful plant species; and (iv) gathering of wood for domestic and irrigation needs.

3. Bou Heudma is located in the region called Bled Talha, from the Arabic name for *Acacia raddiana*.

4. This paradoxical situation can be explained as follows: during the growing season, animals browse on young shoots of vegetation situated outside the reserve. However, the young shoots of the protected plants within the reserve quickly transpire the water supply available in the soil. Consequently, these plants are more likely to die than those exposed to grazing outside the reserve.

5. Progressively, overgrazing favors thus the development of inedible species such as: *Peganum harmala, Asphodelus* spp., *Thapsia garganica, Arthrophytum scopatium, Cleome arabica, Urginea maritima, Stipa retorte, Thymelea hirsuta*, and so on.

6. Save for remains of primitive forests formed of *Pinus halepensis, Juniperus phoenicea*, and *Pistacia atlantica*, the natural vegetation of arid Tunisia is steppic in nature and ideal for stockraising (Akrimi 1990; Boukhris 1973; Henchi 1987). The high and low steppes of central Tunisia encompass steppes of *Artemisia herba alba* and *Artemisia campestris*. Alfa grass steppes (*Stipa tenacissima*) spread over the high plateau of the Dorsale (region of Kasserine), the summits of the mountains of Matmata, Dahar, and Tabbaga. Alfa represents a stage of transition between the forest and the chamaephyte steppes (Quezel 1958). The steppe of *Rhanterium suaveolens* is one of the most extensive in Tunisia but is at the same time the most endangered. The best pastoral species, such as the *Argyrolobium uniflorum, Echiochilon fruticosum, Salsola brevifolia, Aristida plumosa*, and *Stipa lagascae*, are becoming increasingly rare there. The steppe of *Aristida pungens* is considered a degraded form of the *Rhanterium suaveolens* steppe under the effect of aeolian sandiness. The steppe of *Haloxylon salicornicum* occupies the sandy plains in the arid and Saharan bioclimates. The steppes on gypsiferous soils are characterized mainly by *Lygeum spartum* and formations of *Zygophyllum album*. The flats that stretch over vast areas in southern Tunisia are colonized by species such as *Arthracnenum indicium, Artriplex halimus, Franskenia thymifalia, Liminiastrum guyanianum, Salsola tetrandra*, and *Sueda fruticosa*, generally grazed by camels but rarely visited by sheep and goats.

7. Nevertheless, reseeding of pasturelands on a large scale poses serious difficulties. Among these difficulties, some are inherent to the collection of seeds (small size, low density on the stalk, etc.), to which the following are added: weak germinative ability; lack of data on the mixtures of species to be considered; and need for preparation of the soil. Biotechnological development and advances,

namely micropropagation and production of vitro-plants and artificial seeds (Bouzid 1976), could alleviate some of the constraints limiting the rational use of autochthonous species for the improvement of pasturelands, fixation of sand, and conservation of water and soils in degraded zones.

8. At Menzel Lahbib (on the Gabes-Gafsa road, near Sidi Mansour) attempts were made to encourage nomads to settle in a steppe of Arfej (*Rhantherium suavrolens*) that was unable to support tree crops. Nevertheless, these sedentarized nomads attempted arboriculture. The unfortunate result was destruction of the soil and formation of sand dunes that continuously invade the road.

9. In 1966, Le Houérou and Froment estimated the area of pasture of the zone below the Gafsa-Mahres line at 6.8 million ha. At present that territory contains only about 2 million ha of pasture (Chaieb 1989), a decrease of approximately 70 percent.

References

Akrimi, N. 1986. "Désertification et dégradation du sol." Séminaire sur la concili-ation entre le développement et la protection de l'environnement. Tunis: Ministère Agrt.

———. 1990. "Aptitudes pastorales de la végétation naturelle en zones arides tunisiennes et possibilités de son amélioration." *Ecologia Méditerranea* 16:371-382.

Akrimi, N., and A. Abaab. 1991. "Données générales sur la désertification en Tunisie." *Rev. des Régions Aride,*. Numéro Spécial: 9-13. Médenine, Tunisie.

A.N.P.E. 1991. *Traits majeurs de l'environnement en Tunisie.* Tunis: Ministère de l'Environnement.

Attia, H. 1966. "Structures sociales et évolution en Tunisie centrale." *Rev. Tunisienne Sci. Soc.* 3 (6):5-14.

Boukris, M. 1973. *Recherches écologiques et physiologiques sur les plantes gypsicoles de Tunisie.* Ph.D. Thesis, USTL, Montpellier, France.

Boureau, E., Cheboldaef-Salard, J. C. Iger, and P. Louvet.1983. "Evolution des flores et de la végétation tertiaires en Afrique, au nord de l'Equateur." *Bothalia* 14 (3-4)355-367.

Bouzid, S. 1976. "Utilisation de nouvelles techniques d'étude et de multiplication des végétaux." Tozeur (Ministr. Agr. Tunisie): Sém. sur la Rech. Sc. et le Dévelop. des Zones Arides.

Chaieb, M. 1985. *Etude de l'amplitude écologique de quelques espèces pastorales pérennes du sud tunisien en vue de resemis des parcours.* Montpellier, France: D.E.A, Univ. des Sc. Techn.

———. 1989. "Influence des réserves hydriques du sol sur le comportement comparé de quelques espèces végétales de la zone aride tunisienne." Ph.D. thesis, U.S.T.L., Montpellier, France.

CNUD (Conférence des Nations-Unies sur la Désertification). 1977. "Le processus de désertification." *AGECOP Liaison (Sahel Vert)* 38:4-6.

Despois, J. 1940. *La Tunisie orientale: Sahel et basses steppes.* Paris: P.U.F. (2d ed., 1955).

Emberger, L., A. Schoenenberger, M. Gounot, M. Thiault, G. Novikoff, and H. N. Le Houérou. 1957. "Résultats généraux des recherches phytosociologiques faites par le *Service de la Carte des Groupements végétaux* pour le compte de la Tunisie." *Ann. Ser. Bot. Agr. Tunisie* 30:143-189.

FAO. 1980. *Méthode provisoire pour l'évaluation de la dégradation des sols.* Rome: Doc Edit FAO.

Floret, C., E. Le Floch, R. Pontannier, and F. Romane. 1978. *Modèle écologique régional en vue de la planification et de l'aménagement agropastoral des régions arides.* Inst. Reg. Arides. Médenine, Dir., Ress. Eau et Sol Tunis Doc. Techn.

Gammar, A.M. 1989. "Paléoflores Tunisiennes et mise en place de la végétation actuelle," in *Essai de synthèse sur la végétation et la phyto-écologie Tunisiennes,* Fac. Sci., ed. Pp. 197-233. Tunis.

Hamza, A. 1991. "La lutte anti-érosive ancienne dans le bassin versant de l'Oued Zeroud: les leçons de l'Histoire," in *Rev. des Régions arides.* Pp. 87-104. Médenine, Tunisie.

Henchi, B. 1987. *Effets des contraintes hydriques sur l'écologie et l'écophysiologie de Plantago albicansl.* Ph.D. Thesis, Fac. Sc., Tunis.

Ionesco, T. 1975. *Les améliorations pastorales: Méthodologie et réalisation dans le Centre-Sud de la Tunisie.* Sfax: Réunion MAB/EMASAR/UNEP.

Jalel, T. 1991. "Evaluation de l'état actuel de la lutte contre l'ensablement et proposition d'une stratégie d'action." *Rev. des Régions Arides,* Médenine, Tunisie. Numéro spécial:19-30.

Le Houérou, H. N. 1959. *Recherches écologiques et floristiques sur la végétation de la Tunisie méridionale. Première partie: Les milieux naturels, la végétation.* Université d'Alger: C.N.R.S. - IRS.

―――. 1969. "La végétation de la Tunisie steppique (avec références au Maroc, à l'Algérie et à la Libye)." *Ann. Inst. Nat. Rech. Agro.* (Tunisie) 42(5): 620 pp.

Le Houérou, H. N., and D. Froment. 1966. "Définition d'une doctrine pastorale pour la Tunisie steppique." *Bull. ENSAT* (Tunis) 10-11:72-152.

Le Houérou, H. N., and R. Pontanier. 1987. *Les plantations sylvopastorales dans la zone aride de Tunisie.* Tech. note, UNESCO-MAB.

Louvet, P. 1971. *Sur l'évolution des flores tertiaires de l'Afrique nord-équatoriale.* Ph.D. Thesis, Paris.

Martel, A. 1965. *Les confins saharo-tripolitains de la Tunisie (1881-1911)* [2 vols.]. Paris: P.U.F.

Ministère Agriculture. 1985. *Stratégie nationale de lutte contre la désertification.* Tunis: UNEP.

Missaoui, H. 1991. "Aperçu sur le programme national de la conservation des eaux et du sol." *Rev. des Régions Arides,* Médenine, Tunisie Numéro spécial:59-69.

Neffati, M., and N. Akrimi. 1991. "Espèces autochtones à usage multiple susceptibles d'être utilisées pour la revégétation des parcours dégradés en zones arides." *Rev. des Régions Arides* 2: 109 pp. Médenine, Tunisie.

Quezel, P. 1958. *Quelques aspects de la dégradation du paysage végétal au Sahara, en Afrique du Nord.* Athens: Un. Intern. Conserv. Nat.

Tellier, L. 1998. "Note sur la disparition du boisement dans le sud de la Régence." *Bull. Dir. Agr. et Comm.* 9:48-58.

6

Pastoralism and Desertification in Mauritania

Dah Salihi

Mauritania is experiencing such a serious environmental and socioeconomic breakdown that analysts have begun to worry about the survival of this country. The degradation of natural resources has reached a seemingly irreversible state. Desertification is rampant. And climatic change for the worse is perhaps underway. The situation is grave and its implications are catastrophic.

Mauritania's geographical location and geophysical conditions render it prone to periodic droughts and climatic hazards. Yet human activity not natural disaster is the source of Mauritania's environmental problems. Livestock breeders and peasants are fleeing their homes for crowded urban centers such as Nouakchott and Nouadhibou principally because of human-induced impacts on the environment. These impacts have two principal causes. The first consists of an exceptional increase in human and livestock populations, and the second is rooted in harmful land-use practices and the lack of environmentally sensitive development programs.

Although many human activities have adversely affected the environment, this short chapter focuses on pastoralism and range management. It first investigates the causes of desertification and the degradation of Mauritania's natural resources. Then it recommends actions to improve Mauritania's rangeland environment.

The Former Equilibrium and Its Rupture

Traditional Pastoralism: An Adapted System

The traditional Mauritanian pastoral system, established by livestock breeders prior to colonization by the French, evolved over time to accommodate the climatic and edaphic conditions of the region. This system was distinguished by three major characteristics.

The first of these was permanent mobility. Precipitation patterns in Mauritania are irregular and erratically distributed over time and space. As a result, most pastoral grasses shoot up, ripen, and produce seeds very quickly before perishing under the hot desiccating Saharan winds. This results in transitory and patchy rangeland vegetation (Monod 1975). In order to ensure that their animals make use of the fodder available between seed germination and reproduction, herders were obligated to follow the rains wherever they occurred — even into neighboring countries.

The second characteristic was ownership of different animal species (sheep, goats, camels, cattle, etc.). This variety not only allowed for the rational exploitation of diverse rangeland reserves but provided a wide range of animal products that gave the herder economic security and reduced dependency on the outside world. Surplus was exchanged for millet, rice, and other agricultural produce, thus establishing a symbiotic complementarity between herders and cultivators.

The third characteristic of this system was its effective mechanism for maintaining a relatively homogeneous distribution of animals. *E'zekat, lemniha,* and other traditions fostered dispersal of animals throughout the tribal territory, thus avoiding heavy concentrations of animals in restricted grazing areas.[1] Interestingly, there are many similarities between traditional stockraising in Mauritania and scientific principles of range management as practiced in North America.[2]

The Rupture

Colonization began to destroy a viable way of life that, for centuries, enabled Mauritanians to maintain a sustainable environment. Changes initiated by colonial administrations and perpetuated by subsequent national administrations have progressively eroded and radically transformed the traditional pastoral system. Under colonization, pasture to which access had been carefully regulated by agreements between tribes and emirates was reclassified as public domain (Swift 1976). The result has been unsustainable and anarchic exploitation of rangeland resources. The abrogation of traditional grazing arrangements initiated a free-for-all system of rangeland use entailing neglect of the environment — a "tragedy of the commons."

At the same time, administrators encouraged the nomadic populations to settle and cultivate the best lands, thus leaving the most marginal lands for collective pastures. The slogan, "Land belongs to those who cultivate it," incited pastoralists to settle around water points, clear vast areas of gum-trees and acacias, and delegate herd management to shepherds who were obliged to lead herds farther and farther away to find adequate pasture.

For the colonist — preoccupied mainly with pacification, establishing order, and occupation of the territory — this policy was considered essential, as sedentary populations were easier to control. The consequences of such a policy, however, were profound and reached far beyond the immediate impact on the environment.

Because of drought and overgrazing, the vegetative cover that protected and fixed the soil has gradually disappeared. Pastoralists have gradually lost their resource base. The only alternative has been relocating to urban centers and begging for food and work. Little by little, the proud independent spirit of the Mauritanian pastoralist has been waning, replaced by a hand-out mentality.

Until 1970, more than 80 percent of the Mauritanian population were pastoralists whose livelihood consisted of livestock raising. By the early 1990s, most of this population had settled in urban centers. The number of livestock herders has fallen to fewer than 20 percent. Increasingly, livestock owners are businessmen or government bureaucrats who have the means to amass large herds but who lack any expertise in livestock management or environmental protection (Teele 1984). This has led to the concentration of ownership of livestock by a few people (mostly urbanites) who hire former livestock owners to herd their animals. These impoverished herders have little incentive to concern themselves with the long-term health of the rangeland environment.

The Example of Trarza

Trarza, a region located in the west and southwest of the country, provides a poignant example of rural Mauritania's plight. During the 1950s and 1960s, administrators believed that they could help the native populations of western Mauritania by implementing a major development program that focused on improved medical care and the development of water points through digging wells.

These actions led to tremendous growth of human as well as animal populations.[3] The development of new water points also critically altered the pattern of rangeland use (Johnson 1980). New water points increased the exploitable areas — but also increased the periods of utilization. Zones formerly grazed only during the wet season became grazed during the dry season as well, placing permanent pressure on rangeland vegetation and gradually degrading it.

"Modernization" also altered the composition and distribution of herds. Facing new needs and new demands, livestock owners changed the composition of their herds. Ecologically more adapted animals, such as camels and goats, were replaced by more profitable livestock, such as cattle and sheep (Swift 1976).

The first outcome of the government's policy was a significant increase in the number of animals. Due in part to a period of higher-than-normal rainfall, Mauritania witnessed a period of prosperity. Milk, meat, and other foodstuffs were abundant, and the government received substantial revenues from taxes and duties levied on herds. Very soon, however, this prosperity proved ephemeral. The renewable rangeland resources of Trarza were exploited well beyond sustainable levels. With the return to "normal" (low) rainfall levels followed by the onset of prolonged drought, grazing areas became progressively degraded by ever-increasing herds. The vegetative cover that protected an already sandy and light soil disappeared and the humic layers were blown away by increasingly frequent winds. Barren patches of laterite "hardpan" appeared sporadically. Sand dunes formed and began moving, leading to slow but steady sand invasion of agricultural and settled areas. Trarza was the region most severely hit by drought and desertification. As the overexploited vegetation disappeared, animals died by the hundreds of thousands. Famine and massive numbers of human deaths followed. The magnitude of the disaster stunned the world. Unfortunately, unless urgent measures are taken, what can be referred to as "trarzization" will ultimately strike the remainder of Mauritania.

The Foundations of Rational Natural Resource Management

Mauritania is arid in the north, semi-arid in the south. Because of its geographic position Mauritania suffers from a shortage of rainfall, and even more from its irregularity. Rainfalls are brief, intense, and highly localized in time and space. Winds are frequent and dry, soils are typically sandy and light, and high temperatures result in high rates of evaporation and evapotranspiration. These environmental conditions explain Mauritania's traditional pastoral vocation. Even today, meat represents a major part of the diet. Mauritania is one of the largest consumers of meat in the world.[4]

Mauritania's arid environment calls for an approach adapted to this environment. Although the entire country is threatened by desertification, the risks are particularly grave in the regions of Hodhs and Assaba (in the southeast), where the only important expanses of pasture remain and where more than 90 percent of the country's animals are concentrated. It is urgent that new range management practices be adopted. Rational management of Mauritania's natural resources can be achieved most successfully by applying scientific principles to livestock rearing and development projects.

Range Management

Range management is both a science and an art. It attempts to manage use of renewable natural resources in arid and semi-arid lands in order to obtain production sufficient to sustain both humans and animals — without degrading vegetation and the natural ecosystem. In order to be successful, range management principles must be adapted to specific social, economic, and environmental situations. Application of these principles should accommodate traditional approaches to achieve optimal results.

Although precise information on natural fodder production and total livestock numbers in Mauritania is unavailable, it is clear that the present number of livestock is excessive and should be decreased and more evenly distributed over the entire rangeland area. Pastures around wateringplaces should be protected from overgrazing. Establishment of new water points should carefully consider the carrying capacity of the particular zone. Protected reserves should be established to be used for grazing only during periods of drought. The reserved areas could be rotated according to the seasons and the vegetation reproductive cycle.

Completely protected study sites of approximately one hectare (ha) each should be established in each type of vegetation and in each ecological zone. This would allow for estimation of biomass and production of annual and perennial vegetation, thus leading to the calculation of the potential carrying capacity of each zone.[5] For each ecological zone, the most adapted animals should be used. Cattle should be moved frequently from pasture to pasture, especially during sensitive periods of grass reproduction and growth.

The above steps should be taken immediately. Simultaneously, major studies should be initiated to provide an information base allowing for the refinement of range management. Basic studies should be carried out for each environmental zone. These studies should comprise several steps. First, a qualitative and quantitative survey should be conducted of the vegetation and its fodder potential. Next, a zootechnical study (census of livestock, herd composition, pasturing pattern, fodder needs, and so on) should be undertaken. This should be accompanied by a socioeconomic study — the importance of which does not need to be explained (Sandford 1983). It would consist of examining household structure, land-tenure patterns, land-use patterns, household income, drought-coping strategies, the possibility of motivating populations to participate in the struggle against desertification, and so on. A study of water resources should then be conducted, including a complete inventory of water points. Next, a pedological study should be carried out to analyze in detail each plot of pastureland and determine its agricultural and sylvopastoral potential. Finally, an analysis should be undertaken to quantify levels of overgrazing and degradation of rangeland resources.

After these basic data have been established, models of organization and rational management of resources can be developed to accommodate the specific conditions of each pasture zone. Planting and seedling improvement can be undertaken. Programs can be developed to monitor and safeguard water points. Water and soil conservation projects can be established. Cost-effective uses of runoff water can be investigated and implemented.

There should be support for ongoing agricultural research to introduce fast-growing types of fodder, propagate seedlings of useful species in the process of becoming extinct, and introduce fodder (*Medicago, Lolium,* clover) in irrigated and semi-irrigated areas. Pastoretums should be created for research and extension of appropriate techniques to improve pastureland. Research stations should be established in each distinctly different environmental zone to continuously improve rangeland management and extension efforts.

Sound Management of Development Programs

To fight desertification effectively, Mauritania should turn livestock owners into active executors of development projects rather than passive spectators. It is imperative to make livestock owners participate in every phase of development, beginning with their own lands. A recent study (Salihi 1991) has shown that the success of such projects in West Africa depends greatly upon sociocultural, economic, environmental, and technological parameters. Nevertheless, this same study has also shown that project results are more influenced by institutional, administrative, and political considerations than by all other factors put together. Bureaucracies are slow to respond to change. Developers disagree about developmental objectives. And the availability of funds necessary for project continuity is not always certain. This results in projects not being carried out as planned, changes being applied in the course of their execution, or in projects being dropped entirely. High-level support and intra-government cooperation is essential.

Conclusions

Each development project, considered alone, often seems like a drop of water in an immense ocean. Yet the sum total of all projects and programs represents a country's economic, social, and environmental policy. Without integration, and a global vision, there can be no development. A successful project for rangeland improvement in Mauritania would allow natural rangeland vegetation to regenerate and reestablish ecosystem equilibrium. Yet at the same time, it would also reestablish economic opportunities where they traditionally existed, reemploy a sizable percentage of the population, and reconnect Mauritanians with their pastoral traditions — the wellspring of their culture and well-being.

Notes

1. Traditional land-use practices should not be viewed as odd and archaic customs, but rather as activities that are often well adapted to local environmental conditions.

2. These principles include maintaining an appropriate number of animals based on the calculation of carrying capacity; distributing livestock evenly over the pastureland areas; using those areas during the appropriate season, taking into account the stage of vegetative growth; and, finally, using the most appropriate animal species for a given type of vegetation and environment. For further information, see Stoddart et al. (1960).

3. Galaty (1981) estimated that, from 1914 to 1968, cattle in the Sahelian region increased 300-400 percent.

4. For 1,800,000 inhabitants with an average daily consumption of 100 grams (g) per person, the country needs 180 tons daily, approximately 67,500 per year, which amounts to 263,000 head of cattle or 2,630,000 sheep. Bearing in mind this consumption level, and a demographic growth rate as high as 3 percent annually, Mauritania's food security outlook is grim.

5. While waiting for the necessary basic studies to be completed, authorities should apply the general rule: "Take half and leave half" — that is, half of the vegetation could be used while leaving the other half to regenerate.

References

Baum, W. C., and S. M. Tolbert. 1985. *Investing in Development*. Published for the World Bank. London: Oxford University Press.

Galaty, J. G. et al. 1981. *The Future of Pastoral Peoples*. Montreal: McGill University.

Johnson, D. 1980. "UNCOD, Combating Desertification, and the Pastoral Nomad." *Nomadic Peoples* 5:6-10.

Monod, Théodore. 1975. *Les Sociétés Pastorales en Afrique Tropicale.* London: International African Institute (Oxford).

Salihi, Dah O. 1991. *Factors Influencing Success of Donor-Funded Pastoral Projects in the Sahel.* Ph.D. Thesis, University of Arizona, Tucson.

Sandford, S. 1983. *Management of Pastoral Development in the Third World.* New York: John Wiley.

Simpson, J. R., and P. Evangelou. 1984. *Livestock Development in Sub-Sahara Africa.* Boulder, Colo.: Westview.

Stoddardt, S. et al. 1960. *Principles of Range Management.* New York: McGraw-Hill.

Swift, J. 1976. "Some Consequences for the Somali Nomad Pastoral Economy of the Development of Livestock Trading." *Ann. Rev. Anthropology* 6:457-478.

Teele, T. F. 1984. "Development and Management of Livestock Projects in the Sahel Area of Africa," in J. R. Simpson and P. Evangelou, eds., *Livestock Development in Sub-Sahara Africa.* Boulder, Colo.: Westview.

7

Is Sedentarization of Pastoral Nomads Causing Desertification? The Case of the Beni Guil of Eastern Morocco

Abdellatif Bencherifa

This chapter focuses on the relationships between pastoral nomadism and desertification. More specifically, it asks, "Is sedentarization of the Beni Guil in eastern Morocco and their intensified use of land resources causing substantial environmental degradation?" The answer to this question will have major implications for marginal dryland areas throughout North Africa.

Statement of the Problem

Under simple technological conditions, extensive stockraising or pastoral nomadism is probably the optimal resource-use system in North Africa. This is because it allows for flexible adjustments to North Africa's limited and highly variable rainfall. Pastoral nomadism has been a dominant feature of the North African economy throughout history, due to its environmental suitability. However, this form of land use has gradually been receding in importance. Throughout most of North Africa, there has been a similar historical trend of land-use intensification (Bencherifa 1986; Bencherifa and Johnson 1990, 1993). This is a historical trend comprising two related processes. First, extensive pastoral nomadism has been progressively replaced by more intensive agropastoral activities, with cultivation supplementing and partially supplanting nomadic livestock raising. Second, pastoral nomads have gradually become settled or "sedentarized."

Until the mid-1950s, nomad tents remained a common sight throughout Morocco's Atlantic plains (for example, in the Gharb, Zaer, Chaouia, and Doukkala). Even today, these tents can be observed on rare occasions in the Atlantic plains. However, outside of the highlands, they are now a cultural relic. Under the influence of past and present pressures, particularly population growth, extensive pastoral systems have evolved into more intensive, sedentarized agropastoral systems following the Boserupian model (Boserup 1965). This chapter argues that land-use changes among the Beni Guil in Morocco today represent a latter-day instance of this historical trend.[1]

How significant are the *environmental impacts* of this shift from extensive pastoralism to intensive agropastoralism in North Africa in general, and Morocco in particular? Extensive clearing of natural vegetation for cultivation has indeed occurred. In certain areas, there has clearly been accelerated soil erosion. Yet, how significant are the *negative* environmental impacts resulting from land-use intensification, compared to the *societal benefits* that have accrued, including substantial increases in the productivity and carrying capacity of the land? The basic purpose of this chapter is to address this question through drawing on field research undertaken among the pastoral communities of the northeastern high plateaus of Morocco, specifically the Beni Guil confederation.[2]

The Beni Guil were formerly nomads who based their livelihood on herding camels and small ruminants (goats and sheep) over long distances, in accordance with the seasonal distribution of pasture. In the contemporary period, their pastoral system has been undergoing dramatic changes, involving such components as the scale of nomadic migration, the nature of the herds stocked, and the overall relationships of these communities to local resources. The effects of these changes on the physical environment have been substantial.

Nevertheless, this chapter challenges the underpinnings of the dominant perception that changes in natural ecosystems are ontologically detrimental and represent degradation. It analyzes traditional resource-management practices among the Beni Guil as well as current practices, and compares the benefits of land-use intensification to the environmental costs of this intensification.

The problem addressed in this chapter is closely related to the issue of "desertification," which refers to land degradation in low-rainfall and seasonally dry areas. Typical indicators of desertification are the impoverishment of natural vegetation and deterioration of soils. The concept of desertification became internationalized as a result of the devastating famine in the Sahelian region of West Africa, which began at the end of the 1960s. This tragedy was initially blamed on drought and considered a natural disaster.

It soon became apparent to scientists, however, that the Sahelian tragedy was, in fact, an environmental calamity that had resulted from *human actions* — specifically, stockraising and cultivation that were too intensive for the region's relatively fragile environment.

In response to the Sahelian tragedy, the first international conference on desertification was convened in 1977. This was the UN Conference on Desertification (UNCOD). Reports at UNCOD claimed that similar processes of environmental degradation were occurring in most of the world's drylands due to overgrazing, cutting of woody vegetation for fuel and construction, and unsustainable cultivation. Following this conference, UN agencies began to publish statistics on the global extent of desertification. It soon became orthodox wisdom that over a third of the world's land surface was at risk of desertification.

Unfortunately, little actual field evidence was assembled to support this orthodoxy. Recently, "revisionists" have begun to question the validity of much prior desertification research as well as the very concept of desertification (Forse 1989; Helldén 1991; Rhodes 1991). Their critique is based on the facts that:

1. There is no universally agreed upon definition of desertification and, in evoking the image of deserts, the concept is misleading;
2. Many of the key early studies of desertification were flawed because they were conducted during periods of drought; and
3. Areas previously believed to be irreversibly desertified demonstrated remarkable recovery after a single rainy season.

This chapter represents a contribution to the revisionist trend.

Because desertification usually refers to environmental degradation in *dryland environments* where pastoral nomadism was typically the traditional activity, pastoral nomads and their sedentarized descendants are usually blamed for this phenomenon. At first glance, the pattern of land-use intensification among the Beni Guil appears to follow the classical model of desertification derived from the Sahelian environmental tragedy.

However, this chapter argues that, instead, current land-use changes among the Beni Guil replicate a pattern of land-use intensification that has occurred in many other areas in Morocco during the last two centuries. These past changes elsewhere in Morocco have inevitably resulted in alterations to the environment. However, they have not so far resulted in environmental disaster.

To the contrary, the intensification in production systems that has occurred has increased the technological "power" of local communities over their natural resources, sustaining a larger number of people and a more complex social life. While some environmental deterioration has occurred, it is limited in scale and minor compared to the societal benefits resulting from land-use intensification.

The Beni Guil Territory: Past and Present Pastoral System

The Physical Environment

Because of its large size, the Beni Guil territory is far from homogeneous. Instead, it is characterized by significant environmental diversity. The pastoral system of the Beni Guil was well adapted to this diversity. Diversity in environmental conditions helps account for the current distribution of grazing versus cultivated land, seasonality and range of pastoral migration, and other major land-use patterns. This section briefly describes landforms, climate, and natural vegetation of the Beni Guil territory.

Landforms. The Beni Guil territory traditionally encompassed three major physiographic regions. To the north and northwest there is a karstic mountain system known as the *Gaada* that extends from the western Debdou crest to the eastern Jerada.[3] It reaches a maximum elevation of 1,700 meters (m). The eastern high plateaus are immediately to the south. These plateaus comprise the heart of Beni Guil territory. They extend from Ain Beni Mathar township in the north to a series of east-west trending mountains in the south, including Jbel La'rak, Jbel Bouarfa, and Jbel El Kalkh. This section is called locally *Dahra* (the "back side"). Landforms are highly diversified in these plateaus, where elevation ranges from 1,000 m in the north to 1,400 m in the south. The high plateaus are bordered to the east along the frontier with Algeria by a set of large basins, seasonally covered with water. These basins include the *Chott* Tigri and part of *Chott* Elgharbi, which is mostly in Algeria. Finally, south of the high plateaus is a mountain system between Jbel La'rak and Jbel El Kalkh. This system represents an extension of the High Atlas and consists of small mountains reaching 1,500-2,000 m in elevation. They border large basins at elevations between 1,100 and 1,300 m, including Tamellalt and Mengoub in the southwest; Lamsarine and Lamdaouir in the middle; Roknat N'aam and Zoulay in the east; and Tisserfine in the south. This large southern section is locally called *Essahra* ("Sahara") as it borders the vast Sahara Desert to the southeast.

Climate. The Beni Guil territory is dominated by arid conditions. This aridity is a major limiting factor for resource use. In the mountainous *Gaada*, average annual rainfall reaches a maximum of 450 millimeters (mm). In all other parts of the territory, rainfall is marginal, ranging from 240 mm at Ain Beni Mathar in the north to 120 mm at Figuig in the extreme southeast. Of pastoral significance is the fact that the timing of rainfall is different in the *Dahra* and *Essahra*. Because the *Dahra* is exposed to polar fronts, rainfall occurs primarily from December to March. However, its higher elevations have low winter temperatures and are subject to frost. The southern desert-like *Essahra* instead has rainfall peaks in autumn and the beginning of spring. In addition, temperatures are far higher in winter.

Natural Vegetation. Vegetation cover varies with topographic and climatic conditions. In the high elevation section of the *Gaada*, relics of *Quercus ilex* forest are still found. However, arid steppic formations dominate in most parts. Alfa grass (*Stipa tenacissima*) is the dominant vegetation, particularly in well-drained rocky areas. *Artemisia* sp. predominates in heavier soils. However, microenvironments provide pockets of more diverse natural vegetation. Along the wadis and in *maader* (that is, basins where runoff water collects after rainfall), there is relatively luxurious vegetation. Seasonally, the nature and density of vegetation comprising pastoral resources is highly diversified.

The major physiographic and bioclimatic units of the Beni Guil territory provided the general framework for their pastoral nomadic activities. However, within this framework is a diversity of microenvironments that provided significant resource-use opportunities (*wadis, maaders*, streams called locally *siga*, tributaries of large wadis called *sehb*, etc.). In addition, meteorological factors such as cold spells, snowfall, the frequency of spring and summer storms, and so on, had important implications for pastoral life, particularly in the northern part of the territory.

The Classical Pastoral Pattern of the Beni Guil

As mentioned previously, the Beni Guil are a confederation of Arabic-speaking tribes who for centuries practiced pastoral nomadism in the high plateaus and basins of northeastern Morocco. The term "Beni Guil" designates the higher, political level of a typical tribal segmentary unit in which, ideologically, the belief in a common ancestor is perceived as the legitimizing factor.[4] Several tribes make up this confederation, each with a set of subdivisions (Barth 1964; Hart 1981). The tribe level is the level of resource management, as opposed to the confederation level, which has a political function *vis-à-vis* the surrounding tribes (such as the Laamour, Zwa, Doui Mani', and Jarir).

The tribal territory of the Beni Guil is extremely large. Today, it covers approximately 25,000 square kilometers (km²). However, it was even larger in the past, extending into Algeria and encompassing territory that today is under the control of different Moroccan tribes. According to the 1982 census, the total population of the Beni Guil was around 30,000 inhabitants (*Direction de la Statistique* 1982). The current population is probably around 40,000 people. This gives a population density of only 1.6 people/km².

In conventional pastoral nomadic classifications, the Beni Guil can be viewed as authentic Bedouins, both in the pattern of migrations and in the characteristics of their material culture (Johnson 1969; Dyson-Hudson and Dyson-Hudson 1980). They exploited the vegetation resources of different complementary environmental units over a distance of 250-300 km from north to south.[5] Johnson described this type of migration as the "horizontal pulsatory pattern" in his original classification system (1969). Cold winter temperatures in the mountainous northern *Gaada* and the *Dahra* exposed the herds to risks while reducing vegetation growth. During this season, the Beni Guil migrated to the southern *Essahra* as early as the beginning of November. Subsequent hot temperatures and water shortages accounted for their return migration from the *Essahra* to the *Dahra* by March-April. Here, the frequency of storms allowed for good grazing conditions and adequate water resources (particularly along the *wadis* and their tributaries). Ancestral water points served as way stations along the migratory route.

In theory, within the large Beni Guil territory, all members of the confederation have free and equal access to resources. In reality, however, evidence suggests that even in the past not all tribal members had equal access. Each tribe, and indeed each fraction of the tribe, apparently has long had quasi-exclusive rights to territory that are more-or-less acknowledged by other tribal members. As will be described, these territorial rights today provide the geographical matrix for current processes of change from extensive pastoralism to intensive agropastoralism.

From Extensive Pastoralism to Agropastoralism

Changes in the Beni Guil pastoral system, from extensive pastoralism to intensive agropastoralism, have resulted from two major forces. The first factor is the political control exerted over these nomadic groups — initially by the colonial power, then by the post-colonial administration. The second factor involves the general demographic and economic changes in Morocco over the past half century. Intensification has been a progressive adaptive response to changing political and socioeconomic circumstances. The remainder of this chapter examines this intensification and its environmental implications.

Changes in the Spatial Distribution of Tribal Land Resources

The Beni Guil confederation currently consists of sixteen segmentary lineages (Table 7.1). Each lineage has quasi-exclusive access to a different section of Beni Guil territory. Access rights to resources have undergone dramatic change associated with privatization of agricultural and even

TABLE 7.1 Population, Land, and Herd Composition of the Beni Guil Lineages

Tribal lineage	1[a]	2[b]	3[c]	4[d]	5[e]	6[f]
Oulad Mbarek	1,119	2,178	11,141	2,402	118	30
Oulad Belahsen	1,423	2,544	15,458	2,960	350	96
Oulad Fares	3,298	4,387	36,494	7,408	771	35
Oulad Ali Ben Yassin	1,331	2,500	25,602	3,507	336	30
Oulad Youb	1,551	3,884	19,745	2,817	160	30
Oulad Jaber	1,523	5,140	22,648	3,184	235	31
Laalaouna	1,073	4,186	16,423	3,479	371	41
Oulad Ali Bellahssen	585	4,237	10,652	2,517	388	0
Oulad Ahmed Benabdellah	1,973	4,212	35,309	3,663	487	3
Tendrara[g]	816	1,878	7,036	646	431	1
Oulad Chaib	1,260	1,408	12,278	4,338	214	28
Oulad Ben Hmama	422	2,183	3,947	2,329	5	116
Oulad Ramdane	977	1,021	9,545	5,671	176	46
Oulad Hajji	1,460	2,119	16,089	5,263	47	156
Oulad Brahim	942	996	10,832	5,053	299	35
Oulad Abdelkrim	1,960	2,188	20,294	6,149	333	160

[a]Population in 1982, the last year for which census figures are available. These figures are probably still close to reality, because severe droughts during the early 1980s and early 1990s led to large-scale outmigration to urban areas.

[b]The cultivated area in 1989 in hectares.

[c]Total sheep in 1989.

[d]Total goats in 1989.

[e]Total cattle in 1989.

[f]Total camels in 1989.

[g]Only herders in the village are involved.

Source: Data collected by author.

grazing areas. Appropriation of common resources is not only the general rule at the lineage level; it is observed at times at the individual family level. Exclusive-use rights that amount to *de facto* private ownership are openly acknowledged between the sixteen lineages. Such exclusive access to resources are even informally acknowledged by the Moroccan government in the sense that there is no opposition, even though the Beni Guil territory is still officially classified as communal land.[6] This privatization is the end result of a long, cumulative process whereby each group progressively claimed an area of "privileged quarters," formally called *Oualf,* an area with continuous, exclusive usufruct rights by a given group to the exclusion of other groups. The current situation reflects various constraints (social, political, and technological) that have hindered the traditional large-scale migration of herds of camels, goats, and sheep. These constraints are associated with the demographic increase of the total population, not only within the confederation but also in all surrounding tribes. They are also related to political pressures, during and following colonial rule, to exert tighter control over nomads located along sensitive political frontiers.

This factor has had, for the Beni Guil lineages, an unexpected impact on traditional pastoral management. Increased political control entailed greater security, which in turn made "collective" pastoralism less desirable and favored individualism. The trend toward privatization and individualism of resource use is now well advanced among the lower-level segments of the tribe. In the not-distant future, it is expected that individual extended families and even nuclear families will be affected by this trend.[7] Finally, and most important, the former changes took place in a new economic context characterized by an increase in human needs and wants. This has fostered more intensive resource-use systems.

A few Beni Guil groups continue to practice traditional extensive, distant-migration, pastoral nomadism. However, traditional practices are considered to be a relic phenomenon, due to vanish soon. The more general pattern is one of semi- or fully sedentarized Beni Guil communities, each in its own circumscribed *Oualf* territory. Although stockraising is still practiced, small-scale transhumance (localized seasonal migration) is now dominant. Tents are still prevalent, but they are no longer an essential component of material culture reflecting the need to perennially migrate toward new pastures. Rather, they are a surviving component of a culture in change.

The Expansion of Cultivation

The most important land-use change among the Beni Guil is the dramatic expansion of cultivation. The Beni Guil today are more agropastoralists than nomadic herders. In 1982, 73-87 percent of the households within the different lineages were engaged in both livestock raising and cultivation. In 1989, a survey revealed that between 68 and 82 percent of the Beni Guil households owned individual agricultural plots and between 83 and 88 percent also had herds of sheep — a herd animal that is increasing in number while camels and goats are decreasing. This same 1989 survey revealed that between 25 and 35 percent of these households also lived in permanent dwellings. While recent figures are lacking, it is certain that these percentages have increased in recent years.[8]

The expansion of cultivation and of agropastoralism in general is consistent with the current spatial distribution of the population. Each tribal *Oualf* territory, in fact, is composed of a major arable area with specific natural endowments. The cultivated area per lineage varies from slightly fewer than 1,000 hectares (ha) to slightly more than 5,000 ha (column 2 in Table 7.1). The total cultivated area is approximately 45,000 hectares.

Because cultivated fields are rainfed, the geographic location of arable land is not random, but is usually associated with specific sites with additional water resources and better soils. These include areas where runoff water seasonally concentrates or is channeled. Large basins (*maaders*), where runoff water collects and where soil is of higher quality, are extensive in the southern section of the Beni Guil territory, the *Essahra*. For example, the Lamsarine *maader* extends east-west for around 20 km and is approximately 20 km wide. In the northern *Dahra*, smaller basins locally called *daya* are also common. Large wadis and their tributaries (*sehb* and *siga*), where intermittent runoff is channeled, are also moister areas with higher quality soils, where fields are established. In the Oulad Ben Hmama lands in the southwestern border region, agricultural yields are enhanced with irrigation water from wells, using motor-pumps. Here, a stage of full sedentarization has been reached.

Interviews with the Beni Guil have revealed that the better endowed arable areas, which are now cultivated, were formerly the core grazing areas of certain lineages. Their exclusive use for pastoral purposes by certain groups is a well established fact. These areas represent the core areas of sedentarization for the sixteen lineages of the Beni Guil. However, a further stage has developed recently, namely the private appropriation of specific plots at the individual level. In this final stage of privatization, resource management at the level of the nuclear family is replacing the former patriarchal organization of resource use. Cultivation and the subsequent change in value systems based on concepts of private land and territoriality reflect a fundamental shift among the former Beni Guil pastoral nomads. However, livestock raising remains an important component of the production system.

Changes in Livestock Raising

Obviously, the shift from extensive pastoralism into agropastoralism has entailed substantial changes in the livestock raising patterns of the Beni Guil. These changes have been driven by factors such as the curtailment of the Beni Guil territory, the private appropriation of land, the extension of cultivation, and the increase in the number of watering points. Elements of change include the use of trucks for herd transportation and for delivering water to herds in remote areas. Specific changes include the following:

First, large-scale migrations have been replaced by short transhumance movements. Local terminology clearly distinguishes between "moving" the tent from one place to another (*tahwal*), and a nomadic migration (*rihla*).

Only a few large herd owners (originating mostly from the northern lineages) still engage in large-scale migrations as were formerly practiced by the entire Beni Guil confederation.

Second, the composition of herds has changed. Camels have virtually vanished (column 6 in Table 7.1). In addition, despite their relative importance, goats have also decreased in number. Sheep are progressively becoming the animal of choice for Beni Guil agropastoralists. Finally, cattle, although still limited in number (column 5 in Table 7.1) are now more numerous than camels and are an increasingly important part of the herd composition. Cattle are perhaps the best indicator of the shift towards sedentarization, as they are clearly incompatible with large-scale nomadic migrations in desert-like conditions.

Third, social inequalities have increased as large herders with modern machinery are able to control resources in remote areas more effectively.

Finally, in areas where the process of land privatization has not yet occurred, a "tragedy of the commons," initiated by large herders, is taking place along the lines of the well-known model (Hardin 1968), in which common-property resources become degraded because the short-term benefits of individual use outweigh the longer-term negative impacts of collective overexploitation.

Environmental Implications Versus Social Viability

The Vegetation Degradation Issue

The trend toward a more settled life, based on agropastoralism, has clearly resulted in vast land clearing within the Beni Guil territory. This land clearing has triggered major processes of land degradation, including removal of natural vegetation cover, soil erosion, and overgrazing. Of critical importance is clearing and cultivation of the maader depressions, as well as the *sehoub* (sing. *sehb*), both areas with relatively lush natural vegetation. In other areas, particularly in the northern *Dahra*, a type of shifting cultivation is practiced, at the expense of the *Stipa tenacissima* vegetation.

The trend toward sedentarization is usually accompanied by heavy overuse of specific pastoral land around the recently cleared agricultural sites. Overgrazing is a function of both higher livestock numbers and their permanent grazing pressure on rangeland vegetation. Overgrazing leads to changes in the floristic structure of the natural vegetation, a decrease in the total vegetation cover, and general impoverishment of pastoral resources.

In the areas most affected by degradation (for example, in the south-western region called Nabch) wind erosion is resulting in sand dune formation. However, the magnitude as well as the geographic extent of these processes of land degradation are relatively minor, when compared to the social benefits of the shift to more intensive agropastoralism, including higher land productivity and an increased population carrying capacity.[9]

Environmental Change in Societal Context

Environmental debates are often biased toward environmental "preservation" and "conservation" and fail to consider the societal context. In the case of the Beni Guil, traditional land-use patterns became inadequate and unable to support the growing population of the confederation. The shift toward agropastoralism has indeed altered the natural environment. However, it has also allowed for higher land productivity.[10] This shift has also allowed for relatively more stable and improved living conditions for the local population. Finally, the progressive privatization of cultivated land represents better resource management than the "tragedy of the commons" now occurring in areas where pastoral nomadism is still practiced in Beni Guil territory, often with trucks and other modern means. More than "environmental protection" *per se*, there is a clear need for research and extension to ensure the viability and sustainability of the Beni Guil's recently evolved agropastoral system. Such research and extension should focus on drought-coping strategies, improved range-management techniques, and herd improvement.

Conclusions

Analysis of land degradation in dryland environments, such as Beni Guil territory, requires not only that appropriate indicators be identified and documented through field research, but also that an objective assessment of the societal benefits from land-use change becomes incorporated into the analysis. Because resiliency within drylands is now recognized to be greater than previously thought (Mortimore 1988), analyses should particularly focus on a given environment's capacity for regeneration. The best criteria for assessing land degradation will be indicators such as soil loss that are, for all practical purposes, irreversible. Patterns of land-use change among the Beni Guil — from extensive pastoral nomadism to intensive agropastoralism — appear to follow the classical model of desertification.

However, this study has argued that the trend in eastern Morocco instead replicates changes that occurred at earlier periods in many other parts of Morocco. Such land-use changes, by definition, alter the natural environment. However, there is no compelling evidence of environmental calamity in these other areas of earlier agricultural intensification. In fact, most appear to be well-established, stable, productive agrarian environments. As a result, there is no reason to believe that the fate of the Beni Guil environment will be any different.

Notes

1. The origins of this trend in Morocco can probably be traced back to the 19th and early 20th centuries when, in semi-arid areas such as the Chaouia, Doukkala, and Abda, large population communities settled and engaged in agropastoralism. However, this was possible only to the extent that technological change allowed for adaptations to climatic variability. This technological change probably involved the adoption of New World plants such as *Zea mais, Opuntia,* and late-maturing legume crops.

2. Field research was undertaken between December 1989 and August 1990, as part of a development scheme initiated by the Moroccan Ministry of Agriculture. During this period, I benefited from input from Hassan Rachik, Mohamed Hammoumi, and Mohamed Ghanem; their indirect contribution here is acknowledged. I also want to thank the local representatives of the Ministry of Agriculture in Bouarfa, as well as Beni Guil authorities, particularly the former local *caid*, A. My Elbab. The processes described in this paper are similar to those taking place among other northern tribes such as the Beni Mathar, Oulad Abdelhakam, Oulad Ali Bouchnafa, and the Zwa, which were investigated during the same period.

3. This is a toponym referring to the flat plateau-like surface. Today, most of the *Gaada* is used by a northern tribe called Zwa, and the Beni Guil have only limited access.

4. The concept of *Oulad* ("the sons of") is semantically consistent with the tribal segmentary organization and ideology of the Beni Guil. The basic tribal entity is the *qbila*, which is subdivided into high-level segments also called *qbila*, which in turn are subdivided into segments called fractions (*fakhda*). The *fakhda* are subdivided into segments called *adam*, the lowest lineage level. Below this level are extended families called *khayma* (tent).

5. In such large territory, the political function of the confederation is obvious: to ensure that resources can be protected and preserved against surrounding neighbors. Originally, the confederation replicated the model of the five fifths (*khams khmas*), which were the following: Oulad Brahim, Oulad Hajji, Oulad Fares, Oulad Youb, and Oulad Ahmed (Barth 1964; Hart 1981). Today there are 16 *qbilas.* This number might even increase as competition over resources results in increasing claims by lower-level lineages for higher segmentary status.

6. Inter-tribal conflicts within the Beni Guil are now a common fact as a result of these changes.

7. Among the northern neighboring tribes of the Beni Guil such as the Zwa and the Oulad Ali Bouchnafa, this stage has already been fully reached.

8. No quantitative figures can be provided, but a recent investigation by the author confirms the trend.

9. The fact that recurrent drought during the 1980s and early 1990s had far greater detrimental impacts on vegetation cover than land clearing for agricultural purposes also indicates the relatively minor nature of land degradation.

10. While rainfed cultivation in such arid conditions is very risky, the fact that it takes place in humid microenvironments ensures relatively reliable production of cereals. Even when grain yields are poor or non-existent as a result of drought, the cut straw or standing hay are critically important for fodder to sustain the herds during the drought.

References

Barth, F. 1964. *Nomads of South Persia: The Basseri Tribe of the Khamseh Confederacy.* Oslo: Universitets Forlaget.

Bencherifa, A. 1986. *Agropastoral Systems in Morocco: Cultural Ecology of Tradition and Change.* Unpublished Doctoral Dissertation, Clark University, Worcester, Mass.

———. 1988. *Agropastorale Organisationsformen im atlantischen Marokko.* 119:1-13.

Bencherifa, A., and D. L. Johnson. 1990. "Adaptation and Intensification in the Pastoral Systems of Morocco," in J. G. Galaty and D. L. Johnson, eds., *The World of Pastoralism. Herding Systems in Comparative Perspectives.* Pp. 394-416. New York: Guilford Press.

———. 1993. "Environment, Population Pressure, and Resource Use Strategies in the Middle Atlas Mountains of Morocco," In Abdellatif Bencherifa, ed., *African Mountains and Highlands (2). Resource Use and Conservation.* Pp. 101-121. Rabat: Publication de la Faculté des Lettres et des sciences Humaines, Série Colloques et séminaires 29.

Boserup, E. 1965. *The Conditions of Agricultural Growth: The Economics of Agrarian Change under Population Pressure.* New York: Aldine.

Direction de la Statistique. 1982. *Résultats du recensement général de la population et de l'habitat.* Rabat.

Dyson-Hudson, R. and N. Dyson-Hudson. 1980. "Nomadic Pastoralism." *Annual Review of Anthropology* 9:15-61.

Evans-Pritchard, E. E. 1940. *The Nuer.* Oxford: Clarendon Press.

Forse, B. 1989. "The Myth of the Marching Desert." *New Scientist* 4 February: 31-32.

Galaty, J. G., et al. 1981. *The Future of Pastoral Peoples.* Ottawa: International Development Research Center.

Galaty, J. G., and D. L. Johnson (eds.). 1990. *The World of Pastoralism: Herding Systems in Comparative Perspective.* New York: Guilford Press.

Hardin, G. 1968. "The Tragedy of the Commons." *Science* 162(3895):1243-1248.

Hart, D. 1981. *Dadda 'Atta and His Forty Grandsons: The Sociopolitical Organization of the Ait Atta of Southern Morocco.* Boulder: Westview Press.

Helldén, U. 1991. "Desertification: Time for an Assessment?" *Ambio* 20(8):372-383.

Johnson, D. L. 1969. *The Nature of Nomadism: A Comparative Study of Migrations in Southwestern Asia and Northern Africa*. Research Paper No. 118, Chicago: University of Chicago, Department of Geography.

Mensching, H. 1971. "Nomadismus und Oasenwirtschaft im Maghreb: Entwicklungstendenzen seit der Kolonialwirtschaft und ihre Bedeutung im Kulturlandscahftswandel der Gegenwart," in *Siedlungs- und agrargeographische Forschungen in Europa und Afrika*. Pp. 155-166. Wiesbaden: Braunschweiger Geog. Studien 3.

Mortimore, M. J. 1988. "Desertification and Resilience in Semi-arid West Africa." *Geography* n.v.:61-64.

Müller-Hohenstein, K. 1976. *Die ostmarokkanischen Hochplateau: Ein Beitrag zur Regionalforschung und zur Biogeographie eines nordafrikanishen Trockensteppenraumes*. Erlanger: Erlanger Geographische Arbeiten 7.

Nouvel, S. 1919. *Nomades et sédentaires au Maroc*. Paris: Emile Larose.

Rhodes, S. L. 1991. "Rethinking Desertification: What Do We Know and What Have We Learned?" *World Development* 19(9):1137-1143.

Tucker, C. J., H. E. Dregne, and W. W. Newcomb. 1991. "Expansion and Contraction of the Sahara Desert from 1980 to 1990." *Science* 253:299-300.

8

Environmental Degradation in Northern Africa: An Ecological Modeling Approach with Implications for Sustainable Development and Global Change

Christopher S. Potter

Ecological change in arid environments often involves degradation of the soil and desertification — the diminution or destruction of the biological productivity of the land (UNCOD 1978). Whereas periodic drought can exacerbate the process, desertification is chiefly a human-induced phenomenon (Kassas 1985). Although anthropogenic environmental change has occurred in North Africa since Paleolithic times (Le Houérou 1979), sharp, localized declines in land productivity appear to be associated with rapid increases in population sizes (both human and livestock), land clearing, cultivation, and grazing pressure during the twentieth century.

Two decades ago vegetation production in North Africa was estimated at about 25 percent of levels that could be achieved under appropriate management practices (Rodin et al. 1970; Le Houérou 1978). Despite such pessimistic assessments, it has been difficult to estimate the actual extent and severity of environmental degradation over large areas, especially in remote or extremely dry zones where regular ground-based reconnaissance may be limited. The fact is that much survey information for arid environments remains anecdotal and of low reliability (Dregne 1990).

Nevertheless, it is possible to monitor changes in the productivity of vast areas using satellite sensors (see, for example, Box et al. 1989; Justice et al.

131

1985; Tucker et al. 1986, 1983a). As a complement to field surveys, remote sensing technology can significantly improve assessments of environmental change at scales from local to global (Hobbs and Mooney 1990). Reliable, broad-scale estimates of environmental deterioration add new dimensions as well as new responsibilities to policy making. It may be feasible to monitor certain ecological impacts of development investments using satellite observations. Assuming that environmental quality figures prominently in plans for more *sustainable* development, remote sensing technology can provide one objective basis for evaluation of success. Moreover, it has become possible to analyze the problem of desertification on its own terms; that is, considering scales at which regional and global change is taking place. The analysis described in this chapter provides both environmental opportunity and accountability to development practitioners and their constituents.

The purpose of this chapter is threefold. First, it provides background information on techniques for application of remote sensing technology to studies of environmental change. A demonstration of radiative transfer modeling for assessment of potential ecosystem degradation is included as an example for the Northern Africa region. Second, it interprets the results of the remote-sensing based modeling, within the context of sustainable development in North Africa, and reviews general guidelines for dryland restoration. Finally, it outlines a framework for analyzing the impacts of global warming on ecosystems of North Africa as a system of plausible environmental feedback mechanisms.

Review of Earth Remote Sensing

The 1972 launch of the Landsat Multi-Spectral Scanner (MSS) by the National Aeronautics and Space Administration (NASA) provided a new avenue of study for environmental scientists.[1] Satellite observations began to furnish a long-term synoptic view of the biosphere that was extended to the global scale in 1979 by the National Oceanographic and Atmospheric Administration's (NOAA) Advanced Very High Resolution Radiometer (AVHRR). The AVHRR is a satellite-supported, polar-orbiting sensor that produces images of the earth's surface cover at a 1 kilometer (km) spatial resolution (Tucker et al. 1986). These multi-temporal observations have become a common tool for extrapolation of useful ecological indexes over relatively broad scales.

A common remote sensing index is related to the "greenness" of the vegetation cover. It has been called the Normalized Difference Vegetation Index (NDVI). Land classification for the African continent, including deforestation and land conversion, has been derived from AVHRR-NDVI observations (Tucker et al. 1984). Changes in the amount and distribution of green standing vegetation have been assessed (Justice 1986). For crops and grasslands, the greenness index increases with increasing leaf area cover or biomass (Prince and Tucker 1986; Aswar et al. 1989). Reflectance of the underlying surface is an important factor affecting NDVI measurements. Bare soil reflectance can introduce errors of up to 20 percent (Huete 1989). Nevertheless, results from these studies have suggested that, with proper corrections and calibrations of the radiance data, annual agricultural production patterns can be monitored from space.

In a recent application with important implications for North African nations, the AVHRR-NDVI was used with some success to monitor vegetation dynamics during the international campaign to halt the spread of desert locusts (*Schistocerca gregaria*, Forskål) from Sahelian nations into North Africa (reviewed by Showler and Potter 1991; Showler, this volume). Monitoring seasonal dynamics of vegetation greenness by remote sensing offers an early-warning system for detecting responses to drought. It may aid in speeding operations for international relief of famine.

Meaning and Measurement of NPP

A fundamental principle of optical remote sensing related to monitoring the status of ecosystems is that solar radiation incident upon a plant may continue along one of three paths: reflection, absorption, or transmission. Certain remote sensors detect radiation that is reflected by a canopy of the vegetation. The composition of leaf pigments determines the magnitude of reflectance in the visible portion of light spectrum (400-700 nanometers [nm]). Reflectance in the near infrared (NIR) region (720-1300 nm) is controlled to a large degree by the arrangement of cells in the internal portion of leaves.

The comparison of reflectance in the visible to reflectance in the infrared is thought to convey ecologically significant information related to plant photosynthetic activity and the amount of green leaf cover over the soil surface. Experience has shown that incident solar irradiance in the NIR can penetrate through the plant canopy and reflect back up through multiple layers of leaves. The result is an increase in NIR reflectance relative to visible reflectance such that the simple ratio (SR) of NIR-to-visible increases as more leaf layers are added, up to about six layers (Ranson and Williams 1992). Ecologists (particularly those communicating in the English language) define *net primary productivity* (NPP) as the amount of biomass synthesized by plants per unit area/unit time. This term represents a portion of the gross photosynthetically absorbed carbon dioxide remaining after plants meet maintenance respiration requirements. Combined units of grams of carbon per square meter per year (g C m^{-2} yr^{-1}) are commonly reported.

Ecologists and other researchers of desertification point to productivity in general and NPP specifically as among the most significant aggregated indicators of land degradation (Lieth 1975; Steiner et al. 1988; Aber and Melillo 1991). The largest portion of human food sources comes from terrestrial NPP. Humankind now co-opts an amount equivalent to about 40 percent of the planet's annual NPP (Vitousek et al. 1986), with largely unknown consequences for the stability of natural ecosystems and the millions of other species that depend on them.

Several studies have defined a strong relationship between season NPP and satellite vegetation indices (Goward et al. 1985, 1987; Box et al. 1988). For example, in a study of Sahelian grasslands, Prince (1991) demonstrated a strong linear relationship over the annual NPP range on 0-300 g C m^{-2} with confidence interval of 6-16 g C m^{-2}.

It should be noted that NPP is only one component of a more holistic measure of ecosystem status, *net ecosystem production* (NEP), the difference between NPP and respiration of heterotrophic (nonphotosynthetic) organisms. NEP is the sum of changes in organic matter stored in live plants and animals and the soil organic pool. This total carbon balance of the ecosystem can be positive or negative, regardless of changes in NPP alone (Aber and Melillo 1991). While most ecosystems tend toward an NEP of zero over long time periods, disturbances such as fire or land clearing for agriculture can dramatically alter the carbon balance on broad scales.

Methodology

The following section outlines a methodology to assess the productive capacity of ecosystems using satellite observations. Global coverage AVHRR data sets have been applied in this demonstration analysis for estimation of NPP for the years 1983-1984 using a mathematical model that unites satellite sensor observation provided by Kumar and Montieth (1981). NPP may be represented as a function of the capacity of vegetation to convert solar radiation into biomass, which is tied closely to the efficiency of the photosynthetic process. The model is summarized mathematically in Equation 8.1, following the work of Heimann and Keeling (1989).

Equation 8.1 $NPP = e * (0.2793*(SR-1.051)) * S$

where e is the efficiency constant for carbon fixation (g C MJ^{-1}PAR); SR is the simple ratio of near infrared-to-visible AVHRR channel; S is total solar radiation; and (MJ m^{-2} mo^{-1}). Photosynthetic carbon fixation efficiency values (e) in many managed systems range from 0.5 to 1.5 g carbon per MJ photosynthetically active radiation (PAR), depending on plant type and age (Russell et al. 1989). Terrestrial plant canopies (chiefly crops) exhibit values of up to 1.4 g C MJ^{-1} PAR. Although e is generally thought to be a relatively conservative term when considered over diverse vegetation types (Field 1991), secondary effects may operate through temperature, moisture and nutrient stresses so as to reduce the effective e value. This concept has been tested by Potter et al. (1993) using the CASA Biosphere model in global studies of terrestrial production. Results show that typical values of e range from 0.14 -0.30 g C MJ^{-1} PAR in desert and shrub ecosystem types.

The SR term used in Equation 8.1 can be derived through a mathematical transformation of the AVHRR-derived NDVI (Fung et al. 1987). NDVI is related to green leaf cover and absorbed photosynthetically active radiation (Aswar et al. 1984; Tucker et al. 1986). Global coverage data sets for NDVI/SR have been derived from NOAA satellite observations at approximately weekly intervals (Tarpley et al. 1984). For distribution to the global change research community, however, digital data have been composited to monthly scenes (as explained in Justice et al. 1985) and mapped from an original pixel size of 1.1 km (at the equator) to 1°x1° latitude/longitude global grid coordinates. The planetary land surface is thus represented by approximately 21 thousand grid cells. These relatively coarse resolution data are suitable to regional-to-global level analysis on most workstation and high speed personal computers. Full decadal (1980-89) global coverage NDVI data sets at the original 1 km resolution should be available to researchers over the next several years (see Note 1).

The solar radiation fields used in this analysis have been compiled by Bishop and Rossow (1991) for months July 1983 to June 1984. The chief data source is from the International Satellite Cloud Climatology Project C1 at nominal 2.5°x2.5° resolution sampled every three hours for the globe.

All data sets were entered as map layers in a Geographic Information System (GIS). A fully functional raster GIS handles the digitization, transformation, and storage of spatial data arrays. Entry of model variables (Equation 8.1) in the GIS provides the capability for output map layer overlay; weighting or averaging by base (biome type, life zone, or soil type) data bases; and rapid georeferenced isolation of regions or grid cells of interest.

Model Results and Interpretation

The following analysis is provided chiefly to illustrate how remote sensing technology can be used by environmental scientists in monitoring the state of the land surface and its potential productivity. As only a single year of atmospherically corrected data was publicly available at the time of this analysis, all interpretations must be qualified in relation to potential year-to-year variability. Moreover, it should be noted that regional scale temperature or precipitation anomalies (relative to long-term climate averages) in the period of 1983-1984 may be reflected in the plant productivity assessments provided below. As such, no attempt was made to predict interannual patterns in regional NPP, nor should the 1983-1984 results be taken as necessarily typical of previous or subsequent years. The main purpose of the following analysis is to illustrate both the potential and the limitations of optical remote sensing for modeling and monitoring environmental change.

Global Validation of the NPP Model

The model shown in Equation 8.1 was applied to the global data sets for 1983-1984. Following the calibration method of Heimann and Keeling (1989), which set PAR at 50 percent of total solar radiation (McCree 1981), *e* was assigned a spatially uniform value of 0.7 for calculations in the present study. Based on *e* alone, therefore, results from this initial analysis may tend toward the higher probable range of regional NPP assessment (Potter et al. 1993). A global estimate of NPP (derived from Equation 8.1 and summed on a total area basis for all terrestrial grid cells) was approximated at 65 Gt C yr^{-1} (1 Gt = 10^{15} grams) over the years 1983-1984. As expected from the *e* value assignment, this total is somewhat higher than previously remote sensing-based estimates for global NPP (47 to 56 Gt C yr^{-1}) (Fung et al. 1987; Heimann and Keeling 1989; Potter et al. 1993). It is, nonetheless, within the range of probable global values (50-70 Gt C yr^{-1}) commonly cited (IPCC 1990).

Regional Ecosystem NPP — North Africa

The geographic region of interest lies between latitudes 38 and 18 N, longitudes 20 W and 35 E. Annual composited NPP (1988) calculated from Equation 8.1 is shown for the region in Figure 8.1. Forested coastal zones show the highest NPP throughout the year, with annual values greater than 500 g C m^{-2}yr^{-1}. Grasslands, whose regional extent over all of Africa is shown in Figure 8.2 (Matthews 1983), range on average from 100-250 g C m^{-2}yr^{-1} NPP throughout North Africa. Seasonal patterns reveal a "greenup" along the regional margins during the period between January and April, with a "greendown" during the period between July and October (Figure 8.1). The southern margins that border the Sahel appear to lag slightly behind Mediterranean coastal zones in the annual production cycle.

Comparative Potential NPP

In order to put the estimated NPP values shown in Figure 8.1 into a global context, an index of potential productivity was derived. This index used long-term, global coverage (30 year) climate averages (Shea 1986) to

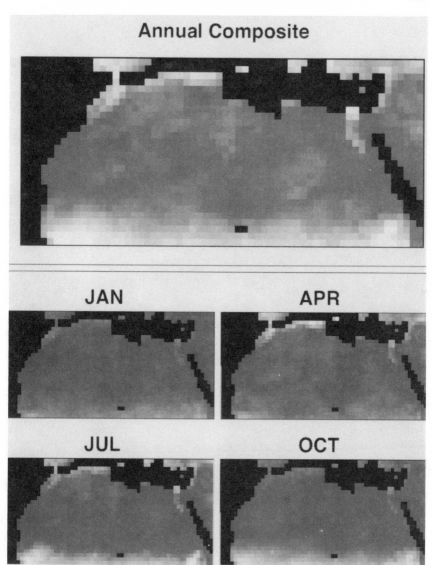

FIGURE 8.1 Net Primary Productivity in North Africa, 1983-1984. Different shades represent different levels of NPP, expressed in grams of carbon per square meter per year (g C m^{-2} yr^{-1}). For the *annual composite*, black represents water; dark gray represents NPP values of less than 100/year; light gray representss NPP values of 100-500; and white represents NPP values greater than 500. For the *seasonal composites*, black represents water; dark gray represents NPP values of less than 20; light gray represents NPP values of 20-100; and white represents NPP values of greater than 100.

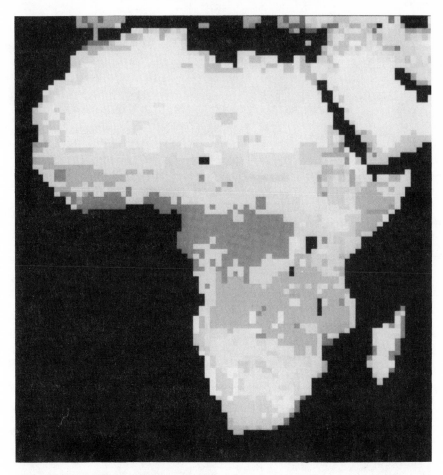

FIGURE 8.2 Vegetation Types in Africa. White represents deserts; light gray represents grasslands and steppes; gray represents dry woodlands and shrubs; dark gray represents moist forests; and black represents water.

Source: Adapted from Matthews 1983.

calculate a comparative *potential* NPP. Leith (1972) generated regression equations for the prediction of NPP on the basis of annual average temperature and precipitation, using measured vegetation data from the International Biological Program (IBP) archives. This relationship was developed from ecosystems that had not been subject to human disturbance, and is therefore interpreted to be a potential productivity estimate in the sense that relatively undegraded systems were represented.

The productivity index was calculated as the ratio of actual NPP (Equation 8.1) to potential NPP over the region at 1°x1° grid cell resolution. This index, which covers a range of 0-100 percent, permits evaluation of the relative productivity at any grid location and comparison of regional trends in NPP. As values approach 100 percent, productivity is assumed to approach the measured average level for climate regimes of that type.

This analysis indicates that, compared to global average ratios for the years 1983-1984, areas within the North African region characterized as evergreen broad-leaved woodland-shrubland and xeromorphic shrubland (Matthews 1983) were not unusually low in terms of annual productivity (Figure 8.3). Average NPP index values for North African woodland/shrubland types ranged from 24-68 percent, compared with the global average range of 29-46 percent for similar ecosystems. Woodlands and shrublands cover around 40 percent of the non-desert areas in the North African region. This analysis does not necessarily suggest that these areas remain entirely undegraded with reference to NPP; rather it indicates that, insofar as 1983-1984 climatic conditions were not significantly different from the long-term regional average (Shea 1986), productivity was not substantially less than in similar systems on a worldwide basis. Nevertheless, it is conceivable that global averages reflect widespread degradation of dry woodland ecosystems.

In contrast, zones dominated by grassland (with some shrub cover) or short grass-meadow ecosystems (Matthews 1983; Figure 8.2) appear to have lost substantial productive capacity, relative to global index averages. During the years 1983-1984, these areas averaged only 15-30 percent of their long-term average potential productivity, whereas global averages for the same ecosystem types displayed around 100 percent of productive potential. Local and regional climatic conditions could account for all or part of this pattern. If, however, grassland areas were not disproportionally affected by drought in 1983-1984 (particularly compared to woodland/shrubland areas), this analysis suggests that degraded grassland vegetation could cover around 7 percent of the total North African region, or up to 40 percent of nondesert areas. These ecosystems correspond roughly to *steppe* and *erme* vegetation types in the French terminology (Le Houérou 1979). Classification of the magnitude of degradation by soil type (Zobler 1986) indicates that cambisols and xerosols have lost the highest relative productivity. These two soil types are found over approximately 36 percent of nondesert areas.

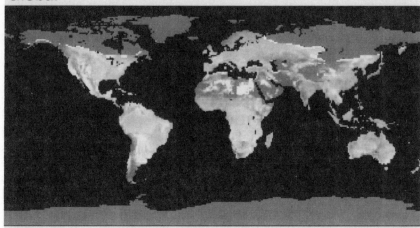

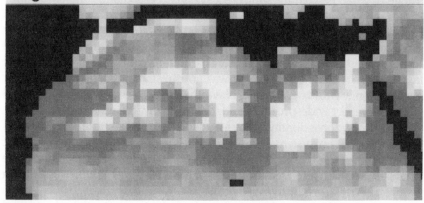

FIGURE 8.3 Relative Productivity Index for North Africa, expressed as percent of potential NPP. Black represents water; dark gray represents NPP values of less than 50 percent; light gray represents NPP values of from 50-100 percent; white represents NPP values exceeding 100 percent.

Geographic Analysis — Probable Zones at Risk

Regional mapping of the NPP index suggests that vegetation cover over large parts of northern Algeria and almost all of southern Tunisia could be substantially (50 percent) below long-term average productive potential (Figure 8.3).

Similar patterns of subaverage productivity can be cited along the pre-Saharan areas east of the Middle Atlas mountains in Morocco. These are qualified conclusions, however, because high interannual variability in climate has a potentially dramatic effect on the greenness index values. Moreover, if dry conditions occur during any given year selected for analysis, much of the land under agricultural usage may be left fallow, so that production is intentionally suppressed for local economic reasons. On the other hand, irrigated areas should reflect management related production increases. The Nile delta areas, for example, reflect high agricultural activity. Because of their inherently low productive capacity (Lieth 1972), desert zones do not show substantial declines in measured NPP.

Limitations of the Methodology

Heimann and Keeling (1989) reviewed potential biases of the modified Kumar and Monteith (1981) NPP model (Equation 8.1). At least two sources of uncertainty exist: 1) the efficiency constant e may vary with plant species or ecosystem stress (water and nutrient) factors; 2) the AVHRR-derived SR term may be altered by frequent cloud cover and low sun angles at high latitude. Only the first of these two possible biases is likely to be significant over the North African region.

While some evidence suggests that e is relatively invariant, factors such as plant disease, drought, nutrient deficiency, and irrigation may alter the seasonal dry matter yield of energy (Prince 1987). Natural, perennial vegetation that experiences significant moisture or nutritional stress may fix carbon during the dormant dry season without impressive visible growth (Running 1990). The implication for the present study is the potential for Equation 8.1 to underestimate NPP slightly during certain months of the year. Assignment of a consistently high e value (0.7) should have balanced this tendency to some extent.

Several factors confine the analysis presented above chiefly to a demonstration of methodology. First, use of AVHRR at relatively coarse spatial resolution precludes detailed differentiation of ecosystem-level patterns of production. For example, it is not possible to say which species of plant is present but only that the area in question is covered with some type of green vegetation. Improved regional and national vegetation mapping is needed to strengthen studies of this nature.

In terms of detecting desertification in its broadest form, it should be noted that the AVHRR sensor would not distinguish areas of natural or primary vegetation from areas where native species have been replaced by alien or weedy species. Secondary regrowth following deforestation may reflect radiation in a manner much like primary plant cover. The sensor should, however, detect changes in leaf cover resulting from the replacement of relatively dense forests by shrub communities.

The loss of ecosystem level productivity is one important indicator of continuing desertification processes, especially in fragile arid environments where any loss of plant cover can take many decades to rehabilitate (Dormaar and Smoliak 1985). Where grassland communities have been given over to agriculture, remote sensing evaluations must consider the seasonality of "greenup" and "greendown" periods to distinguish between natural and managed systems (Justice et al. 1989). Furthermore, environmentally deleterious factors such as sheet erosion of soil and salinization of irrigated lands are difficult to detect with existing satellite sensor technology. High resolution Landsat Thematic Mapper (TM) data are more useful in these cases. Atmospherically corrected AVHRR local area coverage (1.1 km resolution) data may supplement Landsat, but the former is not yet widely available as multitemporal global or regional images.

In this demonstration, conclusions about long-term productive potential of managed areas therefore must remain qualified at best. Environmental degradation is not necessarily a consequence of conversion of natural habitats to human systems of food production, although an argument can be made that risk of production failure is higher under dryland agricultural use (Steiner et al. 1988). An increasing amplitude of year-to-year production levels might be an important indicator of desertification. Future studies using satellite observations in the manner outlined above will provide valuable surveillance of interannual patterns of agricultural production and potential damage to the natural resource base.

Implications for Sustainable Development

Remote sensing has changed the way scientists view the biosphere and accompanying atmospheric interactions, and has helped define the role of humans in global change. The major implications of the previous model analysis are that: 1) woodland and shrubland areas in the North African region should be conserved and protected to the greatest extent possible as a safeguard against loss of the region's remaining productive potential, and 2) grassland (steppe) habitats will require rapid, large-scale restoration management to avoid total ecosystem collapse. Effective, albeit potentially costly, methodology for restoring degraded arid lands has been demonstrated.

Studies on the restoration of drylands elsewhere in the world suggest that mimicking natural soil conditions (moisture and nutrient availability) can significantly improve plant reestablishment and speed recovery of productivity (Bainbridge and Virginia 1990). In many cases, relatively rapid recovery is realized when soil biota (particularly mycorrhizae that increase plant uptake of phosphorus, a limiting nutrient) are reintroduced through human intervention (Allan 1988). In the absence of active management, the recovery time for badly degraded dryland areas is on the order of decades to centuries (Webb et al. 1983). The implication of this ecological reality for sustainable development is that major capital and human resource investments will be needed to rehabilitate better than 40 percent of the degraded nondesert lands in the North African region. Given the apparent state of the landscape with regard to lost productivity, coupled with the long time scales over which soil formation occurs in this environment, these degraded areas will not recover and become environmentally sustainable in the absence of further human intervention and judicious management.

Guidelines for restoration of degraded arid-land soils have been provided by Bainbridge and Virginia (1990) and others. Ideally, development restoration projects should budget for all of the following items:

1. Evaluation of site data on the status of soils, vegetation, wildlife and microclimate;
2. Collection of native seeds and plant material for propagation;
3. Preparation of hardened surfaces for replanting;
4. Direct seeding with mix of plant species;
5. Transplantation of root-inoculated, fast growing native species to protected microsites.

Similar recommendations are likely to be found in the local literature throughout North Africa. The main issue is not *technically* how to rehabilitate the land, but how to reorient development priorities to include restoration of ecosystems.

From a national planning perspective, the analysis presented here provides merely a first step in the conservation and rehabilitation of fragile ecosystems. The relatively coarse spatial resolution of the maps shown in Figures 8.1-8.3 was used primarily to facilitate regional-global comparisons of productivity averages. Corresponding high resolution satellite data sets exist, however, and should be applied in subsequent assessments. Areas identified as potentially degraded in this relatively coarse-grained analysis should be examined using detailed satellite and aircraft observations to pinpoint the most vulnerable remaining natural ecosystems and deteriorating managed sites.

This information should be combined with GIS technology to facilitate a total systems analysis approach to the restoration process. A GIS can incorporate social, economic, and environmental elements in digital map layer overlays to identify areas of probable intervention and successful rehabilitation project activity. As with any technology transfer, however, local training and clearly stated sustainable development objectives must be stressed.

A Framework for Climate Change:
Ecosystem Research in North Africa

Deforestation and desertification in North Africa must be seen within the larger and potentially changing global climate system. The question environmental scientists who can contribute to public policy decisions should be asking is, "If the planet warms, as is predicted by a host of atmospheric general circulation models (AGCM), how will ecosystems in Northern Africa respond in terms of their productivity and long-term stability?" The answer to this question lies in a comprehensive understanding of the coupled global and regional climate system, potential biological feedbacks to temperature, and, perhaps most importantly, human management of the land.

Nearly two decades ago Charney (1975) hypothesized that deforestation in the Sahel was a factor contributing to desertification on the edges of the region. This is a feasible scenario because denuding the vegetation cover increases land surface albedo, causing a net radiative loss compared to adjacent forested areas. Atmospheric circulation patterns may subsequently develop such that heat is imported from aloft and the air column is forced to subside. Together these processes can suppress convective forms of rainfall, possibly leading to increased drought. In the worst case, a positive feedback to plant stress, mortality, and, ultimately, desertification, may be established.

Changes in rainfall distribution and variability will affect soil conditions for plant growth and reestablishment following disturbance. By combining results from climate model experiments, which suggest a warmer regional climate throughout Northern Africa, with paleoclimatic reconstructions, Kellogg (1990) constructed a scenario of probable changes in soil moisture with climate change. For coastal Mediterranean zones, drier than present conditions were predicted, whereas wetter than present conditions may prevail over the vast inland desert areas of the Maghreb countries. Increased frequency of drought in the most important agricultural production areas of the North African region has potentially dire implications for economic development in the Maghreb.

Most computer modeling results suggest that climatic change is likely over vast areas of the globe in the decades to come (IPCC 1990), including reductions in soil moisture over some semiarid zones (Manabe and Wetherald 1986). In a comprehensive study of human ecology in arid areas, Schlesinger et al. (1990) have elaborated on changes that can be expected with increasing desertification and feedbacks to the global coupling of atmosphere-biosphere processes. Based on field studies from the southwestern United States, their major conclusion is that, on a local level, any process that leads to increasing fragmentation of plant and soil resources in either time or space is likely to exacerbate the degradation of semiarid grassland ecosystems. These processes commonly include overgrazing and operation of off-road vehicles, both of which promote soil erosion. Furthermore, when human populations grow and become concentrated into new areas of development, the landscape becomes more heterogeneous, fragmented, and thereby subject to degradation.

In order to relate this hypothesis more specifically to the North African environment, a brief comparative review of the climatology of the semiarid zones is appropriate. Stockton and Meko (1990) pointed out differences between the hydroclimatologic regimes of the southwestern United States and Morocco; these areas differ dramatically with respect to temporal variability of winter precipitation and annual and interannual potential evapotranspiration (low in the United States, high in Morocco in both cases).

These authors also noted that although high spatial variation occurs in rainfall between areas of Morocco, when drought occurs, it frequently affects the entire country. Nevertheless, although the interactive effects of habitat fragmentation and climatic variability remain largely unknown for an expanse such as that covered by the Maghreb, it seems plausible that desertification processes will become more acute in areas of higher rainfall variability.

On the global scale, losses of productivity in arid and semiarid zones may have relatively minor direct impacts on the carbon cycle. Nevertheless, processes associated with the deterioration of drylands can affect global atmospheric patterns through both increased emissions of trace gases and the release of dust during wind erosion. Denitrification, the gaseous loss of nitrogen from soil, may be significant in tropical dry environments (Davidson 1991), which can result in higher greenhouse gas fluxes to the atmosphere. On the other hand, dust from arid regions augments tropospheric aerosol levels, which in turn may lead to climate *cooling* effects (Toon and Pollack 1988). These combined effects on global temperature and precipitation patterns are not yet fully understood.

A conceptual model that shows some of the coupling of terrestrial ecosystem processes to climate change and global atmospheric dynamics

FIGURE 4. MODEL OF SCALE-PROCESS LINKAGES
IN GLOBAL CHANGE

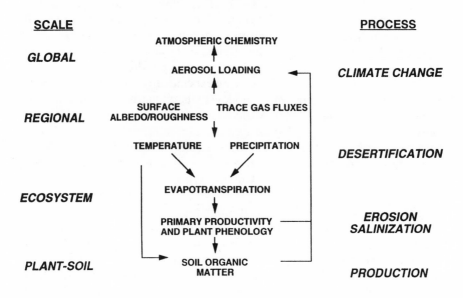

FIGURE 8.4 Model of Scale-Process Linkages in Global Change

is provided in Figure 8.4. The linkages specified, and many others that could be considered, are mainly heuristic reference points for the development of improved computer models of the global environment.

Certain potential feedbacks are particularly relevant in the arid zones and worthy of elaboration here. On the ecosystem scale, temperature increases related to the greenhouse effect may lead to higher evapotranspiration, latent heat loss, and water stress for crops and natural vegetation. For example, alfalfa and date palm may be especially susceptible to moisture shortages (Abderrahman et al. 1991). As production declines accordingly, soil organic matter levels drop, while trace gas emissions and surface albedo increase. The feedback to climate change is thus established, although wind erosion and related aerosol loading may counteract the warming tendency. Much will depend on the role human populations play in tipping the balance toward or away from accelerated desertification.

Conclusions

This chapter has discussed the utility of modeling plant productivity from satellite observations. The methodology outlined here, which combines the monthly greenness index values with the data on solar radiation fluxes and photosynthetic conversion efficiencies, has broad applicability for environmental monitoring at various spatial scales. Although conclusions regarding degradation must be restricted on the basis of availability of regional and local climate records and the coarse spatial resolution of AVHRR data, analysis of 1983-1984 satellite greenness maps suggests a pattern of severe production declines of areas that are or were grassland and grass-shrub vegetation types in the North African region. Degradation of fragile arid and semiarid lands is linked to larger scale processes of global climate change. To predict more accurately the environmental setting for sustainable development, it is critical that research be conducted on the coupling of anthropogenic land use dynamics to changes in the distribution and variability of precipitation at the regional level.

Notes

1. The U.S. Geological Survey will make available multi-temporal Landsat and AVHRR scenes at fairly affordable prices under the Pathfinder program. For more infomation, write to USGS, EROS Data Center, Sioux Falls, South Dakota, 57198 USA.

References

Abderrahman, W. A., T. A. Bader, A. U. Kahn, and M. H. Ajward. 1991. "Weather modification impact of reference evapotranspiration, soil salinity and desertification in arid region: a case study." *Journal of Arid Environments* 20:277-286.

Aber, J. D., and J. M. Melillo. 1991. *Terrestrial Ecosystems*. Philadelphia: Saunders College Publishing.

Allan, E. B. 1988. "The reconstruction of disturbed arid lands: an ecological approach." *AAAS Selected Symposium 109*. Boulder CO: Westview Press.

Aswar, G., M. Fuchs, E. T. Kanemasu, and J. L. Hatfield. 1984. "Estimating absorbed photosynthetic radiation and leaf area index from spectral reflectance in wheat." *Agronomy Journal* 76:300-306.

Aswar, G., R. B. Myneni, and E. E. Kanemasu. 1989. "Estimation of plant canopy attributes from spectral reflectance measurements," in G. Aswar, ed., *Theory and Applications of Optical Remote Sensing*. Pp. 252-295. New York: John Wiley and Sons.

Bainbridge, D. A., and R. A. Virginia. 1990. "Restoration in the Sonoran Desert of California." *Restoration and Management Notes* 8(1):3-14.

Bishop, J. K. B., and W. B. Rossow. 1991. "Spatial and temporal variability of global surface solar irradiance." *Journal of Geophysical Research* 96 (C9):16839-16858.

Box, E., B. N. Holben, and V. Kalb. 1989. "Accuracy of AVHHR vegetation index as a predictor of biomass, primary productivity and net CO_2 flux." *Vegetatio* 80: 71-89.

Charney, J. G. 1975. "Dynamics of deserts and drought in the Sahel." *Quarterly Journal of the Royal Meterological Society* 101:193-202.

Davidson, E. A. 1991. "Fluxes of nitrous and nitric oxide from terrestrial ecosystems," in J. E. Rogers and W. B. Whitman, eds., *Microbial Production and Consumption of Greenhouse Gases: Methane, Nitrogen Oxides and Halomethanes*. Pp. 219-235. Washington D.C.: American Society for Microbiology.

Dormaar, J. F., and S. Smoliak. 1985. "Recovery of vegetative cover and soil organic matter during revegetation of abandoned farmland in a semiarid climate."" *Journal of Range Management* 38(6):487-491.

Dregne, H. E. 1990. "Desertification: man-made impacts on arid lands," in D. R. Haragan, ed., *Human Intervention in the Climatology of Arid Lands*. Pp. 27-38. Albuquerque: University of New Mexico Press.

Field, C. B. 1991. "Ecological scaling of carbon gain to stress and resource availability," in H. A. Mooney, W. E. Winner, and E. J. Pell, eds., *Integrated Responses of Plants to Stress*, Pp. 35-65. San Diego: Academic Press.

Fung, I. Y., C. J. Tucker, and K. C. Prentice. 1987. "Application of advanced very high resolution radiometer vegetation index to study of atmosphere-biosphere exchange of CO_2." *Journal of Geophysical Research* 92:2999-3015.

Goward, S. N., and D. G. Dye. 1985. "Evaluating North American net primary productivity with satellite data." *Advances in Space Research* 7:165-174.

Goward, S. N., D. G. Dye, A. Kerber, and V. Kalb. 1987. "Comparison of North and South American biomes from AVHRR observations." *Geocarto International* 1:27-39.

Heimann, M., and C. D. Keeling. 1989. "A three dimensional model of atmospheric CO_2 transport based on observed winds. II. Model description," in D. H. Peterson, ed., *Aspects of climate variability in the Pacific and Western America* (Geophysical Monograph 55). Pp. 240-260. Washington D. C.: AGU.

Hobbs, R. J., and H. A. Mooney, eds. 1990. *Remote Sensing and Biosphere Functioning*. New York: Springer-Verlag.

Huete, A. R. 1989. "Soil influences in remotely sensed vegetation-canopy spectra," in G. Aswar, ed., *Theory and Applications of Optical Remote Sensing*. Pp. 107-141. New York: John Wiley and Sons.

IPCC. 1990. "Climate change: the IPCC scientific assessment." *Report of the Intergovernmental Panel on Climate Change*. Cambridge: Cambridge University Press.

Justice, C. O., ed. 1986. "Monitoring the grasslands of semi-arid Africa using NOAA AVHRR data." *International Journal of Remote Sensing* 7:1383-1622.

Justice, C. O., J. R. G. Townshend, B. N. Holben, and C. J. Tucker. 1985. "Analysis of the phenology of global vegetation using meteorological satellite data." *International Journal of Remote Sensing* 6(8):1271-1318.

Justice, C. O., J. R. G. Townshend, and B. J. Choudhury. 1989. "Comparison of AVHRR and SMMR data for monitoring vegetation phenology on a continental scale." *International Journal of Remote Sensing* 10(10):1607-1632.

Kassas, M., 1985. "Deforestation, desertification and soil loss." *Desertification Control Bulletin* 12:12-19.

Kellogg, W. W. 1990. "How well can we forecast climate change?" in D. R. Haragan, ed., *Human Intervention in the Climatology of Arid Lands*. Pp. 101-137. Albuquerque: University of New Mexico Press.

Kumar, M., and J. L. Montieth. 1981. "Remote sensing of crop growth," in H. Smith, ed., *Plants and the Daylight Spectrum*. Pp. 133-144. London: Academic Press.

Le Houérou, H. N. 1978. "La désertification du Sahara septentrional et des steppes limitrophes (Libye, Tunisie, Algérie)." *Conseil de Tutelle Colloque Hammamat et Annales Algérie de Géographique* 3(6):2-27.

———. 1979. "North Africa," in D. W. Goodall, R. A. Perry, and K. M. W. Howes, eds., *Arid-land Ecosystems: Structure, Functioning and Management, International Biological Program Volume 16*. Pp. 83-108. Cambridge: Cambridge University Press.

Lieth, H. 1972. "Modelling the primary productivity of the world." *Nature and Resources* 8(2):5-10.

———. 1975. "Primary production of the major vegetation units of the world," in H. Lieth and R. H. Whittaker, eds., *Primary Production of the Biosphere*. Pp. 203-231. New York: Springer-Verlag.

Manabe, S., and R. T. Wetherald. 1986. "Reduction in summer soil wetness induced by an increase in atmospheric carbon dioxide." *Science* 232:626.

Matthews, E. 1983. "Global vegetation and land use: new high-resolution data-bases for climate studies." *Journal of Climate and Applied Meteorology* 22:474-487.

McCree, K. J. 1981. "Photosynthetically active radiation," in O. L. Lange, P. S. Nobel, C. B. Osmond, and H. Ziegler, eds., *Physiological Plant Ecology I. Responses to the Physical Environment. Volume 12A.* Pp. 41-55. Berlin: Springer-Verlag.

Potter, C. S., J. T. Randerson, C. B. Field, P. A. Matson, P. M. Vitousek, H. A. Mooney, and S. A. Klooster. 1993. "Terrestrial ecosystem production: a process model based on global satellite and surface data." *Global Biogeochemical Cycles* 7(4):811-841.

Prince, S. D. 1987. "Satellite remote sensing of primary production: comparison of results for Sahelian grasslands 1981-1988." *International Journal of Remote Sensing* 12(6):1301-1311.

————. 1991. "A model of regional primary production for use with coarse resolution satellite data." *International Journal of Remote Sensing* 12(6): 1313-1330.

Prince, S. D., and C. J. Tucker. 1986. "Satellite remote sensing of rangelands in Botswana. II. NOAA AVHRR and herbaceous vegetation." *International Journal of Remote Sensing* 7:1555-1570.

Ranson, K. J., and D. L. Williams. 1992. "Remote sensing technology for forest ecosystem analysis," in H. H. Shugart, R. Leemans, and G. B. Bonan, eds., *Systems Analysis of the Global Boreal Forest.* Pp. 267-290. Cambridge: Cambridge University Press.

Rodin, L., B. Vinogradov, Y. Mirochnichenko, M. Pelt, H. Kolenov, and V. Botschantzev. 1970. *Etudes géobotaniques des pâturages du secteur ouest du Département de Médéa de la République Algérienne Démocratique et Populaire.* Leningrad: Nauka.

Running, S. W. 1990. In R. J. Hobbs and H. A. Mooney, eds., *Remote Sensing and Biosphere Functioning,* Pp. 65-86. New York: Springer-Verlag.

Russell, G. P., Jarvis, G., and J. L. Monteith. 1989. "Absorption of radiation by canopies and stand growth," in G. P. Russell, B. Marshall, and G. Jarvis, eds., *Plant Canopies: Their Growth, Form and Function.* Pp. 21-39. Cambridge: Cambridge University Press.

Schlesinger, W. H., J. F. Reynolds, G. L. Cunningham, L. F. Huenneke, W. M. Jarrell, R. A. Virgina, and W. G. Whitford. 1990. "Biological feedbacks in global desertification." *Science* 247:1043-1048.

Shea, D. J. 1986. Climatological Atlas 1950-1979. *Surface Air Temperature, Precipitation, Sea-level Pressure and Sea Surface Temperature (45°S-90°N).* Atmospheric Analysis and Prediction Division, National Center for Atmospheric Research, NCAR Technical Note, NCAR/TN-269+STR.

Showler, A. T., and C. S. Potter. 1991. "Synopsis of the 1986-1989 desert locust (Orthoptera: Acrididae) plague and the concept of strategic control." *American Entomologist*:106-110.

Steiner, J. L., J. C. Day, R. I. Papendick, R. E. Meyer, and A. R. Bertrand. 1988. "Improving and sustaining productivity in dryland regions of developing countries." *Advances in Soil Science* 8:79-122.

Stockton, C. W., and D. M. Meko. 1990. "Some aspects of the hydroclimatology of arid and semiarid lands," in D. R. Haragan, ed., *Human Intervention in the Climatology of Arid Lands*. Pp. 1-26. Albuquerque: University of New Mexico Press.

Tarpley, J. D., S. R. Schneider, and R. L. Money. 1984. "Global vegetation indices from the NOAA-7 meteorological satellite." *Journal of Climate and Applied Meteorology* 23:491-494.

Toon, O. B., and J. B. Pollack. 1988. *American Scientist* 68: 268..

Tucker, C. J., B. N. Holben, and T. E. Goff. 1983a. *Intensive Forest Clearing in Rondonia, Brazil as Detected by Satellite Remote Sensing*. Technical Memorandum 85018. Greenbelt, MD: NASA.

Tucker, C. J., C. Vanpraet, E. Boerwinkel, and A. Gaston. 1983b. "Satellite remote sensing of total dry matter production in the Senegalese Sahel." *Remote Sensing of Environment* 13:461-474.

Tucker, C. J., J. A. Gatlin, and S. R. Schneider. 1984. "Monitoring vegetation in the Nile Delta with NOAA-6 and NOAA-7 AVHRR imagery." *Photogrammetric Engineering and Remote Sensing* 50(1):53-61.

Tucker, C. J., J. R. G. Townshend, T. E. Goff, and B. N. Holben. 1986. "Continental and global scale sensing of land cover," in J. R. Trabalka and D. E. Reichle, eds., *The Changing Carbon Cycle: A Global Analysis*. Pp. 221-41. New York: Springer-Verlag.

United Nations Conference on Desertification (UNCOD). 1978. *Round-up, Plan of Action and Resolutions*. New York: United Nations.

Vitousek, P. M., P. R. Ehrlich, A. H. Ehrlich, and P. A. Matson. 1986. "Human appropriation of the products of photosynthesis." *BioScience* 36(6):368-373.

Webb, R. A., H. G. Wilshire, and M. A. Henry. 1983. "Natural recovery of soils and vegetation following human disturbance," in *Environmental Effects of Off-Road Vehicles* Pp. 279-302. Springer-Verlag: New York.

Zobler, L. 1986. "A world soil file for global climate modeling." *NASA Technical Memorandum 87802*. Washington, DC: NASA.

PART THREE

Threatened Ecosystems and Economic Development

9

Endangered Wetlands and Environmental Management in North Africa

Barbara Parmenter

In response to environmental degradation around the globe we are urged to implement strategies of sound environmental management. *Management*, however, is an ambiguous word that often masks more than it reveals. Who are the managers, what and who are being managed, and what does it mean to manage? The ways in which people frame their understanding of the world heavily influence how they answer these questions. The problematic nature of management becomes apparent whenever one actually attempts to "manage" a place. This chapter examines North African wetlands as a case study in environmental management problems and possibilities.

The fact that wetlands cover a tiny percentage of North Africa's land surface (and less than 6 percent of the entire terrestrial globe) increases rather than lessens their significance. Wetlands contain resources that are elsewhere scarce or nonexistent, especially in areas of low rainfall. As focal points of human activity, wetlands may provide not only water for drinking and cultivation but food, in the form of fish and birds; forage for livestock; and fiber and fuel for a variety of needs. From a biological perspective, North African wetlands are oases in an otherwise relatively barren environment, providing habitat and sustenance for diverse communities of animals and plants. The more scarce surface water is, the more critical these areas become. At the same time, however, wetlands are likely to become targets for hydraulic engineering projects that aim to divert water for other purposes. Many of the historically largest wetlands in countries bordering the Mediterranean have been greatly reduced in size or completely drained. These include the Po Delta in Italy, the Ebro Delta and Valencia Lagoon in Spain, the Rhone Delta in France, the coastal lagoons of the Nile Delta in Egypt, Lake Hula in Israel, and the floodplain of the Sebou River in Morocco. As a result of this diminution, the remaining wetlands have become more important.

Wetland Definitions

The term *wetland* refers to a diverse array of water-dependent ecosystems. Lakes, lagoons, swamps, marshes, bayous, bays, estuaries, floodplains, streams, and rivers may all fall under the rubric of *wetland* depending on the definitions employed (Mitsch and Gosselink 1986; Maltby 1986). In French, *marais, marécage, tourbière,* and *étang;* in Arabic, *mustanqa'a, sabkha,* and *mallaha;* and in North African vernacular *merja* and *daya* are all terms referring to wetland habitats. Residents and other users of these areas may never have thought of them as wetlands *per se,* as this term represents a relatively new way of thinking about such places. In English, *wetland* has yet to gain general public usage and creates confusion and controversy as to its precise connotation. Translations in other languages — in French, *les zones humides* and in Arabic *al-aradi al-ratabah* — are likewise vague. The difficulty of assigning precise meaning arises from the fact that wetlands represent an intermediate zone — or more accurately, a continuum between land and water — so that any attempt to establish a single definition must be somewhat arbitrary (Mitsch and Gosselink 1986). One definition of wetlands useful for biologists has been proposed by the U. S. Fish and Wildlife Service. This agency defines wetlands as:

> lands transitional between terrestrial and aquatic systems where the water table is usually at or near the surface or the land is covered by shallow water. ...Wetlands must have one or more of the following three attributes: (1) at least periodically, the land supports predominantly hydrophytes, (2) the substrate is predominantly undrained hydric soil, and (3) the substrate is nonsoil and is saturated with water or covered by shallow water at some time during the growing season of each year (Mitsch and Gosselink 1986: 18).

We should note that in the United States, the definition of *wetland* continues to be the subject of bitter political and legal controversy stemming from the implications for government policy and legislation. This controversy reflects the power of judicial courts in negotiating environmental conflict in the

United States. In other countries the role of the judicial system is negligible. In many of the latter the establishment of definitions based on biophysical characteristics is not as important as the assessment of functional values (for example, fishing, livestock pasturing, hunting, and so on).

Wetland Values and International Conservation

It is these functional values that have formed the basis for wetland conservation efforts over the last 60 years or so. Concern for the maintenance of wetland ecosystems originated primarily with interest in migratory waterfowl protection for the benefit of recreational hunters. Research in the 1930s on waterfowl migration in North America established the concept of flyways as representing aerial pathways taken by waterfowl on seasonal movements between breeding and wintering grounds. This research identified four major corridors that ducks, swans, and geese use to cross the continent (Lincoln 1939; Bellrose 1976). Marshes, ponds, lakes, estuaries, lagoons, and other wetlands act as vital links in these flyway chains by providing food and shelter for birds during their journeys. Because waterfowl are highly valued as gamebirds, wetlands and flyways became closely associated. The maintenance of waterfowl populations necessitates the protection of wetlands that provide way stations along migratory routes.[1]

Ornithologists in Europe employed a similar flyway concept in defining bird tracks between Eurasia and Africa, some of which span more than 5,000 kilometers (km) (Boyd and Pirot 1989). Old World flyway studies, revolving less around gamebird protection, include shorebirds and other waterbird species to represent the full spectrum of wetland-dependent avifauna. The translation of the flyway concept from its formulation in North America to the Old World has been fraught with difficulty. Habitat destruction in Europe dates back far longer than in North America, with wetlands particularly susceptible to disturbance or modification as a result of highly dense human populations.

More frustrating for wetland experts has been the complex political divisions that snarl efforts to coordinate conservation activities within Europe itself, and between Europe and Africa. Cultural, social, and economic differences and disparities further aggravate protection efforts. The conservation of wetlands for birds in one country for the benefit of hunters or bird enthusiasts in another has not proved a sufficient justification for policy or land-use changes.

At the same time, however, ecological research in other fields has revealed other wetland values and reinforced arguments for conservation (Odum 1978; Maltby 1986). Beginning in the 1940s, studies of food chain dynamics have demonstrated that many types of wetlands have high rates of primary production compared with terrestrial systems, in large part the result of the auxiliary energy provided by water flow (Odum 1978).[2]

Although this may not by itself stir great public interest, related values are compelling. High primary production in coastal bays, estuaries, and lagoons sustains commercial and subsistence fisheries, and therefore is of economic importance (Peters, Ahrenholz, and Rice 1979; Britton and Morton 1989). Hydrological studies demonstrate that wetlands may store floodwaters (Ludden, Frink, and Johnson 1983); serve as groundwater discharge or recharge zones (van der Valk 1989); trap sediments and toxins (Howard-Williams and Thompson 1985); and naturally purify limited amounts of human-generated wastes (Chalmers, Haines, and Sherr 1976). Coastal beaches, dunes, and bays protect inland areas during storm surges (Maltby 1986; Odum 1978).

Decomposition of organic matter in wetland muds may play an important role in global recycling of nitrogen and sulfur. Methane gas, a product of marshes where anaerobic conditions are found, may act as a regulator of atmospheric ozone (Odum 1978). Concern for the maintenance of wetland ecosystems has thus expanded from bird protection to encompass other animals and plants, as well as hydrological, physical, and chemical processes that serve human needs.

In response to the emerging recognition of wetland values and the need for conservation efforts that transcend national boundaries, a series of meetings began in the 1960s, sponsored by the International Union for the Conservation of Nature (IUCN); the International Waterfowl Research Bureau (IWRB); and the International Council for Bird Preservation (ICBP).[3] These activities culminated in the Convention on Wetlands of International Importance Especially as Waterfowl Habitat, convened in Ramsar, Iran, in 1971.

Known as the Ramsar Convention, this gathering was the first global treaty to provide a framework for protection of the world's important wetlands, and the first international treaty to deal with a specific ecosystem of any type (Maltby 1986). Morocco, Algeria, and Tunisia are all parties to the Ramsar Convention. As part of the contracting process, each country is required to list at least one wetland as a Ramsar site. Morocco listed four sites when it joined in 1980: Merja Zerga in Kenitra Province, Merja Sidi Bourhaba north of Rabat, Lake Affennourir near Azrou, and Khnifiss Bay (Puerto Cansado). Tunisia also joined in 1980, designating Lake Ishkeul, inland from the Mediterranean coastal town of Bizerte. Algeria listed Lake Oubeira and Lake Tonga, both near El Kala in northeastern Algeria, when it joined in 1983.

To determine whether a particular wetland might be internationally important, the Convention originally advised contracting governments to seek the advice of the nongovermental IWRB, based in England. In 1974, at the second Ramsar meeting in Heiligenhafen, West Germany, specific numerical criteria based on waterfowl populations were adopted (as proposed by the IWRB), together with less precisely defined qualitative criteria (including the uniqueness of a site, its special value for plants and animals, and whether it supports an "appreciable number" of rare or endangered species). Censuses of Palearctic waterfowl, begun by the IWRB in 1967, formed the basis for the quantitative criteria.

Under these criteria, any wetland regularly supporting 10,000 ducks, geese, and swans; 10,000 coots; 20,000 shorebirds; or 1 percent of the flyway or biogeographical population of a waterfowl species or subspecies would be classified as internationally important (Atkinson-Willes 1972; Szijj 1972).[4] Authors of the criteria justified the emphasis on waterfowl on the basis that little information was available on other wetland species.

In the last 5 years, debate over criteria for determining a wetland's importance has broadened considerably. This debate illuminates differences between scientific approaches to wetlands and parallels the evolution of new perspectives on use and management. Discussion has centered on the applicability of numerical waterfowl criteria to areas beyond Western Europe and North America. Three criticisms stand out.

First, a lack of comprehensive and accurate data may prevent valuable wetlands from being listed and protected. Second, quantitative data do not hold for all regions; for example, some bird populations are less concentrated in the tropics than in temperate latitudes, but wetlands they inhabit may be significant.

Finally and most important, representatives of nations from outside Western Europe and North America have called for recognition of wetland values other than wildlife. It is argued that socioeconomic criteria should be included so that sustainable human uses of wetlands may be maintained and protected. This has shifted focus away from preservation of pristine natural wetlands and associated flora and fauna to more comprehensive efforts to maintain systemic functions in a variety of situations and to promote the concept of sustainable use (Ramsar Convention Bureau 1988).[5] At the 1990 meeting of parties to the Convention, revised and expanded criteria were adopted to reflect these evolving concerns (Edward Maltby, personal communication).

Despite this intense debate over the criteria that establish a wetland's international importance, the final decision as to which wetland a government lists under the Ramsar Convention often must be based on limited evidence and political practicality. Although seven North African sites are listed under the Ramsar Convention, there are perhaps several hundred wetlands in the region (depending on the definition employed), a few of which may be more "important" by Ramsar criteria than designated wetlands.

Management Perspectives on North African Wetlands

Interest in the study and maintenance of North African wetlands parallels and is influenced by similar activities elsewhere. European bird enthusiasts realized that migratory bird protection in Europe would have little impact without similar protection in Africa. Morocco, Algeria, and Tunisia lie along the East Atlantic Flyway, a broad corridor travelled by birds migrating between breeding grounds in Eurasia, Greenland, and the Canadian Arctic and wintering grounds in Africa.

The lakes and lagoons of North Africa provide winter homes to a significant proportion of the Old World waterfowl population, including the Eurasian wigeon (*Anas penelope*); teal (*Anas crecca*); pochard (*Aythya ferina*); shoveler (*Anas clypeata*); tufted duck (*Aythya fuligula*); common coot (*Fulica atra*); and greyleg goose (*Anser anser*), the latter found particularly in the wetlands of northern Tunisia and eastern Algeria. All of these are popular gamebirds both in Europe and Africa. Hundreds of thousands of shorebirds also winter in the region, including the black-winged stilt (*Himantopus himantopus*); black-tailed godwit (*Limosa limosa*); bar-tailed godwit (*Limosa lapponica*); dunlin (*Calidris alpina*); ringed plover (*Charadrius hiaticula*); avocet (*Recurvirostra avosetta*); and the very rare slender-billed curlew (*Numenius tenuirostris*), found only at a few coastal sites in Morocco.[6] A far larger number of shorebirds (perhaps several million) use North African coastal wetlands as way stations for food and rest as they journey to winter territories in West Africa. More exotic waterbirds such as the greater flamingo (*Phoenicopterus ruber*) and the spoonbill (*Platalea leucorodia*) also winter in or pass through North Africa. A smaller number of wetland birds breed in the region, including rare species such as the crested coot (*Fulica cristata*); collared pratincole (*Glareola pratincola*); marbled teal (*Anas angustirostrus*); white-headed duck (*Oxyura leucocephala*); African marsh owl (*Asio capensis*); and resident flamingo (Morgan and Boy 1982; Morgan 1982a, 1982b; Kersten and Smit 1984; IUCN Conservation Monitoring Centre 1984; Piersma et al. 1987).

The threats to wetlands, as seen by the bird protection lobby, include drainage projects, dams, hunting, pollution, and disturbance from fishing and grazing. In North Africa, as elsewhere in the world, these activities are accelerating, and many fear that wetlands will be lost before their value can be identified. Morgan and Boy (1982) attempted to develop a rapid survey technique for classifying and assessing North African wetlands to determine quickly and cost-effectively where conservation activities should focus. Based on this analysis they grouped North African wetlands into 11 general classes plus several individual sites not belonging to any obvious class.

Morgan and Boy's classification system includes *chotts* (e.g., Chott Fedjadj and Chott Djerid in Tunisia); *unvegetated sebkhas* (e.g., Sebkhet Sidi el Hani in Tunisia and Grande Sebkhet d'Oran in Algeria); *vegetated sebkhas, type 1* (e.g., Sebkhet al-Sedjoumi in Tunisia and Sebkhet Djendli in Algeria); *vegetated sebkhas, type 2* (e.g., Sidi Moussa wetland complex in Morocco); *seasonal mesohaline wetlands* (e.g., Merja Daoura, and Merja Sidi Mohammad Ben Mansour in Morocco); *oases* (e.g., Oued Segui in Tunisia and Chegga Oasis in Algeria); *freshwater mountain lakes* (e.g., Dayat al Hachlaf, Dayat Ifrah, and Ageulmame Sidi Ali in Morocco); *oligohaline lowland lakes* (e.g., Lake Oubeira in Algeria and Lake Kelbia in Tunisia); *seasonal Phragmites and Scirpus lacustris marshes* (e.g., Lake Tonga, Garaet el-Mkhada, and Marais de la Macta in Algeria, and Marai Bas Loukkos in Morocco); (e.g., Marais de Soliman and Lac Zerkine in Tunisia); and *marine wetlands* (e.g., Lac Melah in Algeria, Lake Ishkeul in Tunisia, and Merja Zerga in Morocco). Individual sites not belonging to any class include reservoirs, salinas, and several small mixohaline sites.

This classification system is based on physical parameters (area, salinity, precipitation, evaporation, inflow/outflow, substrate, and depth); vegetation (species and coverage); invertebrates (zooplankton and zoobenthos species counts); and waterfowl (species counts). Of the 62 wetland sites surveyed, Morgan judged 22 to be of international or North African importance. His criteria included the effectiveness of the wetland as a conservation unit; its representativeness; diversity of species and habitats; waterfowl numbers (similar to Ramsar criteria); rarity of species and sites; research use; and educational and tourist potential (Morgan and Boy 1982; Morgan 1982a, 1982b).

A second source of interest in North African wetlands comes from fisheries researchers, although they rarely use the term *wetland* and their concerns are quite different. For several decades fisheries specialists have studied the lakes, lagoons, estuaries, and coastal waters of the region for their fishing potential. Indeed, much of the ecological information available on these wetlands comes from fishery-related studies. The primary purpose of these studies is to understand physical and biological characteristics in order to manipulate them to increase fish production. From the fisheries perspective, management includes the introduction of new fish species and the regulation of the fishing industry. Thus, although fishery managers are concerned about environmental quality, fisheries do not necessarily depend on the maintenance of "natural" habitats or the protection of indigenous fish.

In the late 1970s the Tunisian Institut National Scientifique et Technique d'Océanographie et de Pêches (INSTOP) hosted a UNESCO-sponsored meeting of experts to discuss lagoons, deltas, and salt marshes of the southern Mediterranean as ecosystems with high biological yields. The meeting initiated a regional effort by marine and fishery scientists to review and evaluate existing knowledge of eutrophic coastal ecosystems, and to establish a coordinated program of study and management. The goals of this program were to "control exploitation of natural biological production" including algae, mollusks, crustaceans, and fish; to develop intensive and semi-intensive aquaculture; and to "control protection and development" (UNESCO 1979: 9). The research program defined pollution, drainage, and uncontrolled exploitation as the major threats, although part of the program also studied the impact of fish-eating birds on fish resources. An initial review of existing information carried out under this program revealed a substantial body of literature concerning the hydrology and hydrochemistry of coastal wetlands and the biology of commercially important fish species (Kerambrun 1986).

The differences between the bird and fishery perspectives are profound. Most bird research concerning wetlands has been performed by foreigners. Fishery science research, while initiated by colonial governments, is now conducted primarily by North African specialists. There appears to be little coordinated cooperation between the two groups, although researchers concerned with birds have relied on fishery-related studies for biological and hydrological data. Both groups wish to manage wetlands, but for radically different purposes. Fishery scientists desire to control and increase natural production to meet what they see as important economic and nutritional needs. This may include the radical alteration of wetlands for fish farms and the introduction of exotic species. On the bird protection side, the original participants in the Ramsar Convention aimed to preserve relatively natural and pristine wetlands from any kind of development, or if necessary, manipulate them to be more attractive to migratory birds.

Both fishery scientists and bird protectionists face an uphill battle against more powerful governmental agencies where agricultural and industrial interests hold sway. From these latter perspectives wetlands represent a waste of space and precious water resources. Beginning in the colonial period, large-scale drainage projects targeted regions like the Gharb Plain where seasonal flooding of the Sebou River formed vast marshes or *merjas*.

Colonial drainage projects required the dismantling of traditional water management systems and the usurpation by the central government of all water resources including rivers and wetlands. To accomplish this, French colonial administrations in Morocco, Algeria, and Tunisia issued various legislation prior to 1920 placing rivers, lakes, and marshes in the public domain (Swearingen 1987; Mekouar 1988; El Amami 1983).

Together with hydraulic engineering projects, centralized control of water transformed the Moroccan wetlands into agricultural landscapes, which government authorities considered more appropriate and efficient. The advice given by a French engineer to protectorate authorities in Morocco to allow "not a single drop of water to flow into the sea" affirms a near messianic faith in the beneficent powers of science to overcome the perceived deficiencies of nature (Swearingen 1987).

The outcomes have varied. The Gharb Plain has become Morocco's breadbasket — but at the cost of uprooting the land's original inhabitants and transferring tenure first to a French and later Moroccan elite (Swearingen 1987). El Amami (1983) argues that in Tunisia centralized control of water and massive transfers of water from inland regions to the coast — beginning with the French and continuing under Tunisian leadership — have had disastrous consequences. Massive expenditures have resulted in "an inhuman, eroded agricultural region and community dependence on a 'technostructure' born of the need to 'manage' these major [hydraulic] works." Nevertheless, the assertion that water not used for agriculture or industry is water wasted still echoes across northern Africa and throughout much of the world.[7]

This faith in engineering and the pursuit of landscape transformation were integral to the Enlightenment mindset, which held that nature can and should be manipulated and improved upon to perpetually increase benefits to humanity. Nevertheless, the application of these principles by agricultural authorities and engineers seriously threatens ecological functions valued by groups such as fishery scientists and conservationists. All see their positions as eminently rational and scientifically based. Yet profound differences exist not only in their conclusions but in the basic ways they frame their questions. For conservationists wetlands are jewels to be protected as part of a far-flung network of migratory birds. For fishery experts wetlands are factories of protein production in need of careful control and management. For agricultural authorities and hydraulic engineers wetlands are wastelands and obstructions to a more efficient and productive use of space and resources.

These external groups often ignore or override the perspectives of local wetland communities. For the people who dwell in and around them, wetlands offer a range of resources including fish, shellfish, aquatic plants, and waterfowl. Pasturing of livestock on marsh grasses is often a significant component of wetland economies. Small communities in wetland areas traditionally exploit a wide array of available resources, maintaining a diverse and relatively reliable subsistence base of small-scale production and consumption. Diodorus of Sicily remarked on this way of life in Egypt during the second century A.D., observing that the Nile marshes abounded in plants, fish, and fowl. The marshes, Diodorus wrote, "render the poor self-sustaining, for not only do they afford a varied diet, ready at hand and abundant for all who need it, but they also furnish not a few of the other things which contribute to the necessities of life."[8]

In North Africa grazing, fishing, hunting, and plant collecting were the traditional axes around which wetland economies revolved, particularly in floodplains, lowland marshes, and lagoons. Célérier (1922a, 1922b) described in detail the marshy landscape of the Gharb Plain prior to the drainage of its numerous seasonal marshes and the damming of the Sebou River. In winter and spring the meandering Sebou would overflow its banks, creating vast flooded marshlands called *merjas* (meadow or pasture). Célérier estimated the total area of the *merjas* at 60,000 hectares (ha) (1922a). In summer the waters dried up but left luxuriant pastureland plus dense thickets of reeds and rushes called *hydras* by the French. He noted that "the excess of water in an important region of Morocco is a veritable paradox which has naturally had a profound impact on the inhabitants" (Célérier 1922a: 111).

But a paradox for whom? Not apparently for the residents of this floodplain, who by Célérier's own account made a good living from the *merjas*. Hunting and fishing provided substantial revenues for local people. Eels were particularly abundant and well adapted to the environment of the *merjas*. "Birds of every size and color" were to be found in the region, especially marsh birds. Reeds and rushes (*birdi, diss,* and *smar*) formed the basis of a cottage industry, being widely used in the construction of boats, mats, and houses. More substantial dwellings were built using bricks made of local clay. The summer pasturing of livestock, especially cattle, constituted the most important part of the *merja* economy. The *merjas*, wrote Célérier, became oases in summer, with lush vegetation and plentiful water. Local residents held the rights to this pasturage but allowed in the stock of more distant uplands. Célérier (1922) quoted an official count of 37,000 head of cattle on the marshes during one season.

Although this wetland economy was apparently thriving, Célérier attributed its richness to the abundance of resources rather than human ingenuity. The adaptation of local residents to this marshy environment was symptomatic of their fatalistic indolence, in Célérier's opinion, and prevented them from improving the situation — for example, by erecting barrages and dikes to drain the marshes. But his own arguments make little sense — if local residents were doing so well, why alter the environment? Célérier acknowledges the "excellent revenues" enjoyed by the inhabitants of the Sebou floodplain but argues that much more could be done with the area. With French colonists pressing for land, French authorities believed that the *merjas* could be put to more efficient use for colonization while still allowing local inhabitants to make a living (Célérier 1922b). Complicated legal maneuvering made the transfer of land to French hands possible and eventually paved the way for drainage of most of the *merjas* (Swearingen 1987).

We see then that conservationists are only the latest would-be managers to come to the wetlands of North Africa. There is a long history of people, both local residents and outsiders, who have sought to shape these places according to their perceptions and frameworks of understanding. All of these people may be thought of as "managers," in that they all wish to manipulate the environment to produce desired outcomes. All work according to their own local rationality while seeing others as irrational, stubborn, "indolent," or hopelessly unrealistic. How, then, do these various "managers" interact today in managing remaining wetlands?

The Merja Zerga, Morocco

The Merja Zerga on the Atlantic coast of Morocco is one of the few surviving *merjas* in the Gharb region. As a coastal lagoon, its character differs fundamentally from more inland merjas in that it contains water year-round and has a connection to the sea.

Merja Zerga receives fresh water from the Oued Drader and the Nador Canal and during high tides is flooded by seawater. More than 10,000 people live in or near the lagoon, where they raise sheep and cattle, fish, and farm (Fender 1987). It is one of the most important wetlands for migratory birds on Morocco's Atlantic coast (Kersten and Smit 1984). The Ministry of Agriculture declared Merja Zerga a "Réserve Biologique Permanente" in 1978 and listed it as one of Morocco's Ramsar sites in 1980. The Réserve covers approximately 7,160 ha, of which 3,740 are lagoon or marsh habitat (Fender 1987b). The Ministry of Agriculture's declaration did not define what a *biological reserve* means nor did it prescribe a purpose for preservation. Presumably, the declaration resulted from international pressure to conserve migratory birds.

From the beginning the Merja Zerga Réserve has suffered from lack of attention and funding. Direct responsibility for the Réserve lies with the Direction des Eaux et Forêts, under the Ministry of Agriculture. Agricultural and water authorities have traditionally been concerned with the intensification of landscape use and the eradication of wetlands, as discussed above, so that their lack of interest in a wetland reserve is easily understandable.[9] Bureaucratic complexity also hampers protection efforts at Merja Zerga. A tidal lagoon, Merja Zerga varies in salinity in different places and at different times. The Direction des Pêches et Maritime holds authority over the brackish parts of the lagoon. The Ministry of Interior is responsible for portions of the area. Local communes control much of the grazing lands adjacent to the lagoon (Mohammed Aissi, personal communication). Thus although Eaux et Forêts is technically authorized to manage the reserve, it cannot take management actions without agreement from these other institutions. Pressure for such agreement must come from higher up, and it is at this higher level that interest in the reserve is generally absent.

From 1978 to 1985 conservation activities at Merja Zerga consisted primarily of occasional waterbird counts in conjunction with flyway studies by organizations such as the International Council for Bird Preservation (ICBP) and the International Waterfowl Research Bureau (IWRB). These studies confirmed the reserve's importance as a major international wetland for waterbirds. In 1985, Eaux et Forêts appointed a warden for the reserve who received conservation education training in England through the efforts of the ICBP. Around this same time, the United States Peace Corps program began sending volunteers to the reserve to work with the warden in researching and developing management plans.

Although the reserve has received attention both within Morocco and internationally, to date little has been done there of an official nature. The warden and Peace Corps volunteers trained in biology and ecology have identified the following activities of local people as the main direct threats to Merja Zerga: heavy overgrazing by livestock; fishing; collection of marsh plants (mostly *Juncus* spp.); hunting; and poor farming practices. As the presumed goal of the reserve is protection of migratory birds, their management recommendations consist mostly of banning or severely restricting these activities to preserve the natural ecology of the lagoon and marsh systems (Hassan Kachiche, personal communication; Fender 1987b). Given the dynamics of the situation at Merja Zerga, it is understandable and even predictable that conservation has made little progress. The spectrum of players are operating within frameworks that prevent communication, cooperation, and understanding.

The Ministry of Agriculture has little interest in a nature reserve and has limited power to affect land use at Merja Zerga in any event. The warden is marooned at the reserve with weak administrative support, meager funding, and little to do. Peace Corps volunteers deal with the management problem within the frameworks in which they have been trained but have no social or political standing to affect change. They likewise lack a historical and social perspective on wetland economies and land tenure. Although there is vague talk of compensation and other initiatives to ensure the well-being of residents, implementation of proposed management plans would certainly be detrimental to local livelihoods. One must presume that residents would resist these restrictions, thereby endangering the entire enterprise.

The situation at Merja Zerga exemplifies the complex nature of environmental management. Who are the managers? The warden, Peace Corps biologists, and wetland specialists all see their role as management. They focus especially on managing local residents in order to maintain the natural ecology of the lagoon and marsh habitat. But these villagers have been "managing" the lagoon and its marshes for decades (and possibly centuries). Shifting sand dunes periodically block the connection between the lagoon and the sea (Morgan 1982). Were it not for local villagers who clear the obstruction, the natural ecology of the lagoon would have changed radically. Ironically, the bird that has caused the most excitement at Merja Zerga in recent years is the slender-billed curlew (*Numenius tenuirostris*). This little-known shorebird is one of the most endangered birds in the Old World, and Merja Zerga is its only known regular wintering site. The curlew is seen most often on heavily overgrazed meadows and in fallow agricultural fields. Thousands of black-tailed godwits (*Limosa limosa*) and other waders also use the grazed areas. Thus reserve management plans to ban or limit grazing in order to allow the natural ecology of the marsh to regenerate itself might have a deleterious impact on these birds (van den Berg 1990).

Agricultural authorities and hydraulic engineers are likewise managers. The construction of the Nador Canal in 1953, which partially drained the Merja Daoura into Merja Zerga, caused the rapid formation of a new delta in the southern end of the lagoon. Engineering modifications of the Oued Drader feeding the lagoon from the west have decreased sediment deposits from that source (Mohamed Berriane, personal communication). The large plantations of eucalyptus in the area have altered soil and runoff conditions. Given these many adjustments — made by local residents possibly for centuries and by engineers over the last few decades — we would find it difficult to define the "natural" state of the Merja Zerga lagoon.

What, then, is the object of management? The answer is that all the various actors are managing continuing processes — ecological, economic, physical, and cultural — at multiple scales. Nevertheless, our compartmentalization of knowledge and authority works against weaving these processes and scales together. Engineers, bureaucrats, ornithologists, fisherfolk, and farmers have yet to develop a common language for understanding one another's perspective.

Ishkeul National Park, Tunisia

Experiences at Lake Ishkeul in Tunisia further illuminate these issues. Ishkeul National Park covers 12,000 ha of northern Tunisia just inland from Bizerte. The park, declared in 1980, includes Lake Ishkeul and its marshes together with Djebel Ishkeul. The same area is also a listed site under the UNESCO World Heritage, Ramsar, and Biosphere Reserves conventions. It is the only place in the world to be listed on all three of these conventions (Hollis 1986). Together with the Camargue in France and the Coto Doñana in Spain, Ishkeul is considered one of the Mediterranean region's premier wetlands. As the object of an international campaign, conservation at Ishkeul has received extensive international funding, and both Tunisian and foreign scientists have over a number of years carried out wide-ranging studies at the lake (Hollis 1986).[10]

Despite this relative success, the conservation of Lake Ishkeul faces very difficult management questions. The main threats to the lake come from the construction and planned construction of dams on the rivers that feed the lake. Computer modelling was used to analyze the potential impacts of these dams and alternative scenarios. The construction of all six dams will increase salinity in the lake and dry out much of the marsh area. Some birds, such as flamingos (*Phoenicopterus ruber*), may be attracted to these new conditions; but a large proportion of the estimated 250,000 waterbirds that use the lake each winter will most likely no longer be able to find suitable habitat (Hollis 1986). Government hydraulic engineers and irrigation authorities respond that the river water that now empties into the lake is needed for human consumption and agricultural development, and that water diversion is in the best economic interest of the country. Acknowledging that bird protection is not a compelling argument for government authorities charged with development needs, scientists working on Lake Ishkeul have begun to analyze its productive values in order to develop economic justification for wetland maintenance.

In doing so they have turned to traditional uses such as fishing and grazing, the very activities that would-be managers at Merja Zerga wish to restrict. These small-scale economies require low financial and technological inputs. When the profits and costs of fishing and grazing are compared with those of irrigation schemes in the area, the calculations show that the traditional lake activities are of higher economic benefit. In addition, the researchers argue that the irrigation schemes have frequently run over budget; have failed to produce at anticipated levels; and have incurred damaging social and economic side-effects (Thomas et al. 1991).

Other benefits also accrue to the lake and its marshes. Raw sewage from the town of Mateur is discharged into the Oued Djoumine, which flows into Ishkeul. When the river flowed freely, it carried this sewage into Ishkeul's reedbeds, which naturally broke down the wastes. Today, with the construction of a dam across the Djoumine, there is not enough water to carry off the sewage and so it concentrates in the remaining stagnant water. Mateur will likely have to build a sewage treatment plant to deal with this new pollution problem (Thomas et al. 1991). In addition, the attractiveness of the lake and marshes for waterfowl, especially geese, helps prevent these birds from feeding in cultivated lands, thus saving the expense of pest control and crop damage. Added to potential income from tourism to the national park, the economic benefits from maintaining the wetland ecosystem are plentiful (Thomas et al. 1991). To realize these benefits, however, requires understanding and negotiating multiple uses and recognizing that management is a continually evolving process. The work at Lake Ishkeul is doubly important in that it points out the values of wetlands in general. As mentioned earlier, conservationists have identified more than 20 North African wetlands of international or regional importance, most of which have no protection at all. Some of the most important, for example, the salinas at Sidi Moussa in Morocco, have been substantially altered by people but still provide excellent habitat for migratory birds (Morgan 1982b; Kersten and Smit 1984). If the only focus of wetland conservation is on preservation of some illusory natural system within the borders of official reserves, these other wetlands may be sacrificed to damaging *ad hoc* development.

Conclusions

Environmental management rarely functions as planned. Laurent Mermet, a French wetland expert, notes that any group with a stake in an area promotes its own "local rationality." Frequently the result is a chaotic situation in which it is difficult to determine who is causing the problem and who is trying to manage it (Mermet 1990). As scientists and others concerned with environmental management delve deeper into how to maintain valued ecosystems, they repeatedly come up against this problem. The response has often been to locate the problem with local people or with influential interested parties such as government agencies, as we have seen in the cases of Merja Zerga and Lake Ishkeul.

A recent international conference on the role of people in wetland management highlights this dilemma.[11] The majority of contributors attributed the problem of apathy toward wetland conservation to a low level of local environmental awareness, and secondarily to a paucity of social science data and skills on the part of would-be managers. Proposed solutions included more intensive environmental education, public consultation in policy making, and expanded social science research to complement biological data; in other words, doing more of what is already being done.

A significant minority of experts at the conference felt, however, that scientific and governmental organizations were themselves part of the problem and that they need to reevaluate their own approaches. It was argued that we would do better to treat management as a learning process rather than as a set plan, as we are unlikely ever to know enough about all the factors affecting any given environment. An integral part of this learning process must be the exploration of various perspectives and the questioning of one's own position (de Groot and Zanen 1990). This approach to wetland management requires a more profound comprehension of political, social, cultural, and economic processes occurring in and around wetlands and other valued environments. These factors often are poorly understood and undervalued, and few studies have examined wetland societies in their environmental context. Sectoral studies do exist but are focused on specific aspects of resource use. There is, for example, a substantial ethnological literature on artisanal fisherfolk on a variety of waters. Conducted mostly by anthropologists, these studies detail among other things fishing techniques and methods for the distribution of catch (for example, Forman 1967; Gunda 1984; McCay 1978). More recently, fishery scientists and economists have begun reevaluating traditional fishing practices as potentially useful paths in economic development projects (Emmerson 1980; Johannes 1981; Kapetsky 1981). As researchers at Lake Ishkeul have demonstrated, wetland conservationists must actively involve themselves in these issues or risk becoming irrevelant.

Wetlands have always been utilized, manipulated, and transformed by human activities. The persistence of North African wetland communities encompassing both people and wildlife manifests a remarkable resilience and adaptability. Shorebirds gather on sewage ponds and salt pans. Flamingos take rapid advantage of heavy rains to nest in temporarily flooded *sabkhas*; local residents fish, farm, hunt, and pasture livestock in and around coastal lagoons, making a living from a variety of small opportunities. In some areas such as Merja Zerga and Lake Ishkeul, these opportunities now include working as guides for foreign birdwatchers.

The existence of these places in a mostly arid region need not be paradoxical. Rather they perform important functions that need to be understood from a variety of perspectives. Wetland losses necessitated by agricultural and industrial development can be mitigated with increased attentiveness to these functions and to the values they represent across a spectrum of interests.

Notes

1. In the United States, flyway management was a primary motivation in the establishment and expansion of the National Wildlife Refuge system under the authority of the U.S. Fish and Wildlife Service. Wetlands form the core of many of these refuges.

2. The ecologist writing in 1941 was Raymond Lindeman, who studied food cycle dynamics in Cedar Bog Lake, Minnesota. Eugene Odum (1978), the ecologist who with his brother Howard Odum has researched and promoted wetlands as naturally productive habitats, offers a brief account of the development of perceived wetland values in North America, citing Lindeman as a pioneer on the ecological side.

3. Project Mar, in collaboration with the International Waterfowl Research Bureau (IWRB) and the International Council for Bird Preservation (ICBP), focused primarily on shallow water ecosystems because these faced the most immediate threat from drainage, diking, and reclamation. Project Aqua dealt with the limnology and hydrology of freshwater and brackish areas "of agreed international importance for research, education or training." Project Telma studied and

protected peatlands of "international importance to science." All three projects shaped interest in wetlands on a global scale, but migratory bird protection remained the main concern in the Ramsar Convention as initially drafted (Luther and Rzèyska 1971; Carp 1972; Maltby 1986).

4. Under the criteria adopted at Heiligenhafen, a wetland is considered internationally important if it: i) regularly supports 1 percent (at least 100 individuals) of the flyway or biogeographical population of one species of waterfowl; or it ii) regularly supports either 10,000 ducks, geese, and swans; 10,000 coots; or 20,000 waders; or iii) supports an appreciable number of an endangered species of plant or animal; or iv) is of special value for maintaining genetic and ecological diversity because of the quality and peculiarities of its flora and fauna; or v) plays a major role in the region as the habitat of plants and of aquatic and other animals of scientific or economic importance (Atkinson-Wiles et al. 1982: 1021-1022).

5. Discussions and recommendations concerning criteria are found in a number of documents from the 1987 Proceedings of the Third Meeting of Contracting Parties to the Ramsar Convention. See especially W.G. C.3.2. and C.3.3; REC. C.3.1 and C.3.3; INF C.3.7., C.3.9, C.4.11, C.3.20, C.3.28, C.3.29 (Ramsar Convention Bureau 1988).

6. *Shorebird* is the North American collective term for a variety of wading birds; Europeans generally use the term *wader* for this group.

7. In Egypt plans are being studied to construct bunds across the mouths of the Rosetta and Damietta Nile branches and redirect flow into the brackish delta lakes, which would become large freshwater reservoirs (*al-Ahram* 28 November 1988).

8. *Diodorus of Sicily.* Loeb Classical Library, Book I, Ch. 34. Translated by C. H. Oldfather. London: William Heinemann.

9. The placement of responsibility for wetland protection under authorities traditionally hostile to wetlands is by no means limited to Morocco or North Africa. In the United States, wetland conservation and permit handling for development is the responsibility of the Army Corps of Engineers, which was previously dedicated to massive alteration of the nation's river and wetland systems.

10. Baseline scientific work and management plan development at Ishkeul performed by teams from University College London and the Camargue station of the Conseil National de Récherches Scientifiques was funded respectively by the Commission of European Communities and the French Ministry of the Environment.

11. "The People's Role in Wetland Management," an international conference sponsored by the Centre for Environmental Studies at Leiden University, held in Leiden, Netherlands, 5-8 June 1989 (Marchand and Udo de Haes 1990).

References

Atkinson-Willes, G. L. 1972. "The International Wildfowl Censuses as a Basis for Wetland Evaluation and Hunting Rationalization," in E. Carp, ed., *Proceedings, International Conference on the Conservation of Wetlands and Waterfowl, Ramsar Iran, 30 January - 3 February 1971.* Pp. 87-110. Slimbridge, England: The

International Wildfowl Research Bureau.

Atkinson-Willes, G. L., D. A. Scott, and A. J. Prater. 1982. "Criteria for Selecting Wetlands of International Importance," in M. Spagnesi, ed., *Proceedings of the Conference on the Conservation of Wetlands of International Importance Especially as Waterfowl Habitat, Cagliari, Italy, 24-29 November 1980. Supplemento alle Ricerche di Biologia della Selvaggina 8(1)*. Pp. 1017-1042. Bologna: Instituto Nazionale di Biologia della Selvaggina.

Bellrose, F. 1976. *Ducks, Geese and Swans of North America.* 2d ed. Harrisburg, Penn.: Stackpole.

Boyd, H., and J.-Y. Pirot, eds. 1989. *Flyways and Reserve Networks for Water Birds.* IWRB Special Publication No. 9. Slimbridge, England: International Waterfowl and Wetlands Research Bureau.

Britton, J. C., and B. Morton. 1989. *Shore Ecology of the Gulf of Mexico.* Austin: University of Texas Press.

Carp, E., ed. 1972. *Proceedings, International Conference on the Conservation of Wetlands and Waterfowl, Ramsar, Iran, 30 January - 3 February 1971.* Slimbridge, England: IWRB.

Célérier, J. 1922a. "Les 'Merjas' de la Plaine du Sebou."*Hespéris* 2 (1922):109-138.

———. 1922b. "Les 'Merjas' de la Plaine du Sebou." *Hespéris* 2 (1922):209-239.

Chalmers, A. G., E. B. Haines, and B. F. Sherr. 1976. *The Capacity of a Spartina Salt Marsh to Assimilate Nitrogen from Secondarily Treated Sewage.* Atlanta: Georgia Tech.

de Groot, W. T., and S. M. Zanen. 1990. "Overview Paper: Enhancing Participation of Local People," in M. Marchand and H. A.Udo de Haes, eds., *The People's Role in Wetland Management: Proceedings of the International Conference, Leiden, The Netherlands, June 5-8, 1989.* Pp. 515-527. Leiden: Centre for Environmental Studies.

El Amami, Slaheddine. 1983. "Changing Concepts of Water Management in Tunisia." *Impact of Science on Society* 33(1):57-64.

Emmerson, D. K. 1980. *Rethinking Artisanal Fisheries Development: Western Concepts, Asian Experiences.* World Bank Staff Working Paper No. 423. Washington, D.C.: The World Bank.

Fender, Wade. 1987a. *Merja Zerga Biological Reserve: Preliminary Statement for Management.* Unpublished Report. United States of America Peace Corps and Direction des Eaux et Forêts/Maroc.

———. 1987b. *Merja Zerga Biological Reserve: Preliminary General Management Plan.* Unpublished Report. United States of America Peace Corps and Direction des Eaux et Forêts/Maroc.

Forman, S. 1967. "Cognition and the Catch: The Location of Fishing Spots in a Brazilian Coastal Village." *Ethnology* 6:417-426.

Gunda, B., ed. *The Fishing Culture of the World: Studies in Ethnology, Ecology and Folklore.* 2 vols. Budapest: Akademiai Kiado.

Hollis, G. E. 1986. *The Modelling and Management of the Internationally Important Wetland at Garaet El Ichkeul, Tunisia.* IWRB Special Publication No. 4. Slimbridge, England: IWRB.

Howard-Williams, C., and K. Thompson. 1985. "The Conservation and Management of African Wetlands," in P. Denny, ed., *The Ecology and Management of African Vegetation.* Pp. 203-235. Dordrecht: Junk.

IUCN Conservation Monitoring Centre. 1984. *Draft Directory for Wetlands of International Importance.* Kew, England: Protected Areas Data Unit, IUCN Conservation Monitoring Centre, The Herbarium, Royal Botanic Gardens.

Johannes, R. E. 1981. *Words of the Lagoon: Fishing and Marine Lore in the Palau District of Micronesia.* Berkeley: University of California.

Kapetsky, J. M. 1981. "Some Considerations for the Management of Coastal Lagoon Fisheries." *FAO Fisheries Technical Paper* 218.

Kerambrun, Pierre, compiler. 1986. "Coastal Lagoons Along the Southern Mediterranean Coast (Algeria, Egypt, Libya, Morocco, Tunisia): Description and Bibliography." *UNESCO Reports in Marine Science* 34. Paris: UNESCO.

Kersten, M., and C. J. Smit. 1984. "The Atlantic Coast of Morocco," in P. R. Evans, J. D. Goss-Custard, and W. G. Hale, eds., *Coastal Waders and Wildfowl in Winter.* Pp. 276-292. Cambridge, England: Cambridge University Press.

Lincoln, F. C. 1939. *The Migration of American Birds.* New York: Doubleday.

Ludden, A. P., D. L. Frink, and D. H. Johnson. 1983. "Water Storage Capacity of Natural Wetland Depressions in the Devils Lake Basin of North Dakota." *Journal of Soil and Water Conservation* 38:45-48.

Luther, H., and J. Rzèyska. 1971. *Project Aqua: A Source Book of Inland Waters Proposed for Conservation.* Oxford: Blackwell Scientific Publications.

Maltby, E. 1986. *Waterlogged Wealth.* London: Earthscan.

Marchand, M., and H. A. Udo de Haes, eds. 1990. *The People's Role in Wetland Management: Proceedings of the International Conference, Leiden, The Netherlands, June 5-8, 1989.* Leiden: Centre for Environmental Studies.

McCay, B. 1978. "Systems Ecology, People Ecology, and the Anthropology of Fishing Communities." *Human Ecology* 6:397-422.

Mekouar, Mohamed Ali. 1988. *Recueil D'Etudes in Droit Ecologique: Environnement, Société et Développement.* Casablanca: Afrique Orient.

Mermet, L. 1990. "Participation, Strategies and Ethics: Roles of People in Wetland Management," in M. Marchand and H. A. Udo de Haes, eds., *The People's Role in Wetland Management: Proceedings of the International Conference, Leiden, The Netherlands, June 5-8, 1989.* Pp. 92-99. Leiden: Centre for Environmental Studies.

Mitsch, William J., and James G. Gosselink. 1986. *Wetlands.* New York: Van Nostrand Reinhold.

Morgan, N.C. 1982a. "An Ecological Survey of Standing Waters in North West Africa: II. Site Descriptions for Tunisia and Algeria." *Biological Conservation* 24: 83-114.

———. 1982b. "An Ecological Survey of Standing Waters in North West Africa: III. Site Descriptions for Morocco." *Biological Conservation* 24:161-182.

Morgan, N. C., and V. Boy. 1982. "An Ecological Survey of Standing Waters in North West Africa: I. Rapid Survey and Classification." *Biological Conservation* 24: 5-44.

Odum, E. P. 1978. "The Value of Wetlands: A Hierarchical Approach," in P. E. Greeson, J. R. Clark, and J. E. Clark, eds., *Wetland Functions and Values: The State of Our Understanding.* Pp. 16-25. Minneapolis: American Water Resources Association.

Peters, D. S., D. W. Ahrenholz, and T. R. Rice. 1979. "Harvest and Value of Wetland Associated Fish and Shellfish," in P. E. Greeson, J. R. Clark, and J. E. Clark, eds.,

Wetland Function and Values: The State of our Understanding. Pp. 606-617. Minneapolis: American Water Resources Assoc.

Piersma, T., A. J. Beintema, N. C. Davidson, O. A. G. Munster, and M. W. Pienkowski. 1987. "Wader Migration Systems in the East Atlantic," in N. C. Davidson and M. W. Pienkowski, eds., *The Conservation of International Flyway Populations of Waders.* Pp. 35-56. *Wader Study Group Bulletin 49,* Suppl. *IWRB Special Publication 7.*

Ramsar Convention Bureau. 1988. *Proceedings of the Third Meeting of the Conference of Contracting Parties, Regina, Saskatchewan, Canada, 27 May to 5 June 1987.* Gland, Switzerland: Ramsar Convention Bureau.

Swearingen, Will D. 1987. *Moroccan Mirages: Agrarian Dreams and Deceptions, 1912-1986.* Princeton: Princeton University Press.

Szijj, J. 1972. "Some Suggested Criteria for Determining the International Importance of Wetlands in the Western Palaearctic," in E. Carp, ed., *Proceedings, International Conference on the Conservation of Wetlands and Waterfowl, Ramsar, Iran, 30 January - 3 February 1971.* Pp. 111-119. Slimbridge, England: IWRB.

Thomas, David H. L., Fethi Ayache, and G. Edward Hollis. 1991. "Use and Non-use Values in the Conservation of Ischkeul National Park, Tunisia." *Environmental Conservation* 18(2):119-130.

UNESCO. 1979. "Coastal Ecosystems of the Southern Mediterranean: Lagoons, Deltas and Salt Marshes: Report of a Meeting of Experts, Tunis, 25-27 September 1978." *UNESCO Reports in Marine Science 7.* Paris: UNESCO.

van den Berg, Arnoud B. 1990. "Habitat of the Slender-billed Curlews in Morocco." *British Birds* 83:1-7.

van der Valk, P., ed. 1989. *Northern Prairie Wetlands.* Ames: Iowa State University.

10

Forest Degradation in Morocco

Abdelmalek Benabid

Morocco's distinctive land forms and climate characteristics are reflected in a varied and unique flora. Its high mountain ranges have a complex structure, resulting in many different microenvironments. The Mediterranean climate, which dominates in most parts of the country, is strongly influenced by the Atlantic Ocean, creating a wide bioclimatic spectrum.

Depending on location, the average annual rainfall varies from 30 millimeters (mm) to 2,000 mm. All bioclimatic zones present in the Mediterranean region are found in Morocco (Emberger 1955, 1964; Daget, 1977a, 1977b; Donadieu 1977). This accounts for the extreme diversity of Morocco's vegetation. Morocco's forests comprise more than thirty major tree or woody species and thirty secondary species. Forest species are found in all of the country's bioclimatic zones. Overall, forests occupy an area of around five million hectares. In addition, alfa grass steppes, which contain many different species of shrubs, extend over another three million hectares. Finally, sparse stands of *Acacia* occupy an area of around one million hectares in the Saharan regions.

During the last few decades, vegetation formations of all types in Morocco have been subjected to intense pressure by human activities, including stockraising. Most of Morocco's forests have become degraded to varying degrees. For many forest ecosystems, the natural balance has been irreversibly disrupted. This is particularly true for fragile ecosystems in marginal ecological zones. Due to degradation and clearing activities, Morocco's total forest area has gradually declined. Major causes of degradation and deforestation include overgrazing, fuelwood gathering, timber harvesting, and land clearing for cultivation and urban expansion. The application of forestry techniques developed for more temperate zones has also had a detrimental impact on Morocco's forests (Benabid 1985).

This chapter begins with a brief description of Morocco's forest zones and principal forest species. Then it briefly discusses causes of deforestation and relates these to contemporary socioeconomic activities in Morocco. Next, it examines processes of forest degradation and provides a profile of the current condition of Morocco's forests. The chapter concludes with general recommendations on ways to stop forest degradation and restore Morocco's forest ecosystems.

Biological Diversity of Morocco's Forest Ecosystems

There are six major forest zones in Morocco, each comprised of distinctive associations of trees and shrubs. These are the Lower-Mediterranean, the Thermo-Mediterranean, the Middle-Mediterranean, the Upper-Mediterranean, the Mountain-Mediterranean, and the Oro-Mediterranean zones (Figure 10.1). A brief description of each zone is provided, followed by comments on pine forest in Morocco.

The Lower-Mediterranean

The Lower-Mediterranean forest zone in Morocco contains succulents and aphyllous (leafless) elements in addition to Mediterranean species (Benabid 1976). This zone extends over a large area in Morocco's southwest (Benabid 1982). It has dramatically declined as a result of human-induced degradation and deforestation.

The well-known argan tree (*Argania spinosa*), found only in Morocco, is a key component of the Lower-Mediterranean. Indeed, argan is the most extensive and diversified species within this zone. Argan forests are found in the coastal region from Safi to Ifni, in the Souss Plain, and along the western slopes of the High Atlas and Anti-Atlas. Argan's stand density is low; however, its ecological range is broad, extending from sea level up to 1,400 meters (m) elevation (see Figure 10.1). Argan trees prefer warm to temperate bioclimates with arid to semi-arid conditions (rainfall between 100 mm and 400 mm). They grow well in all types of soils.

Formations of acacia (*Acacia gummifera*, *A. raddiana*, and *A. ehererbergiana*) are also a key component of this forest zone. *Acacia gummifera* formerly covered large expanses in the Marrakech region. Today, remaining specimens are largely confined to sacred sites such as cemeteries and maraboutic shrines, where they are protected. *Acacia raddiana* and *A.*

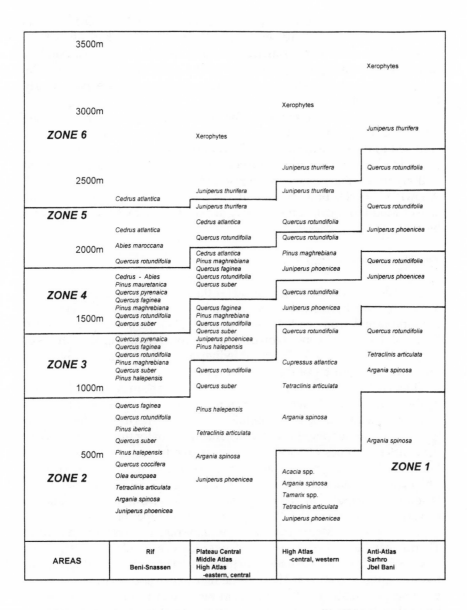

FIGURE 10.1 Major Forest Zones in Morocco. Zone 1 is the Lower-Mediterranean; Zone 2, the Thermo-Mediterranean; Zone 3, the Middle-Mediterranean; Zone 4, the Upper-Mediterranean; Zone 5, the Mountain-Mediterranean; and Zone 6, the Oro-Mediterranean.

Source: Benabid 1985.

ehererbergiana are found mainly in flood plains of the Wadi Draa and its tributaries; that is, in Saharan temperate bioclimates where they have access to groundwater. Tamarisk formations (*Tamarix aphylla* and *T. canariensis*) are also specific to ephemeral wadis and small basins where the water table is close to the surface. These formations are particularly important in Morocco's Saharan regions.

Two other major tree species in the Lower-Mediterranean zone are the thuya and the juniper. Thuya (*Tetraclinis articulata*), a species largely confined to the southwestern Mediterranean basin, is found more extensively in Morocco than anywhere else. It is often found in areas forested with argan, and is also extensive in eastern Morocco and the central plateau. A lowland species of juniper, *Juniperus phoenicea*, is also common in the Lower-Mediterranean zone in sandy areas with warm, semi-arid to arid bioclimates.

The Thermo-Mediterranean

The Thermo-Mediterranean is by far the most extensive forest zone in Morocco, both horizontally and vertically, covering both lowland and mountain areas, from sea-level up to around 1,700 m (Figure 10.1). It is also the most diversified zone. However, apart from remaining formations of thuya, juniper, and oak, Thermo-Mediterranean forests presently cover only around a quarter of their former range.

Thuya is a key species in the Thermo-Mediterranean zone. Although it is also found in the Lower-Mediterranean zone, thuya is most strongly associated with warm to temperate, semi-arid Thermo-Mediterranean bioclimates. Its adaptability and resistance account for thuya's presence in very different types of soils. The cypress tree (*Cupressus atlantica*), also known as the Atlas cypress, is another key Thermo-Mediterranean species. This cypress is endemic to Morocco. It prefers semi-arid environments and is found principally in the Nfiss valley in the western High Atlas at elevations from 900 m to 1,400 m. It grows in all types of soils.

As in the Lower-Mediterranean zone, *Juniperus phoenicea* is present in the Thermo-Mediterranean in warm, dry, sandy areas. Cork oak (*Quercus suber*), which is found exclusively in the western part of the Mediterranean basin, is another common Thermo-Mediterranean species in Morocco. It is found principally in Morocco's northwest; that is, in areas with more humid bioclimates and cool to temperate temperatures. However, pockets of this tree are also found in the High Atlas and eastern Middle Atlas. Cork oak grows almost exclusively in acidic soils. Other principal Thermo-Mediterranean forest species are green oak (*Quercus rotundifolia*); two other species of oak (*Q. faginea* and *Q. coccifera*); argan; two species of pine (*Pinus iberica* and *P. halepensis*); and a wild olive (*Olea europaea*).

The Middle-Mediterranean

Located altitudinally above the Thermo-Mediterranean zone, the Middle-Mediterranean zone extends over a smaller area but has denser forest stands. Juniper (*Juniperus phoenicea* ssp. *turbinata*) is optimally found in this forest zone, although its adaptability and resistance allow it to appear in other zones. *J. phoenicea* replaces thuya where continental conditions become too severe for this latter species. It also replaces green oak in lower rainfall areas. It is extensive on south-facing slopes of the High, Middle, and Anti-Atlas ranges.

Green oak (*Q. rotundifolia*) is extensive in the Middle-Mediterranean zone, though it is also common in the Thermo-Mediterranean, Upper-Mediterranean, and Mountain-Mediterranean zones. This evergreen's great adaptability and resistance allow it to colonize all types of soils and bioclimates — from semi-arid to hyper-humid, and from temperate to extremely cold. Green oaks are mainly found between 600 m and 2,700 m in elevation. Overall, they constitute roughly one-fourth of Morocco's forested areas. Other major Middle-Mediterranean forest species are deciduous oak (*Q. pyrenaica, Q. faginea,* and *Q. suber*) and two species of pine (*P. pinaster maghrebiana* and *P. halepensis*).

The Upper-Mediterranean

The Upper-Mediterranean forest zone is immediately above the Middle-Mediterranean in elevation. It covers approximately the same area as the Middle-Mediterranean but is more diverse. In drier areas, this zone is forested with green oak or juniper (*J. phoenica*); in more humid areas, it is forested with deciduous oak and conifers. A key species in this zone is the deciduous oak, *Quercus faginea*. This hardy species is also present in the Thermo-Mediterranean and Middle-Mediterranean zones, ranging from sea level up to 1,800 m. It colonizes all kinds of soils in subhumid to hyperhumid and warm to cold bioclimates.

Another deciduous oak closely associated with the Upper-Mediterranean zone is *Q. pyrenaica*. This oak is less wide-ranging than *Q. faginea*. It is largely confined to the central and western parts of the Rif Mountains, where it is also present in the Middle-Mediterranean zone. *Q. pyrenaica* prefers humid to hyperhumid conditions but avoids calcareous soils. When climatic conditions are favorable to deciduous oak forest, *Q. faginea* and *Q. pyrenaica* are usually found in association. However, the former species is more likely to be found in deep colluvial soils, while the latter is better adapted to thinner soils and colder environments. Coniferous species often found in the Upper-Mediterranean at higher elevations are the Atlantic cedar (*Cedrus atlantica*); an endemic species of fir, *Abies maroccana;* and two different species of pine (*P. clusiana mauretanica* and *P. pinaster maghrebiana*).

Mountain-Mediterranean

The Mountain-Mediterranean zone is the primary home of coniferous trees in Morocco. However, conifers are concentrated in the more humid parts of this zone. Elsewhere, wherever precipitation is not sufficient to support conifers, green oak is the dominant tree. In markedly dry areas, juniper (*J. thurifera*) replaces green oak. The Atlantic cedar (*C. atlantica*) is a key species in the Mountain-Mediterranean zone. Among the four species of cedar, *Cedrus atlantica* is the most western species and is endemic to Algeria and Morocco.

C. *atlantica* is believed to have been much more extensive in North Africa in the past, and is widely considered the region's most majestic and noble tree. Today, extensive areas of Atlantic cedar are found only in Morocco. Stands of this tree grace Morocco's summits between 1,500 m and 2,500 m in cool to very cold, humid bioclimates. Atlantic cedar is present in the central Rif, the Middle Atlas, and the eastern High Atlas. It extends into other forest zones, including the Upper-Mediterranean and occasionally the Oro-Mediterranean. Cedars grow on all types of strata, but prefer acidic soils.

The endemic fir, *Abies maroccana*, is also found in the Mountain-Mediterranean zone. Stands of this fir are concentrated near the high peaks of the western Rif in cold and humid bioclimates. This fir also is present in the Upper-Mediterranean zone. In lower elevations of the Mountain-Mediterranean zone, it is mixed with *Q. rotundifolia* (green oak) or *Q. faginea*. However, at higher elevations, pure stands of this fir are found. They gradually thin out and are replaced by cedar near the summits.

The Oro-Mediterranean

The Oro-Mediterranean is the forest zone highest in elevation. At lower levels, its consists of open stands of juniper (*J. thurifera*). This juniper extends over most of the summits of the eastern Middle Atlas and the east-central High Atlas. It grows on all types of soils in bioclimates ranging from semi-arid to subhumid and cold to extremely cold. At higher levels, between 2,800 m and 3,200 m in elevation, juniper disappears and is replaced by thorny xerophytic shrubs, which extend up to 3,800 m. Beyond this elevation, only alpine tundra is found.

Pine Forests

Four species or varieties of pine are found in Morocco. Small stands of *Pinus halepensis* (Aleppo pine) and *P. pinaster* var. *maghrebiana* are found in the Rif, the Middle Atlas, and the High Atlas. However, Aleppo pine is more extensive in eastern Morocco. *P. pinaster* var. *iberica* and *P. clusiana* var. *mauretanica* are present in Morocco only in the western Rif. Phytosociological studies by the author (Benabid 1984a) have shown that pines are not climax forest species in Morocco. Instead they are species that become established in degraded forest ecosystems.

Causes of Deforestation

Morocco's forests, and its natural vegetation in general, are being subjected to heavy pressure from humans and livestock. This pressure is becoming so intense that many areas, even in the humid northern Rif, are beginning to undergo a process of desertification. Leading causes of deforestation are overgrazing, excessive cutting, and forest clearing for cultivation and urban expansion. Moroccan forestry officials estimate that approximately 30,000 hectares (ha) are deforested each year. Mismanagement of forests is also a significant factor behind forest degradation in Morocco. This section briefly summarizes the leading causes behind deforestation and forest degradation.

Overgrazing and Excessive Cutting

Herds of livestock in Morocco's forests far exceed the grazing capacity of these forests. Overgrazing and cutting of saplings and branches for fodder are probably the leading cause of forest degradation and disappearance in Morocco. Of particular importance is the fact that new seedlings or saplings are browsed or cropped off before they can form new trees, leading to the creation of "fossil forests" throughout vast areas of Morocco. Ironically, these forests appear to the untrained eye to be healthy. However, they are comprised exclusively of mature trees, without any successors. As a result, massive deforestation from disease or old age can be anticipated in the future.

Overgrazing also greatly reduces the biodiversity of natural vegetation in forest areas. Unauthorized forest cutting for fuel, charcoal manufacture, fencing, and construction are other leading causes of deforestation. Illegal timber harvesting is a particular threat to stands of Atlantic cedar, because this cedar is highly prized for construction of ornate decorative ceilings and craft manufacture.

Forest Clearing for Cultivation and Urban Expansion

As in many other parts of the developing world, forests are disappearing to make room for people. Vast areas of Morocco's forests have been cut during the past several decades to create new agricultural land, both fields and orchards. (Editors' note: More recently, extensive forest areas in the Rif — perhaps up to 50,000 ha — have been cleared to create plots for illegal cultivation of marijuana, known locally as *kif*). In addition, large areas of forest have been cleared to prepare terrain for urban construction. For example, a large expanse of argan forest was cleared to construct Agadir's airport. Unbridled urbanization along the Mediterranean and Atlantic coasts (see chapter by Berriane, this volume) is also occurring at the expense of forest areas.

Mismanagement of Forests

Moroccan forestry officials have traditionally used forestry techniques developed elsewhere for other forest environments, particularly for forests in northern Europe. In general, these techniques (clear-cutting, for example) are inappropriate for Morocco's forests. As a result, Morocco's forest ecosystems have suffered. Inappropriate forest-management techniques have disrupted the natural forest ecosystem in various ways. These techniques have introduced undesirable changes in microclimatic conditions at the forest floor, leading to greater erosion, decreased humus, and drier soils. They have brought about a marked decrease in forest productivity and accelerated aging of climax forests. And they have interrupted natural regeneration processes.

Forest Degradation Processes

There has been a critical deterioration of forest ecosystems in Morocco during the past few decades. Some forest ecosystems have gradually disappeared. Others have been profoundly degraded in structure and biodiversity to the point where natural forest regeneration is difficult if not impossible. Processes of forest degradation leading to desertification have been well studied by Barbero et al. (1990). This study, which encompasses the entire Mediterranean region, is valid for Morocco as well. It demonstrates that the frequency and intensity of impacts from humans and livestock result in different stages of forest degradation, which together form a continuum (Figure 10.2). According to the typology developed, forest degradation begins with a process of "matorralization," proceeds through "dematorralization," "steppification," and "therophytization," and ends with a process of "desertification." These stages will be briefly examined.

Matorralization

Matorralization is a term coined from the French vegetation term, *matorral*, which refers to a degraded form of Mediterranean scrub vegetation.

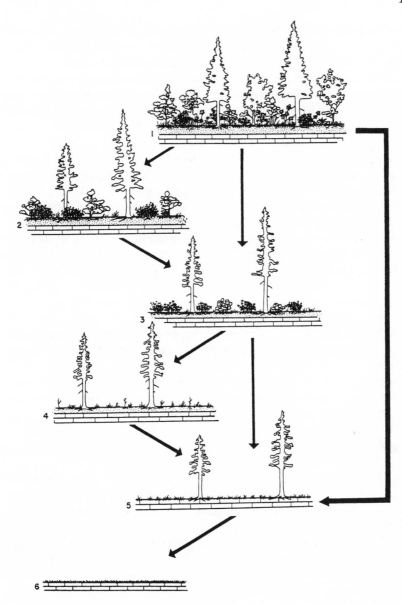

FIGURE 10.2 Forest Degradation Processes. Stage 1 represents climax forests; 2 represents matorralization; 3 represents dematorralization; 4 represents steppification; 5 represents therophytization; 6 represents desertification.

Source: Adapted from Barbero et al. 1990.

Matorralization occurs when the climax forest is opened up through grazing and cutting. In the more open conditions created, climax forest species have difficulty regenerating because evapotranspiration increases, soils become drier and more barren, tree seeds find it harder to become established, and seedlings are subject to water stress, which lowers their survival rates. As a result, the disturbed forest areas are invaded by more xerophytic, low-growing brushy species with hard-surfaced leaves, which can tolerate the more hostile conditions.

Matorralization can be observed in all of Morocco's forest bioclimates, from very humid to arid. In humid and sub-humid regions of northern Morocco, for example, low-lying drought-resistant sclerophylous forests have replaced deciduous or coniferous forests. In drier regions, the former climax species have been replaced by more heliophytic and xerophytic species, which do not need shade to become established and can thrive in eroded soils. Typical species in matorralized areas include *Pinus halepensis*, *Cytisus* sp., *Calycotome*, *Ephedra*, *Rosmarinus*, *Juniperus*, and *Euphorbia* sp.

Dematorralization

As degradation of forests proceeds, larger matorral species are gradually replaced by smaller, more drought-resistant species, creating a lower, more open, more degraded scrub formation. Key species of this stage include *Cytisus* sp. (particularly genista) and *Rosmarinus*. Rapid invasion by these species is due to their rapid growth, large seed production, and a greater tolerance of drought-like conditions.

Steppification

Further degradation leads to *steppification*. In this stage, matorral species are replaced by a sparser cover of more xerophytic plants better adapted to the extreme aridity induced by the progressive deterioration of ecological conditions. Typical species in this stage in Morocco include *Stipa* sp., *Artemisia* sp., *Antirrhinum* sp., and *Thymus* sp. These species gradually become dominant due to their regular and sustained seed production and their emission of toxic substances that inhibit the growth of other species. The "forest" now has very limited biodiversity.

Therophytization

As the vegetation cover becomes thinner, soil becomes drier and more barren of organic matter and conditions become increasingly inhospitable for most plant species. Further deterioration of ecological conditions leads to the gradual disappearance of woody vegetation. Apart from the surviving mature "fossil" trees, all that remains is a sparse cover of tough annual species. These annuals can survive in the hostile degraded environment because they germinate, grow, and flourish during the short periods favorable to their vegetative activities. *Therophytization* has disastrous implications for the environment and for socioeconomic activities depending on this environment. For example, the lack of vegetative cover leads to rapid runoff, which results in the drying up of water tables.

Desertification

The ultimate stage of forest degradation is *desertification*. This stage is characterized by the disappearance of "fossil" trees due to aging and lack of water and nutrients essential for sustenance. At the end of this stage, virtually all traces of the former forest have disappeared and the landscape is essentially barren. This stage can be reversed in humid and subhumid bioclimates. However, in arid and semi-arid bioclimates, restoration of the former forest cover is practically impossible. In these areas, true deserts have been created, and the land has little or no socio-economic value.

Present Condition of Morocco's Forests

Recent phytosociological studies make it possible to summarize the present condition of Morocco's forests. This section provides a brief synopsis, using the previously discussed typology of forest degradation stages, and adding "climax forests" as a point of departure.

Climax forests are relatively well preserved forest ecosystems. In this stage, forest structures and architecture are well balanced. There are normally three different levels or stories of vegetation present: the forest canopy, a secondary level consisting of small trees and shrubs, and the forest-floor cover consisting of low-lying perennials and annual grasses. Studies have shown that this multi-storied architecture provides the optimal edapho-climatic conditions for the regeneration of climax forest species such as cedar, fir, juniper, oak, argan, and thuya. Unfortunately, climax forest is no longer very extensive in Morocco. Limited areas of climax forest, however, can still be found in both the Rif and the Atlas mountains, particularly in the Middle Atlas and the central High Atlas. In *matorral forests*, natural regeneration of climax species still occurs and pine species have difficulty becoming established. Matorral forests are extensive in Morocco. In general, most of the forests of the Rif, the western and eastern High Atlas, and the Anti-Atlas can be classified as matorral forests.

Dematorralized forests are common in the Rif, the eastern Middle Atlas, the High Atlas, and the western Anti-Atlas. These are all regions where forest clearing has been extensive. Cleared areas have usually been invaded by aggressive species such as *Cytisus* (especially genista) and *Rosmarinus*. In these dematorralized areas, natural regeneration of many climax species, including cedar, fir, and oak, is rare. However, certain other climax species, such as juniper, thuya, and argan, can become re-established if the forest is protected from further degradation. Pine can quickly become established in dematorralized areas, provided that the necessary edapho-climatic conditions are present.

Steppicized forests are becoming extensive in eastern Morocco, in the eastern High Atlas, and in the Anti-Atlas. They are also beginning to appear in some valleys of the eastern Rif and other parts of the Atlas mountains. In these highly degraded environments, natural regeneration of any climax forest species — even heliophytic and xerophytic species such as juniper, cypress, thuya, and argan — is extremely rare. On the other hand, pine can become established in these environments, though its establishment is often compromised by degraded soils.

Therophytization is present in virtually all of Morocco's forests. As previously noted, therophytized areas are ecologically highly disturbed and highly simplified. The remaining forest consists of stands of "fossil" trees, which will ultimately disappear, and a relatively barren forest floor. In such areas, natural regeneration of the forest is virtually impossible. Unfortunately, many thousands of hectares of Moroccan forest have reached this stage and are now being transformed into biological deserts.

In sum, the overall condition of Moroccan forests is not good. Extensive areas of forest have disappeared, and most remaining forests have undergone varying degrees of degradation. The productivity, species composition, and regenerative processes of most remaining forests have been profoundly disrupted. Forest areas have undergone radical changes in microclimatic conditions; geochemical cycles have been altered; soils have become drier and more barren; and the underlying water tables have been lowered, often dramatically.

Conclusions

Unfortunately, deforestation and forest-degradation processes in Morocco are likely to accelerate. As Morocco's human and livestock populations continue to increase, the pressure they exert on forests will become ever more onerous. The condition of Morocco's forests is now reaching a crisis stage. Both from environmental and socioeconomic perspectives, urgent measures are needed to halt further deterioration of these forests. With appropriate measures, forest deterioration can be arrested and even reversed. These measures will include reforestation and implementation of improved forest management techniques.

As previously noted, an estimated 30,000 ha are *deforested* each year in Morocco. However, to counteract this loss, between 30,000 and 40,000 ha of new forest are *planted* each year. It would therefore appear that reforestation more than compensates for forest loss. Unfortunately, reforestation has not been very successful in Morocco. Overall, the average success rate for reforestation operations does not exceed 50 percent. In certain areas, the success rate is as low as 20 percent. And some reforestation operations have been complete failures. In these areas, one sees barren hillsides with a stippling of reddish-brown dead seedlings. Reforestation failure has typically occurred because exotic, non-adapted tree species have been planted. Either their seedlings could not become established or, if they did become established, they were subsequently devastated by insects or diseases. Examples of the latter have included decimation of pine plantations by caterpillars and of eucalyptus plantations by *xylophages* (Benabid 1984b). A final problem is that reforestation is usually undertaken with the wrong objective — short-term economic gain rather than regeneration of the natural forest.

In general, Morocco's forestry officials should concentrate on reforestation with *native* forest species, which are already fully adapted to Moroccan conditions and which should have a much higher survival rate. In addition, officials should place far greater emphasis than has traditionally been the case on fostering *natural regeneration* of climax forest species.

Exotic species such as pine and eucalyptus may have a valuable role to play in reforestation or afforestation projects designed to combat desertification or establish commercial plantations for charcoal manufacture, timber, and paper pulp. However, these exotic species should not be used to replace matorral forest. They should be used only when the land is relatively barren — that is, in highly degraded dematorralized, steppicized, or therophytized areas. In such areas, it is highly recommended that artificial planting be restricted to parallel strips, instead of blanketing the entire area of intervention, in order to allow for natural regeneration of native climax species in between the strips. Mixed planting of exotic and native species for a multipurpose reafforestation has led to spectacular results in some areas in Morocco.

Creativity and experimentation is required. For example, planting a moderately dense pattern of Aleppo pines in a matorral of *Rosmarinus* or alfa grass could assist in the reconstitution of climax forest species such as juniper, thuya, and green oaks. At higher elevations, the same operation, with other pine species instead of Aleppo pine, should lead to the recolonization of a mixed formation of cedar and green oak. Improved soil management techniques would also help in the reconstitution of climax forests in certain types of matorral.

Forestry officials should acknowledge that forestry management techniques developed in other countries for different bioclimates will usually not be directly appropriate for Morocco. Further studies and experiments are needed to determine the most appropriate management techniques for each forest type in Morocco. In general, outside of artificial plantations, forestry officials should avoid clearcuts and instead employ methods of selective cutting that consider the light and shade requirements of the tree species in question to optimize their natural regeneration and productivity. These requirements should also be considered in reforestation and thinning operations to restore climax forests.

Because overgrazing in Morocco's forests is one of the major causes of forest degradation, policies must be developed to reduce herd sizes in forests to help forests regenerate naturally. Developing such policies will be a major challenge. One way to reduce grazing pressure on forests is to improve natural pastures outside of forest areas through rangeland management. In addition, forage-crop production could be emphasized (for example, as an integral part of an improved crop-rotation system) to reduce the need for forest grazing. In forest areas themselves, native species with high fodder content could be planted to reduce pressure on tree seedlings and to improve microclimatic conditions for seedling establishment and growth. Improved forest management of the extensive green oak forests in Morocco could substantially improve the pastoral value of these forests.

In order to succeed, efforts to restore Moroccan forests must adhere to two basic principles: (1) forest management techniques should be completely adapted to the local ecosystem, in order to ensure the forest's sustained regeneration and productivity and to preserve its biodiversity; and (2) appropriate means should be developed to accommodate the conflicting needs for forest conservation, on the one hand, and forest-resource use (grazing, timber, fuelwood, etc.) on the other.

References

Barbero, M., G. Bonin, R. Loisel, P. Quezel. 1990. "Changes and Disturbances of Forest Ecosystems Caused by Human Activities in the Western Part of the Mediterranean Basin." *Vegetatio* 87:151-173.

Benabid, A. 1976. *Etude phytoécologique, phytosociologique et sylvo-pastorale de la tétraclinaie de l'Amsittène*. Thèse Univ. Droit, Econ., Sci., Aix-Marseille III.

———. 1982. "Bref aperçu sur la zonation altitudinale de la végétation climatique du Maroc." *Ecologia méditerranea* VIII A and 2:301-315.

———. 1984a. "Etude phytoécologique des peuplements forestiers et préforestiers du Rif centro-occidental (Maroc)." *Travaux Inst. Scient., Sér. Botan.* 34. (Rabat).

————. 1984b. "A propos de l'écologie des essences forestières du sud-ouest australien méditerranéen. Application au Maghreb." *Ann. Recherche Forest. Maroc* 24:58-99.

————. 1985. "Les écosystèmes forestiers, préforestiers et présteppiques du Maroc: diversité, répartition biogéographique et problèmes posés par leur aménagement." *Forêt méditerranéenne* VII(1):53-64.

————. 1990. "Dégradation des écosytèmes forestiers marocains." *Colloque International: Pollution, Environnement et Développement*. Rabat.

Daget, P. 1977a. "Le bioclimat méditerranéen: caractères généraux, modes de caractérisation." *Vegetatio* 34:1-20.

————. 1977b. "Le bioclimat méditerranéen: analyse des formes climatiques par le système d'Emberger." *Vegetatio* 34:87-103.

Donadieu, P. 1977. "Contribution à une synthèse bioclimatique et phytogéologique au Maroc. *Bull. Inst. Agron. Vétér. Hassan II.* (Rabat).

Emberger, L. 1955. "Une classification biogéographique des climats." *Rev. Trav. Lab. Bot. Zool. Fac. Sci. Montpellier, Sér. Botan.* 7:3-43.

————. 1964. "La position phytogéographique du Maroc dans l'ensemble méditerranéen." *Al Awamia* 12:1-15.

11

Disappearing Species: The Case of the Monk Seal in Algeria

Zitouni Boutiba

The monk seal (*Monachus monachus*) is the most endangered species in the Mediterranean. This pinniped has become the symbol in the fight of many environmental associations to combat pollution and protect the natural environment. This fight is regarded by many as critical: If the monk seal cannot be rescued from extinction in the Mediterranean, then prospects are dim for many other endangered species and for preservation of biodiversity in general.

The existence of the Mediterranean monk seal along the coast of Algeria was first reported by Loche (1840) in his *Classification des Oiseaux et Mammifères d'Algérie*. The second mention of the monk seal is in Trouessart (1905), who signalled its presence in Algeria, Morocco, and Tunisia. In 1919, Doumergue reported a sighting of the monk seal offshore near Oran. It was not until 1927 that Gavard undertook the first study of the biology and behavior of this mammal, following the capture of three specimens (two females, one pregnant, and a young male) in the Oran area in 1926. The three seals soon died because they could not survive in captivity. The corpse of the male was sent to the University of Algiers; there, Dieuzeide (1927) undertook a detailed study of its anatomy. In his *Exploration Zoologique de l'Algérie de 1830-1930*, Seurat (1930) mentions the presence of the monk seal along the coast of Algiers. On the basis of these facts, Algeria was included in King's (1956) early general studies on this species. Five years later, Santa (1961) reported the presence of the monk seal along the coastline of Oran. It was not until the 1970s that the distribution and habitat of the species along the Algerian coast began to be known through studies by Boulva and

Cyrus (1974); Chebab and Bouabdelli (1978); Bougazelli (1979); and Lloze (1979). These authors provided a good basic understanding of the distribution of the monk seal population between Béni Saf (Wilaya of Tlemcen) and Cap Ténès (Wilaya of Chlef). This population was estimated at 100 individuals by Boulva (1979) and Lloze (1979).

Around the same time (1970s), evidence for the decline of the monk seal population first appeared. This led some authors to raise the question of the survival of this species while others undertook research to understand the evolution of its population. Bahri (1974) and Jacquin (1974) denounced the deliberate massacre of this sea mammal by local fishermen. Boulva (1979) and Bougazelli (1979) emphasized the threat of extinction that this species, abundant along the whole of the Algerian coast in the 1960s, was now facing. At that time, the monk seal was no longer observed along Algeria's west coast (Bougazelli 1979; Boulva 1979). On the east coast the species was observed infrequently (Bougazelli 1979; Avella 1987). Indeed, the last observation goes back to 1974 (Marchessaux 1987). However, recent work has noted the regular presence of the species along the west and central coasts. Additionally, for the last 10 years research has been systematically undertaken to record the evolution of Algeria's monk seal population and gather together observations made along the entire Algerian coast (Boutiba et al. 1988; Lefevre et al. 1989; Boutiba 1990).

This chapter reviews recent research and summarizes results. The objective of this research, which involved a systematic exploration of the coastline and nearby offshore areas, was twofold — to interview the greatest number of people with precise knowledge of the Mediterranean monk seal and its habits, and to document the presence of the monk seal along the coast, whether at sea or on land. These outings also made it possible to count and autopsy corpses washed up on shore; count caves and shelters used as habitat by this sea mammal; set up a network of reliable observers along the Algerian coast; and gather sizable data on the biology, ecology, and ethology of the species.

Equipment and Methods

Data Collection

From September 1986 to September 1990, many investigations of the Mediterranean monk seal were undertaken along the coast of Oran and Algiers from Merdat Ben Mhidi in the west to Dellys Beach in the east (Figure 11.1).[1] We interviewed more than 450 fishermen (sport and commercial) who regularly go out to sea, and some 60 yachtsmen. This

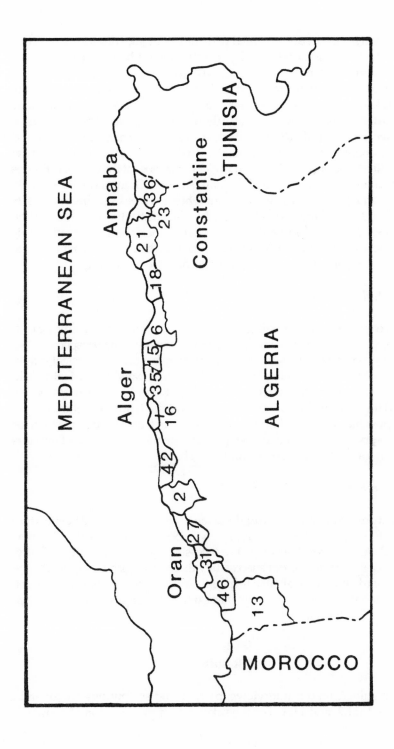

FIGURE 11.1 Location of the Investigated Coastal Areas

information has been supplemented with the testimonies of various maritime authorities (Customs, Coast Guard, port authorities, fisheries officials); as well as members of the security services (*gendarmerie*, etc.).

In the course of our investigations, which lasted 90 days and covered more than 900 kilometers (km) of coastline, a campaign was undertaken to sensitize people to the problem of the survival of the monk seal species. It sought to reach fishermen and coastal administrators, university teachers, secondary and primary school students, and others. We also interviewed oceanographers at the Institut des Sciences de la Mer in Algiers, and those at the Centre d'Etudes et de Recherche sur la Pêche in Bou Imaïl (Algiers), Oran, and Béni Saf in an attempt to make them more aware of the plight of the monk seal. In our contacts we have distributed more than 3,000 copies of a sensitization and information leaflet, *Let's Save the Monk Seal*. In the event of a monk seal observation, this leaflet makes it possible for people to contact us directly and communicate details. A network of volunteer informants has also been set up.

Field Patrols

The coastal portions accessible by land were surveyed many times, albeit infrequently. A total of 110 days or 650 hours of systematic prospection (5-6 hours/day on average) was devoted to exploring the coast. The coastal sectors of the western and central regions were visited by means of a 4 x 4 all-terrain vehicle. Failing that, we used our own vehicle. Every 200-250 meters (m) we stopped for about 10-20 minutes on beaches and cliff roads. Sometimes, as far as was possible, we climbed down sea cliffs in search of a strategic position for better observation. On other occasions we descended to the base of the cliffs to explore caves, shelters, creeks, and small bays.

Outings at Sea

Twenty missions at sea were undertaken to areas of monk seal habitat (two in 1986, four in 1987, four in 1988, seven in 1989, and three in 1990). Areas explored were inaccessible by land but accessible by sea, albeit with difficulty. All missions were carried out successfully thanks to logistical support of the Coast Guard and the invaluable help of fishermen and yachtsmen. Each sea mission lasted 3-6 hours. All took place when the sea was calm. These sea outings occurred in all seasons.

Results

The results from our interviews, patrols, and sea outings are given in Tables 11.1, 11.2, and 11.3. For the sake of clear presentation of results, it seemed practical to divide the Algerian coast into three main sectors corresponding to geographic regions. These sectors included the West Coast (Oranie); Central Algeria (Algérois); and the East Coast (Constantinois) (Figure 11.1).

Assessment of Findings

The west and central coasts (from Cap Milonia in the west to Azzefoun in the east) are the two main areas along which we undertook systematic and detailed surveys (tables 11.1 and 11.2). Only for these two areas are our data sufficiently numerous to be considered comprehensive.

On the west coast we counted, on average, 56 monk seals distributed over 20 areas in 1987; 25 individuals in 17 areas in 1988; and 18 individuals in 1989 and 15 in 1990 in 11 areas. Interestingly, in the same region Lloze (1978) counted as many as 102 monk seals in 30 different localities (Table 11.1). Over a 12-year period we noted a sharp decrease in both the number of monk seals and the number of areas in which the species is to be found.

On the central coast, data published by Bahri (1974), Bougazelli (1979), and ourselves (Table 11.2) enabled us to record, 10 years ago, 14 observations in more than 11 localities. However, in 1988 and 1989 we counted only 5 individuals in 3 localities (Boutiba 1990) and only a single individual in 1990 in the area of Bou Haroun (Wilaya of Tipaza). The situation is, therefore, similar to that observed on the west coast — a clear decline in monk seals and areas of habitat.

In sum, between the late 1970s and the early 1990s, there has been a spectacular drop in the number of monk seals and they have disappeared from many areas that at one time hosted the species.[2] The methods of data collection used do not provide a scientifically reliable and complete census of the monk seal population because of the latter's secretive habits and its distribution over a coastal stretch of almost 900 km. Nevertheless, we can say that the data provide a relatively reliable picture of the critical situation of the monk seal in these major coastal areas. A number of tentative conclusions emerge.

On the west and central coasts, the monk seal population is now fragmented into tiny groups or isolated individuals. Comparing our data with those of Lloze (1979) and Bougazelli (1979) reveals that a number of areas in which the monk seal used to live are now deserted. For example, Draz Illes and Ras Tarsa in the Wilaya of Tlemcen, which until recently were inhabited by groups of 8-10, are now completely deserted. In the same way a group of 6 monk seals at Cap Falcon, mentioned in Boutiba et al. (1988), has been absent since 1989. (Incidentally, this date marks the beginning in this area of a development project.)

In the eastern part of the west coast, the monk seal is not found anywhere

TABLE 11.1 Monk Seal Geographic Distribution Along the Western Coast of Algeria (in Oran Region, from Cap Milonia to Souahlia Bay)

Places (West > East)	Number of Individuals (by year)					Habitat
	1978	1987	1988	1989	1990	
Wilaya of Tlemcen						
Cap Milonia[a]	15	1	--	--	--	grotto
Ras Kla[b]	1	1-2	--	1	1	grotto
Palomas Island	2	--	--	--	--	grotto
Ghazaouet Harbor	2	1	1	--	--	harbor
Neil	1	--	--	--	--	shelter
Cap Tarsa[c]	1	10	1	--	--	grotto
Sidi Ouchaa	1	1	1-2	1	--	grotto
Honaine El Mokrane[d]	--	3	1	1	--	grotto
Wilaya of Ain Témouchent						
Ouardania > Rachgoun	--	1-2	1-2	1-2	1	grotto[e]
Rachgoun Island	--	2	1	--	1	grotto[f]
Port of Béni Sat	3	1	--	2	--	harbor
Cap Oullassa - Camerrafa	--	--	--	2	1	creek[g]
Cap Figalo	2	5-6	--	--	--	grottos
Bou Zadjar	10[h]	1	--	--	--	grottos
Wilaya of Oran						
Maddaght	6	6[h]	2-3	--	--	grotto[i]
Cap Blan	3	2	2	--	--	grottos
Habibas Islands	1	2	1	1	1	grottos
Fourais Islands	--	--	--	--	--	rocks
Plane Island	1	--	1	--	--	rocks
Cap Falcon	3	2	--	--	--	grottos
Oran[j]	1	--	--	--	--	grottos
Pointe de l'Aiguille	6	1	1	1	1	grottos
Cap Ferrat	2	--	1	1	--	grottos
Cap Carbon	1	--	--	--	1	grottos
Wilaya of Mostaganem						
Cap Rouge	1	--	--	--	--	grotto[k]
Stidia	4	--	--	--	--	beach
Port of Mostaganem	--	--	--	--	--	port
Cap Ivi	1	6	1	--	--	grottos
Oullis	2	1	--	--	--	beach

(TABLE 11.1 continued)

Places (West > East)	Number of Individuals (by year)					Habitat
	1978	*1987*	*1988*	*1989*	*1990*	*Habitat*
Achachaa (ex: Picard)	15	--	--	--	--	beach
Kef El Asfer	3	--	2	2	2	grotto[i]
Petit port - Sidi El Adjel (ex: Port Mesnard)	--	4-5	3-4	3-5	2-5	grottos
Wilaya of Chlef						
Cap Khrémis	3	--	1	--	--	grotto
Colombi Island (beach)	3	--	--	--	--	grotto
El Marsa	1	--	--	--	--	grotto
Kef Kalaa	1	--	--	--	--	grotto
Pointe Rouge	1	--	--	--	--	grotto
Béni Haoua	1	1	--	--	--	grotto
Cap Ténès	3	--	1	--	--	grotto
Ténès	1	--	--	--	--	
Souahlia Bay	--	1	1-2	--	1	grottos
TOTAL	102	54-58	22-28	17-19	14-16	

[a] Ras El Ouareye
[b] Plage des sels
[c] Draz Illes
[d] The port
[e] Plus 2 shelters
[f] Plus 3 shelters
[g] Plus cliff
[h] Young individuals present
[i] Plus creek
[j] Rocher de la Vieille
[k] Plus beach

Sources: 1978 data are from Lloze (1979, Table 1). Other data collected by author.

in the vast zone stretching between Cap Falcon (to the west of Oran) and Achachaa (northeast of Mostaganem). It is also no longer seen along the coast of the Wilaya of Chlef.

By contrast, we have noticed the settling of small groups of isolated individuals in areas in which the species was not previously reported to

TABLE 11.2 Monk Seal Geographic Distribution Along the Coast of the Region Around Algier Between Damous and Azzefoun

Places (West > East)	Number of Individuals (by year)			Habitat
	1979	1989	1990	
Wilaya of Tipaza				
Damous (Seiche)	1	--	--	grotto
Goucaya (beach)	2	--	--	grotto
Cherchell	1	--	--	grotto
Bou Haroun[a]	2-8	2	1	grotto
Bou Ismail	1	--	--	
Wilaya of Alger				
Dhémil (beach)	1	--	--	beach
Alger Bay	1	--	--	creek + beach
Pointe Pescade	--	2	--	
Cap Mtifou	1	--	--	creek
Wilaya of Tizi Ouzou				
Dellys (beach)	1	1	--	beach
Azzefoun	--	--	--	creek
TOTAL	11-17	5	1	

[a]Port and "Grotte des Veaux Marins"

Sources: 1979 data are those reported in Bougazelli (1979). Other data collected by author.

live, or rarely so. Thus, in the Wilaya of Mostaganem, the Sidi Adjel colony (northeast of Mostaganem) is apparently new. The monk seal, most likely driven away from its old sites by human activity, has settled in less frequented, isolated areas.

In the case of Sidi Adjel, individual monk seals could have come from neighboring areas of this site. (Cap Ivi, Oullis, Kef El Asfer in the west, and Cap Khrèmis, Béni Haoua, and Kef Kalaa in the east). The results shown in table form clearly indicate that the decline noted in the west coast (from Ghazaouet to Cap Ivi) by Boutiba et al. (1988) is continuing, if not accelerating. We can consider that the sea monk population is decreasing exponentially following the classic equation:

TABLE 11.3 Observations of the Monk Seal Along the Eastern Coast of Algeria, Region of Constantine, from the Béjaïa-Port to the Frontier with Tunisia, Summer 1988

Place (West > East)	Number Observed
Wilaya of Béjaïa	
Béjaïa-Port	--
Tichi	--
Ziana Mansouria	1
Wilaya of Jijel	--
Ras Attia	2
Wilaya of Skikda	
Bay of Collo	2
La Marsa	--
Cap de Per	--
Wilaya of Annaba	
Chetaïbi	1
Wilaya of El Tarf	
El Kala	2
Frontier with Tunisia	--
TOTAL	8

Source: Data collected by author.

Equation 11.1 $$N_t = N_o\, er^t$$

N_t represents the population at time t; N_o is the reference population; e is the base ($e = 2.7183$); and r is the instantaneous increase (or decrease) in the rate of the population at time t, the time expressed here in years. The following equation allows the approximate calculation of r when we have two or more estimates of a population obtained in two different years:

TABLE 11.4 Seasonal and Annual Frequency of *Monachus monachus* Observations Along Western and Central Coasts of Algeria, 1987-1990[a]

	1987	1988	1989	1990	Total
Winter	18	11	3	3	35
Spring	19	8	8	3	38
Summer	30	17	15	8	70
Autumn	19	14	2	6	41
Total	86	50	28	20	184

[a]Every death is counted as an observation.

Source: Data collected by author.

Equation 11.2 $$r = \frac{\ln (N_o / N_t)}{t}$$

Using these equations, we can see that, from 1978-1990, numbers of monk seals along the west coast of Algeria fell by an average of 15 percent/year.[3] By contrast, from 1987-1990 there was an annual decrease of 35.5 percent.[4] Along Algeria's central coast, the monk seal population was estimated to be 11-17 individuals in 1979 (Bougazelli 1979; Boutiba 1988, 1989). In 1990 this population had apparently dropped to a single individual.[5] These two examples illustrate the sharp fall in population numbers, which were originally low.

This situation seems true of all monk seal groups and demonstrates the fragility of these small populations. During the last 12 years the apparent annual extinction rate averaged 18 percent for the two large coastal regions. We believe that the actual extinction rate is around 15 percent/year. Probably 3-4 percent of the monk seals believed to have disappeared in fact migrated to areas where living conditions were more favorable, either to the Chaffarine Islands in Morocco or the islands of Galite in Tunisia.

Table 11.4 also reflects the dramatic fall in population. The monk seal is observed throughout the year, with the highest frequency in the holiday season. The relatively low number of monk seals observed during the other three seasons is undoubtedly related to bad weather, which limits the number of sea outings and makes access to coastal areas more difficult.

Causes of Disappearance

From Loche's (1840) observations concerning the monk seal in his *Classification des Oiseaux et Mammifères d'Algérie*, one can assume that this seal lived throughout Algeria's coastal areas in the nineteenth century but that it was seen less often along the coastline of Constantinois than along the coastlines of l'Oranais or l'Algérois. The presence of monk seal colonies in these latter regions is confirmed at the beginning of the twentieth century in the reports of Trouessart (1905); Doumergue (1919); Gavard (1927); Dieuzeide (1927); and Seurat (1930). Today, however, the monk seal is confined mainly to the west coast, along which some 15 seals are still surviving in small groups or as isolated individuals. The survival of this tiny population here can be explained by the shape of its 500 km coastline, which, *a priori*, seems more favorable to the species than the other two coastal regions. The west coast is highly irregular, and access by land is difficult at many points. Furthermore, high cliffs make up around three-fourths of the coastline. At the base of these cliffs are many caves and small creeks, ideal shelters for the survival of the species. The waters bordering this coast are under the influence of Atlantic currents, which favor high trophic production, ensuring sufficient food resources year round.

The presence along the western coastline of many islands (Rachgoun, Laïlla Habiba Island, Fournis, Plane, Cap Falcon, and Arzew) favors the permanent presence of the monk seal population. Indeed, these insular areas, far from densely populated coasts, have abundant food resources and offer deep and sheltered caves favorable to the settling of the species. If we exclude a few exceptions, the fishermen of the west coast do not kill the monk seal: they consider it a companion, a friend to respect and fear at the same time. According to local legend, "He who kills a monk seal will have bad luck."

Local coastal residents cite cases that verify this legend. There is the story of the fisherman whose ship was wrecked in 1962 a few days after he had killed a monk seal. There is also the story of the fisherman who, after deliberately killing a monk seal that had helped itself to his catch, disappeared at sea in 1966. Forty-eight hours later he was found dead. Avella (1987) estimates that 90 percent of the fishermen in the Maghreb do not show any hostility toward this mammal.

Nevertheless, there is a minority who have contributed to the monk seal's decline. Such ill-intentioned people do not hesitate to kill the monk seal, which they view as a competitor capable of ripping apart their nets to feed on their fish. Reports indicate that the monk seal has been intentionally eliminated by means of firearms and/or explosive devices (Jacquin 1974; Bahri 1974; Boutiba et al. 1988).

Moreover, fishing techniques commonly used represent a permanent danger to the monk seal. Frequently it drowns when entangled in fishing nets. Indeed, eight such deaths were registered between 1987 and 1990 on Algeria's west central coast.

The sharp fall in the monk seal population can also be explained by many other factors. Pollution of Algeria's marine waters is increasing, as in the rest of the Mediterranean. The effects of this pollution on *Monachus monachus* are not well known (Marchessaux and Duguy 1977). It may be that coastal oil pollution forces the monk seal to desert the coast that it once occupied (*IUCN* 1976). Thus, the pollution of the Arzew Gulf may well have caused the disappearance of the species from the coast east of Oran. In the same way, coastal pollution of the Algérois (central Algeria) is likely the main cause of the extinction of the monk seal population there.

In light of the importance of tourism to the Algerian economy, touristic infrastructure is developing considerably, particularly along the coast, which means that the coast is busy almost all year round. The increasing number of yachts, the movement of which is totally uncontrolled, also threatens the species by disturbing individual monk seals in their habitat. Indeed, the monk seal is extremely sensitive to such disturbance. In some cases such disturbances may have caused entire colonies to disperse, hampering species reproduction. Continual disturbance may explain the high death rate among offspring. Baby monk seals are abandoned by mothers who flee disturbances. The setting up of industrial sites and new ports, the expansion of old ones, and the building of roads to hitherto inaccessible beaches and creeks contribute to the modification of the coastal environment and the decline of the monk seal.

Conclusions

The monk seal is the most endangered animal species in the Mediterranean. Comparison of recent observations with previous estimates reveals a dramatic decline in the population of monk seals. The recorded number of monk seals in 1978 was 102 individuals, while in 1990 there were only 16, which amounts to a decrease rate of 18 percent/year on the west and central coasts. Few monk seals are believed to still exist on Algeria's east coast. The decline of the monk seal in Algeria has reached a crisis stage, even though the species has been protected officially since August 1983 (Presidential Decree No. 83-509). This legal protection, which was late in coming, has not been able to prevent the destruction of monk seals.

People are responsible for the extinction of the monk seal through direct killing (shooting and use of explosives); disturbance (tourism, rapid coastal expansion); and indirect action (accidental capture in fishing nets, pollution). It is therefore critically important that protective measures be immediately reinforced in areas where the species still survives and that a campaign be carried out immediately to sensitize the public — fishermen and tourists in particular — to the looming threat of monk seal extinction. Several ideas have been advanced for the preservation of remaining Algerian monk seals. A formal request to create natural reserves has been presented. Two reserves have been suggested — one (Rachgoun Island Reserve) around Béni Saf, and a second (Habibas Islands Reserve) southwest of Oran. It is our belief that an additional proposition should be made to compensate fishermen for damage caused to their fishing nets by monk seals.

In many Mediterranean countries, not only in Algeria, the monk seal has become the symbol of the struggle to preserve the environment. Preservation of the monk seal depends on a number of factors, the most essential being respect for this animal. Its friendliness toward humans makes it an easy target; thus the best way to protect it is to avoid disturbing it. If the monk seal can be saved, this will indicate that we have gone one step further toward achieving a higher environmental consciousness. On the other hand, if this defenseless mammal becomes extinct, all of society will have to share the blame.

Notes

1. The mission on the Constantine coast is not taken into account in this work. Only one mission was completed on the coast of Constantine for a number of reasons: remoteness, lack of means of transport, poor accommodations, and so on.

2. The comparison of our data with Lloze's (1979) data on the west coast and those of Bougazelli (1979) on the central coast must be undertaken with caution. Our respective fieldwork (data collection, coast survey, and sea outings) was undertaken with significant differences in time span by different researchers and in dissimilar conditions.

3. $r = -0.160$.

4. $r = -0.439$.

5. An operation similar to the one above gives the Instantaneous Regression Rate $r = -0.210$; that is, an annual decrease of 21.3 percent.

References

Avella, F. J. 1987. "Man versus monk seal in North Africa: a preliminary report." *Third International Conference on the Monk Seal, Antalya, Turkey.* Pp. 1-11.

Bahri, R. 1974. "Epargner les derniers phoques de la Méditerranée." *Algérie actualité.* P. 465.

Bakalem, A. 1980. "Pollution et source de pollution marine d'origine industrielle sur la côte ouest algérienne: étude préliminaire." *Vème journées Etud. Pollut. Cagliari, C.I.E.S.M (1980):*195-200.

Bougazelli, N. 1979. "Quelques données sur le phoque moine d'Algérie (*Monachus monachus*)," in K. Ronald and R. Duguy, eds., *The Mediterranean Monk Seal, Proceedings of the First International Conference, Rhodes, Greece, 2-5 May 1978.* Pp. 175-78. Oxford and New York: Pergamon Press.

Boulva, J. 1979. "Mediterranean monk seal." *Mammals in the Seas, FAO Fisheries*

Series II (5):95-100.

Boulva, J., and J. L. Cyrus. 1974. "The Mediterranean monk seal, *Monachus monachus*, in Northwest Africa (Tunisia to Mauritania)." *XXIVème Congres-Assembl. Plenière de Monaco*, December 6-14, p. 2.

Boutiba, Z. 1990. "Observations récentes de phoques moines (*Monachus monachus*) sur le littoral centre algérien (région d'Alger)." *Mammalia* 54(4):663-664.

Boutiba, Z., B. Souabria, and D. Robineau. 1988. "Etat actuel de population du phoque moine (*Monachus monachus*) sur le littoral ouest algérien (région d'Oran.)" *Mammalia* 52(4):549-559.

Chebab, R., and M. B. Bouabdelli. 1978. "Etude statististique et éthologique de Monachus monachus (Hermann 1779) sur le littoral ouest algérien." *Mém. D.E.S. Univ. d'Oran, Alg.* 1-32+11:1.

Dieuzeide, R. 1927. "Sur quelques points d'anatomie du phoque moine de la Méditerranée (*Monachus albiventer Bold*)." *Bull. Stat. Aquac. Pêches Castiglione, Algeria* 2:215-249.

Doumergue, F. 1919. "Exhibition d'un phoque moine à Oran." *Atlas P.L.M. Bull. S.A.G.O.*: 1.

Gavard, J. 1927. "Observations sur le phoque moine Monachus albiventer (Bold.) faite au laboratoire de Castiglione." *Bull. Stat. Aquac. Pêches Castiglione, Alg.* 2: 175-211.

IUCN. 1976. "League for the conservation of the Monk Seal," *Newsletter No. 1.* Ontario, Canada: Univeristy of Guelph, College of Biological Science.

Jacquin, M. 1974. "A propos du phoque moine ou veau marine." *Ens. Sc. Nat. Oran., Alg.* 12:2.

King, J. E. 1956. "The monk seals (genus *Monachus*)." *Bull. Br. Mus of. Hist.* 3:201-56.

Lefevre, J. R., F. Moutou, Z. Boutiba, and D. Derrar. 1989. *Déclin du phoque moine Monachus monachus sur les côtes algériennes entre Cap Falcon et Ras Kéla: Les mesures d'urgence préconisées.* Marseille: GIS Posidonie Publ.

Lloze, R. 1979. "Répartition et biologie du *Monachus monachus* (Hermann 1779) sur la côte oranienne," in K. Ronald and R. Duguy, eds., *The Mediterranean Monk Seal, Proceedings of the First International Conference, Rhodes, Greece, 2-5 May 1978* (U.N.E.P. Technical Series), Vol. 1. Pp. 91-93. Oxford and New York: Pergamon Press.

Loche, V. 1840. *Exploration Scientifique de l'Algérie (Histoire des Mammifères marins).*

Marchessaux, D., and R. Duguy. 1977. "Le phoque moine, *Monachus monachus* (Hermann 1979), en Grèce." *Mammalia* 41:419-439.

———, 1987. *Etude de l'évolution du statut du phoque moine en Tunisie et dans l'archipel, de régionale UNEP.* Marseilles: GIS Posidonie.

Santa, S. 1961. "Les poissons et le monde marin des côtes de l'Oranie." *Soc. géogr., archéol. province d'Oran, Alg.* 1: 315.

Seurat, L. G. 1930. *Exploration zoologique de l'Algérie de 1830-1930.* Paris: Masson et Cie.

Trouessart, E. 1905. *La faune des Mammifères de l'Algérie, du Maroc et de la Tunisie,* Vol. 10. F.R. de Rudeval: Imprim. Edit. Paris.

PART FOUR

Quality of Life
and
Environmental Protection Issues

12

Pollution and the Deteriorating Quality of Life in Tunisia

Belgacem Henchi

Over the last 25 years Tunisia has witnessed rapid demographic and economic growth. This has placed a heavy burden on natural resources and the environment. Consequences of this growth include pollution and a general decline in the quality of life. This chapter reviews the factors contributing to this condition, summarizes steps taken to remedy it, and suggests further preventative actions.

The Social and Economic Context

There are four major socioeconomic trends in Tunisia that have had a significant impact on the environment. The first of these is population growth. Heavy pressure has been exerted on Tunisia's natural resources as a result of the doubling of Tunisia's population since 1960. At the country's independence in 1956, there were approximately 3.8 million inhabitants. In 1992, the population was estimated to be 8.4 million, with an annual growth rate of about 2.2 percent. This increase has been accompanied by economic growth — and by significant changes in the geographical distribution of the population, the structure of economic activity, and income and consumption patterns. In turn, each of these factors has greatly affected the environment.

As is the case in many other developing countries, the population is undergoing transition from quite high levels of fertility and death to much lower levels. Declines in fertility and mortality during the last 20 years have been striking compared with those in other countries of the region.

Although the growth rate has been decreasing, it will require several decades to attain a rate of equilibrium (2.1 children per woman) and even more time to achieve a stable population. Long-term strategies to develop resources should plan for a population at least double the current one.

A second trend is rapid urbanization. The rural population comprised 67 percent of the total population in 1956. However, as a result of internal migration, this rural population represented only 43 percent of the total in 1992. Parallel to this rural exodus, there has been massive migration from the country's interior toward the coastal zones, which are more highly developed.[1] A higher natural population growth rate and limited possibilities for work in rural areas are the main causes of migration from the countryside to the cities. Both the seasonal nature of work and land tenure status contribute to underemployment in rural areas. In addition, the greater variety of jobs in urban areas and the widely shared belief that income and living standards are much higher there (for example, easier access to education and other social services) are factors that weigh heavily on the decision to relocate. Unfortunately, many new urban dwellers end up in shantytowns on the outskirts of cities, with neither work nor opportunities.

The third trend is industrialization, which has caused pollution of Tunisia's land, air, freshwater resources, and marine areas, endangering public health. The final trend is development of tourism. Tourism strengthens the pressure exerted on fragile coastal ecosystems (see the chapter by Berriane, this volume) but has positive effects as well. For example, the quality of beaches in Tunisia's touristic resorts is more carefully controlled than elsewhere.

Pollution and Its Sources in Tunisia

Industrial Pollution

Industrialization in Tunisia has not been subject to adequate regulations to prevent pollution. As a result, pollution from industrial activity has reached alarming proportions. Tunisia has an industrial complex comprising approximately 10,000 factories, mainly in the regions of Tunis, Bizerte, Sousse, Mehdia, Sfax, Gabes, and Gafsa. Of these, some 1,200 are highly polluting (Banque Mondiale 1989). Roughly 20 large public industrial units also contribute to industrial pollution in Tunisia. One of these, SIAPE, has thus far discharged 40 million tons (t) of phosphogypsum into the sea, as well as 110 t/day of sulfur dioxide (SO_2) and 80 t/day of fluorocarbons into the atmosphere (Ben Abdallah 1986; Ben Abdallah, Boukhris 1991; Henchi 1992). This has resulted in pronounced environmental deterioration around Sfax and Gabes. Similar pollution surrounds mining towns in the Gafsa region.

Tanneries are highly polluting. Numbering about 30, the tanneries each year discharge 650,000 cubic meters (m³) of waste waters laden with chromium, sulfur, cyanides, pigments, and other substances (Ministère du Plan 1990). The food industry, comprising 1,150 factories, including 200 oil processing plants, discards massive volumes of grossly polluted waste water. For example, the oil processing plants (which primarily produce olive oil) annually discharge 450,000 m³ of organic waste (Banque Mondiale 1989). Fruit and vegetable canneries annually release approximately 20 million m³ of waste water laden with organic material and dangerous microorganisms (ONAS 1990a; Ministère du Plan 1990). Detergents are also a factor in pollution; Tunisia uses 22,000 t/year of solid detergents and 10,000 t/year of liquid detergents (Ministère du Plan). Pollution caused by textile and paper-pulp mills is equally critical.

Urban and industrial activities, along with traffic, directly harm Tunisia's atmosphere. About 40,000 t of SO_2 and 30,000 t of fluorocarbons are released each year into the lower atmospheric layers near Sfax and Gabes by phosphate processing concerns (Banque Mondiale 1989). The iron plant of El Fouledh daily releases major quantities of particulate matter with heavy concentrations of iron. Combustion of 100,000 t of hydrocarbons annually in Tunisia pollutes the ambient air through the SO_2 released (ANPE 1989). Tunisia's 3,000 quarries and six cement plants pollute the environment with significant quantities of highly alkaline dust, since each ton of cement produced releases 22.5 kilograms (kg) of dust into the atmosphere (Henchi 1992). Most quarries are located near the major urban centers. This concentration near urban areas helps minimize transport costs of building materials.

Unfortunately, this proximity has intensified environmental problems. These problems include pollution of water through dust caused by crushing; noise pollution from explosions and the operation of crushing rollers; severe pollution of agricultural areas in the vicinity of those quarries; erosion from excavations on slopes; and obstacles to expansion of cities. Industrial pollution imperils many sensitive environs such as the Gulf of Gabes, wetland areas, and certain underground aquifers. This is notably the case with the Sfax and Kasserine aquifer, which supplies the irrigated area of Oued Edderb. Traces of mercury from the paper-pulp plant ("La Cellulose") can be detected in the aquifer several kilometers away from the dump site.

Out of 4,000 industrial plants generating polluted water only 13 percent are connected to purifying stations; the remaining units discharge directly into their surroundings without any treatment (Ministère du Plan 1990). The region most seriously affected is south of Greater Tunis (the industrial pole of Ben Arous).

Industrial-based pollution has also affected marine resources. The Gulf of Gabes has undergone serious deterioration as a result of phosphogypsum discharges laden with heavy metals (Cd, Zn, Cu, Pb, and others). Pollution by hydrocarbons also causes serious harm to the marine environment. This pollution originates principally in port activity, especially that related to unloading and loading in the main harbors, which lack adequate devices to fight accidental pollution.

Urban Pollution

The problem of household waste and sewage is acute in Tunisia's cities. It represents at present the most important source of pollution, degradation of the environment, and deterioration of Tunisia's quality of life. Tunisia's urban population is estimated at 4.8 million — 57 percent of the country's total population. The urban population is expected to reach 7.2-7.8 million inhabitants (about 70 percent of the total) by the year 2001. Growth of the urban population has been accompanied by an increase in activities that pollute. The volume of discharged waste water is constantly increasing.

Household Waste Water. Untreated household waste water constitutes a health threat that affects cities and even rural villages. Easily 50 percent of the urban population as well as an undetermined percent of the rural village population continue to discharge waste water freely into the environment, causing both pollution and public-health hazards.[2] Water-borne diseases are common. However, no cases of cholera have been recorded in recent years. Furthermore, infectious hepatitis has been stabilized. Nevertheless, rates of occurrence of this latter disease remain high compared with those in developed countries. Regions in the south have much higher rates of hepatitis and other waterborne diseases than the national average.

Solid Waste. The most recent estimates show that the volume of household refuse collected each year is close to 1.2 million tons (Ministère du Plan 1990; Labidi 1991). It is composed primarily of organic substances, glass, plastic, cloth, paper scrap, and metals. Save for some communes, household refuse is not dumped into controlled public refuse sites. Consequently, it becomes a direct source of insalubrity and filth. The most preferred spots for refuse dumping are ravines, beds of wadis, and marshes.

No sorting of rubbish is performed at these dumps, except at Henchir El Yahoudia, where only part of the recyclable rubbish is recovered. Insects and rodents proliferate in the dump areas, increasing the risk of epidemics. Garden waste (7,000 t/year in the city of Tunis alone and 20,000 t/year total elsewhere) as well as debris from building demolitions (100,000 t/year) add to disposal problems (Ministère du Plan 1990).

Hazardous Waste. The primary source of hazardous waste is industry; a small quantity, however, comes from hospitals and other sources. Most of this waste is collected and stored together with household refuse, without any preliminary sorting according to hazard (inflammability, toxicity, radioactivity, presence of pathogens, explosiveness, and so on). This results in critical risks to the environment and health of the neighboring population. An example of such wastes is bleaching clay from the enterprise SOTULUB. SOTULUB recycles used lubricating oils at a rate of 10 t/year, using bleaching clay as a filter (Ministère du Plan 1990). At present, these clays, which are laden with various dangerous substances (PCBs and heavy metals), are stored within the factory without any particular precautions. The main problems with hazardous wastes relate to their inadequate collection, transportation, and storage.

Agricultural/Rural Pollution. Agricultural pollution is generated through utilization of fertilizers, pesticides, and other chemical inputs. These products are spread by runoff waters following rain and can contaminate water supplies. Increased use of such products in agriculture during the last few years has increased worries about pollution of water as well as soil. Consumption of fertilizers has increased nearly tenfold since 1965 (Ministère du Plan 1990). Consumption is highest in the north of the country (approximately 80 percent of the total); the central region is second with 15 percent (Badra 1992; El Ghezal 1984). Fertilizers are used mainly to increase yields in rainfed cereal production.

The use of pesticides is also rapidly increasing. Pesticides are used primarily for the production of olives, citrus, and cereals. The hectarage of olive groves treated with pesticides increased from 38,000 ha in 1981-1982 to 274,000 ha during the 1984-1985 season (Ministère du Plan 1990). Precise data on pesticide imports are unavailable, mainly because chemical products are imported in various forms and because their concentrations vary. With the collaboration of the Ministry of Public Health, the Ministry of Agriculture controls importation, formulation, sales, and transport of pesticides until they have reached the agricultural users. But as private importers/distributors are often involved, it is feared that unsafe storing and handling may be creating public-health risks. The packaging and labeling of chemical products should be improved, and end-users should be properly informed about the harmful effects of chemical products intended for use in agriculture.

This brief overview of sources of pollution illustrates the significance of this phenomenon to the degradation of the country's environment. The impact of these various sources of pollution on the environment is readily apparent with regard to land, fresh water, and marine resources. However, few studies have been conducted to quantify levels of pollution. Likewise, data on air quality in Tunisia currently yield only an approximation of pollution levels, as data are not gathered regularly nor with a highly accurate system. At present only two mobile laboratories are available, one belonging to the INM (National Meteorology Institute) for Tunisia as a whole, and the other affiliated with the Municipality of Tunis.

From available information, it appears that the most polluting agent in Gabes is SO_2, followed by oxides of nitrogen and particles in suspension. These polluting agents originate in the phosphate and cement industries. In Sfax, there are considerable concentrations of NO_2 and SO_2. High concentrations of particles can be found in Bizerte because of cement-producing factories. Several specific industrial polluting agents (ammonia, fluorine, chlorine, hydrochloric acid, sodium carbonate, oxides of iron and lead, and mercury) have not been measured by the INM laboratory simply because it lacks the necessary equipment. The absence of legal limits for discharges from industry prevents effective air quality control and is a major cause of the deterioration of air quality.

Air pollution is likely to become an increasingly serious problem for public health in the next few years, mainly because of urbanization, industrialization, and demographic growth. Air pollution has already caused many cases of respiratory disease, which affects old people and children in particular. A health study carried out in the region of Gabes has shown that more than one-third of the occurrences of respiratory ailments and absenteeism from school could be avoided if pollution were lowered to a reasonable level. The effect of pollution on public health is one aspect of the deterioration of the quality of life in Tunisia. Other forms of this deterioration are considered in the following section.

Deterioration in the Quality of Urban Life

Tunisia has witnessed sustained urbanization during the past few decades. Presently the urban population exceeds 4.8 million inhabitants, 57 percent of the country's total population. The urban population has increased at an annual rate of 4.4 percent since the last census of 1984. It is concentrated along the coast where the majority of industries, tourist compounds, and services are located. Approximately 77 percent of the total urban population lives in coastal cities. A sizable percentage of this population consists of recent immigrants from the countryside.

Despite efforts to improve the quality of housing and urban services, many Tunisians still live in deplorable conditions. This is particularly the case with recent immigrants to the city. These immigrants usually settle in older quarters of the cities — the medinas — or in squatter settlements on the outskirts. In the medinas, existing houses are divided up and redivided, and several households share the same lodging despite their great numbers. Serious overcrowding is accompanied by deplorable hygiene conditions that are the result of a flagrant shortage of sanitation and kitchen facilities.

This overcrowding leads to the deterioration of buildings, many of which are historically important. In squatter settlements the basic infrastructure is insufficient, and such districts often lack sanitation and social services. It is difficult to comprehend the adjustment problems facing new migrants. Most consider themselves "marginal" inhabitants of the city, mainly because of their comparatively low urban income. The progressive loss of identity is often accompanied by deep anxiety and tension.

Due to government programs to address housing issues, there has been some reduction in overcrowding in the medinas, as shown by indicators such as the average size of urban dwellings and the number of persons living in each room or house. However, this has resulted more from an increase in the number of spacious urban dwellings (three or more rooms) than from a decrease in the number of small lodgings. The number of single-room urban units decreased only slightly (4 percent) between 1975 and 1984, while the number of urban dwellings of five or more rooms increased more than 110 percent during the same period (Banque Mondiale 1989). Indeed, the majority of urban families (54 percent) were still living in one- or two-room houses in 1984, an increase of 85,000 families during the above-mentioned period (Banque Mondiale 1989). Families with the lowest incomes have the smallest houses, despite the fact that they have greater numbers of children than families with higher income levels. Overall improvement of urban lodging has benefited primarily families with high levels of income and secondarily those with medium incomes. As for the categories with the lowest levels of income, improvements have been very limited.

Because of immigration from the countryside, the proliferation of squatter settlements (called "bidonvilles" in North Africa) in the peripheral zones of cities has been striking in recent decades. This has especially been the case in Tunis, where over the last 15 years some 80 squatter settlements have been established, with a total population of around 300,000 (Banque Mondiale 1989). Altogether, these squatter settlements occupy some 16 square kilometers (km²). Squatter settlements develop arbitrarily and haphazardly, without any prior planning. In addition, despite their cluttered appearance, housing densities are relatively low.

Thus, valuable urban space is wasted and vital greenbelt areas surrounding Tunisia's cities disappear. Housing densities in bidonvilles in Tunis are only around half those in official housing schemes. In Sfax, these densities are even lower. The lack of orderly layout and low densities make provision of sanitary services — sewer lines and piped water — relatively expensive. Most squatter settlements, however, lack both sewer systems and running water. Many even lack sources of safe drinking water. Most houses have simple latrines or discharge their waste into cesspools along the bidonville's unpaved lanes. Implications for public health in these squatter settlements are obvious. Water-borne and insect-vectored diseases are common.

Squatter settlements are an unfortunate and extreme symptom of the decline in Tunisia's quality of life and the degradation of its urban environment. More general problems are traffic congestion, noise pollution, visual blight, disappearance of green spaces in the built-up environment, and the previously discussed air pollution, water pollution, waste disposal problems, and litter.[3]

Achievements in Environmental Protection

Protection of the environment and preservation of natural resources have long concerned the Tunisian government. Since the historic change in national leadership on November 7, 1988, environmental protection has become an essential component of the country's economic and social development policy. Government concern for the environment is reflected in the budgets allocated for environmental cleanup and protection efforts. These have included restoration projects, preventative actions, and programs to increase environmental awareness.

An array of actions targeting pollution — specifically urban sanitation problems — have been carried out for more than three decades. Improved management of urban sewage is a major focus of national environmental protection policy. Presently, 75 percent of household waste from coastal urban areas and 100 percent of that from touristic establishments are connected to public sewage systems (ONAS 1990a). Twenty-four water-treatment plants thus far operative enable the annual processing of 80 million m^3 of waste water, making it possible to irrigate thousands of hectares while protecting the environment (Saïd, Koundi 1990). The Office National d'Assainissement (National Sanitation Office) is attempting to increase the number of water-treatment plants to 65. This would make it possible to supply 150 million m^3 of filtered water to irrigate 20,000 ha (ONAS 1991).

To respond to the urgent character of waste disposal problems, which have grown to alarming proportions in Tunisia's urban centers as a result of rapid urbanization, a national sanitation program was launched a few years ago. This program is developing national strategies for disposal of household and solid industrial waste, often in conjunction with regional town-planning schemes.

These schemes call for the establishment of monitored collective dumping grounds for municipalities. Short-term dumping grounds for dangerous and toxic industrial wastes are also being developed. Some are part of action plans to curtail the proliferation of squatter settlements and the anarchic expansion of cities. These plans seek to revise procedures for urbanization and rehabilitation of squatter settlements, as well as to increase the number of green spaces.

Parallel with programs targeting pollution, campaigns to increase environmental awareness have been launched since the change in national leadership in 1988. Emphasis is on protection of the environment as a national duty. More specific consciousness-raising campaigns have been organized for the education of children, manufacturers, and summer-resort tourists. NGOs (non-governmental organizations) working in the environmental arena in Tunisia have also helped to increase public awareness of environmental problems.

Conclusions

In sum, despite formidable challenges, the Tunisian government has taken significant steps to address problems of pollution and the decline in quality of life. Among these steps are the drafting of environmental legislation and regulations adapted to Tunisian conditions; the development of urban sewage systems; the increased production of natural gas as a source of electricity, with consequent reduction of atmospheric pollution; the improvement of housing densities and urban services, such as electricity, sanitation, and water potability; the rehabilitation of pollution-sensitive zones, such as critical wetlands; and improved collection and disposal of household waste.

Nevertheless, major constraints persist. Among these are insufficient public and industrial participation in efforts to improve urban cleanliness; high costs involved in clean up of existing industries; disregard of regulations in force; the weakness of regulatory mechanisms; the great number and dispersed nature of small polluting units, which hamper cleanup efficiency; the shortage of financial means for industrial clean up; the proliferation of squatter settlements and difficulty in exercising integrated urban land-use planning; and the lack of infrastructure for the collection and disposal of household and industrial waste, both solid and liquid.

Notes

1. Each year, approximately 125 ha of fertile agricultural land is destroyed by urbanization in Tunis alone (Ministère du Plan 1990).

2. Approximately 100 million m³ of household waste water per year are discharged outside of the public sewer systems (ONAS 1990a, 1990b).

3. In Tunis, for example, green spaces account for 126 ha total — that is, 0.9 m²/inhabitant. Shortage of green spaces is even more acute in Sfax, where they cover only 20 ha — that is, 0.6 m²/inhabitant (Ministère du Plan 1990).

References

ANPE. 1989. "Etat de l'Environnement en Tunisie." Unpublished report of the Agence Nationale de l'Environnement (ANPE), Government of Tunisia.

Badra, B. 1992. "Mode de Vie et Projet de Développement de la Population Forestière de Jendouba." Report published by the Centre d'Etudes et de Recherche Economiques et Sociales (CERES), Tunis.

Banque Mondiale. 1989. *Rapport sur l'Environnement et Plan d'Action National: Cas de Tunisie.* Washington, D.C.: World Bank.

Ben Abdallah, F. 1986. *La Pollution à Sfax.* Publication of the Centre Régional de Documentation Pédagogique de Sfax. Vol. 37 (February).

Ben Abdallah, F., and M. Boukhris. 1991. "Sur les teneurs en fluor des feuilles et des fruits des quelques plantes croissant dans les environs d'une usine de production d'acide phosphorique et d'engrais." *Bull. Sc. Nat.* (Tunisia) 20:n.p.

El Ghezal, A. 1984. *Préservation du Milieu Naturel et Développement Economique en Tunisie.* Thèse de spécialité, Université Paul Valéry Montpellier III.

Henchi, B. 1992. "Etude de l'état de l'environnement et la protection des ressources naturelles en Tunisie." *Arab Journal of Sciences* 19:28-42.

Labidi, M. 1991. "Conservation de l'Environnement et Démographie Urbaine." Bulletin No. 5, Cellule Central de l'Environnement et du Développement Durable du RCD, La Kasba, Government of Tunisia.

Ministère du Plan. 1990. *Plan de Développement Economique et Social.* Commission Sectorielle de Protection de l'Environnement, Ministère du Plan, Government of Tunisia.

ONAS. 1990a. "Rapport sur l'Etat de l'Assainissement Urbain en Tunisie." Report published by the Office National de l'Assainissement, Ministère de l'Environnement, Government of Tunisia.

———. 1990b. "Les Stations d'Epuration en Tunisie." Proceedings of the Séminaire International sur la Gestion de l'Environnement Industriel, Tunisia. Published by the Office National de l'Assainissement, Ministère de l'Environnement, Government of Tunisia.

———. 1991. "Rapport d'Activité de l'Office National de l'Assainissement." Report published by the Office National de l'Assainissement, Ministère de l'Environnement, Government of Tunisia.

Saïd, M., and A. Koundi. 1990. "La réutilisation des eaux épurées et des boues résiduaires en Tunisie." Unpublished paper presented at the 2ème Symposium International de Marseille sur la Protection du Milieu Marin contre la Pollution Urbaine, Marseille.

13

Desert Locust Control, Public Health, and Environmental Sustainability in North Africa

Allan T. Showler

Control of the desert locust, *Schistocerca gregaria* (Forskål), can present environmental hazards in North Africa, the Sahel, Sudan, the Horn of Africa, and a broad expanse of Asia from the Arabian Peninsula to northwest India (Steedman 1988). During normal recession periods, densities of this locust are low and it presents little or no threat to human society. However, after periods of drought, when green vegetation re-emerges, rapid population buildups and competition for food occasionally result in a transformation of the locust population referred to as phase transformation (Showler and Potter 1991).[1]

Following this transformation, locusts often form dense migratory bands and swarms that can invade and devastate agricultural areas. A single swarm of adults can comprise billions of locusts, with up to 80 million per square kilometer (km^2) over an area of more than 1,000 km^2 (Steedman 1988). In one day, a swarm of locusts can fly 100 km in the general direction of prevailing winds. Bands of nymphs can march about 1.5 km per day. Large-scale swarm outbreaks often involve hundreds of swarms, and the locusts' recession range expands to envelop the Middle East, India, the sub-Sahel from Guinea to Tanzania, and parts of southern Europe (Pedgley 1981).

Each locust can consume its weight (2 grams [g]) daily in leaves, fruit, flowers, seeds, and bark. Most green vegetation is devoured (with the possible exception of coffee). Crops at risk include millet, maize, rice, sorghum, sugar cane, barley, cotton, fruit trees, vegetables, wheat, and rangeland grasses. As North Africa is a major food-producing region (Steiner et al. 1988), governments are compelled to protect valuable cash and food crops from the menace of locust swarms. Wheat and barley crops are particularly susceptible to desert locust invasions: locusts can attack the stems and cause total grain loss. Fruit trees are also vulnerable to attack; defoliation can affect fruit yields for years. Large areas of rangeland can be lost to swarms where forage is often at a premium (Potter and Showler 1990). Published accounts of locust invasions of North Africa date back to 811 A.D., when swarms reached Italy. The record, though probably incomplete, indicates that locust plagues in North Africa have occurred in most centuries since then (Bois 1944, 1948).[2]

Historic estimates of crop damage caused by desert locust swarms provide a framework for evaluating potential agricultural losses in North Africa. In Ethiopia 167,000 metric tons of grain were lost in 1958, an amount sufficient to feed 1 million people for a year. The value of all crops lost to locusts in Morocco, 1954-1955, was about $70 million (Steedman 1988).

To estimate potential crop losses in the absence of chemical control, Potter and Showler (1990: 159) constructed a hypothetical situation focused upon Tunisia:

> If one assumes that the heaviest desert locust infestations come in the central and southern portions of the country around Kasserine and Gafsa, as they did in spring 1988 (Khoury et al. 1989), a total of about 552,000 ha devoted to grain production would be at risk to locust damage. This surface area is less than the maximum amount of land that the crop protection service was prepared to treat in 1988 (approximately 1,000,000 ha [Khoury et al. 1989]). Converting area cultivated to crop production, the net worth of grain that could be easily lost to desert locust consumption during such an invasion equals about twenty-nine million dollars (INS 1987). To put these potential losses into perspective, the amount of arable land devoted to grain cultivation in Tunisia was approximately 1,363,000 ha in 1986 (INS 1987). This harvest normally represents seventy-two million dollars of net annual cereal production. Under the scenario presented above, Tunisia could lose 40 percent of its yearly wheat and barley production if desert locust swarms were not controlled and they completely consumed grain crops in the principal infestation zones of the central and southern regions. Looking at potential crop losses due to desert locust impacts in another context, Tunisia received between 59,000 and 210,000 metric tons of food aid annually from 1972 to 1984 (FAO 1985). These figures represent from fourteen to forty-eight million dollars per year of grain donated by the international community. It is therefore reasonable to conclude that desert locust swarms are capable of consuming a cereal harvest equivalent in value to the current annual food aid received by Tunisia.

A decision not to attempt to control the desert locust is considered by many to be morally irresponsible given the ever-present threat of malnutrition and famine in Africa. Inaction is also politically unacceptable in agrarian nations wherein crop production is vital to the survival of farmers and the government alike. This chapter summarizes recent methods utilized in various campaigns to control this economically significant insect, focusing particularly on their implications for public health and the environment.

Plague and Control Campaign 1986-1989

In 1986 desert locust swarms from Sudan and Ethiopia moved west across the Sahel. More breeding occurred around the foothills of the Adrar des Iforas of Mali; the Aïr Mountains of Niger; the Tibesti of Chad; the Red Sea Hills of Sudan; and to a lesser extent, in Senegal, Mauritania, Morocco, Saudi Arabia, and southern Algeria until early 1989 (Showler and Potter 1991). Morocco was infested in 1987 with swarms arriving from Western Sahara and southern Algeria. By March 1988 the infestation of Morocco was five times more severe than the previous year. Algeria was invaded by swarms from Mali, Mauritania, Morocco, and Western Sahara beginning in September 1987; and southern Algeria harbored substantial breeding areas that were largely undetected in the vast and rugged terrain (Showler and Maynard 1988). Cavin (1988) estimated that the 1988 infestation of Algeria covered 2.4 million ha; 25 percent emanated from breeding areas in southern Algeria and 75 percent arrived from adjacent countries. Tunisia was invaded by locust swarms from Algeria from 15 March-14 May.[3] One swarm in Kairouan covered 800 olive trees (100 ha) with 50,000-60,000 locusts per tree, 4.4 million locusts total (Showler 1992). Some swarms continued from Tunisia toward Italy but drowned enroute (Potter and Showler 1990). Showler and Potter (1991) identified four key factors that contributed to the demise of the last plague:

1. A storm front from West Africa carried swarms across the Atlantic to the Caribbean in October 1988 (most drowned, and survivors died out on land from the Virgin Islands to Trinidad and Tobago);
2. A cold 1988-1989 winter in North Africa halted the expected eastward movement of swarms along the Mediterranean coast before they could be turned south to the Sahel by spring winds;
3. Dry weather across the Sahel and Sudan reduced vegetation and breeding sites; and
4. Swarms were sprayed in North Africa before they could breed and move on to the Sahel.

Desert locust swarms were located using information from many sources. Predictive models using the African Real Time Environmental Monitoring and Information System (ARTEMIS) for cold cloud measurements were able to assess weather by satellite imagery, and data collected in other ways were operational. Nevertheless, these models were not always accurate (Showler and Potter 1991). Greenness maps produced by National Oceanic and Atmospheric Administration (NOAA) satellite-based sensors that capture images of the relative quantities of green foliage do not locate actual swarms; they do, however, aid in identifying areas potentially favorable to locust breeding and aggregation. In this way, visual survey efforts, whether by ground or by air, can be streamlined for maximizing efficiency.

While greenness maps were very useful, they were not available to all North African countries during some critical times.[4] Despite the availability of sophisticated tools, there is no technology to substitute for visual surveillance.[5] Locust swarms were reported by military post personnel; professional scouts in ground vehicles and aircraft; forest service lookouts; and nomads (Khoury et al. 1988; Showler and Maynard 1988). Scouting by ground and air was, however, limited as a result of the dispersal of swarms throughout vast areas of remote and inaccessible terrain (Showler and Maynard 1988). Reports from neighboring countries on locust activity allowed North African nations to anticipate and prepare for the arrival of new swarms.

When swarms entered Algeria and Morocco from northern Mauritania and Western Sahara, armed conflict[6] prevented such early warnings. In general, a relatively short lead time for locating and treating swarms before they descended upon croplands exacerbated the sense of urgency for rapid response.

Insecticide use was the only technology available to combat locust swarms under the circumstances. Decisions to apply pesticides were, however, made primarily on the basis of immediate political necessity rather than long-term, environmentally sound crop protection strategies. The most commonly used insecticides in North Africa were malathion; fenitrothion; dichlorovos[7] (organophosphates); and deltamethrin (a pyrethroid). Carbaryl (a carbamate), although donated to at least one North African country and considered relatively benign environmentally (Table 13.1), was not applied because of mixing and formulation problems (DAC 1992). Use of organochlorine compounds, such as benzene hexachloride (BHC), was discontinued because of concerns about environmental persistence.

In Morocco, 1.8 million ha were sprayed, nearly 1.7 million ha of which were treated aerially (DAC 1992); by November 1988, up to 81,000 ha were being treated per day (Showler and Potter 1991). In Tunisia, 360,000 ha

TABLE 13.1 Relative Toxicity of Antilocust Insecticides to Nontarget Organisms

Chemical Name	Chemical Family	Persistence	Bioaccumulation	Birds	Mammals	Fish	Aquatic Invertebrates
Bendiocarb	C	M	M	M	M	M	M
Carbaryl	C	L	L-M	L	L	L	L
Chlorpyrifos	OP	M-H	M-H	—	M	L-M	H
Cypermethrin	PY	M-H	H^c	—	L	H	H
Diazinon	OP	M	M	M-H	L	M	H
Dieldrin	OC	H	H	H	H	H	M
Fenitrothion	OP	L	M	H	L	L-M	H
Cyhalothrin	PY	M	H^c	L	H	H	H
Lindane	OC	M-H	H	M-H	M	M	M
Malathion	OP	L	L	M	L-M	L	L

aL = low, M = medium, H = high, — = no data.

bC = carbamate, OP = organophosphate, OC = organochlorine, PY = pyrethroid.

cBased on log P.

Source: Adapted from TAMS/CICP 1989.

were sprayed, 247,000 of which were treated aerially. In Algeria, about 145,000 ha were treated during the fall of 1988 alone; 30 percent was sprayed aerially and 70 percent by ground (Showler and Maynard 1988).

North African countries have more resources for locust control operations than Sahelian countries and did not experience simultaneous grasshopper outbreaks. Therefore, control efforts could be mobilized with greater concentration and efficiency than in the Sahel. Operations were usually conducted prior to 0900 hours before swarms began to fly for the day. Terrestrial spraying was done using an exhaust nozzle[8], conventional mist unit, or fogger unit most commonly mounted on pickup or Unimog trucks. Tractor-pulled spray rigs using nozzles affixed to pressure hoses were occasionally used in orchards.

In many cases, farmers were given backpack sprayers to protect their crops with relatively low-toxicity pesticides[9] but overexposure of applicators to the pesticides was, and remains, an inherent concern (Potter 1988). Aerial applications involved conventional boom sprayers or ultra-low volume (ULV) sprayers mounted on a variety of aircraft.[10] Morocco, for example, had 56 aircraft — 42 airplanes and 14 helicopters — by the end of the plague. Large planes (DC-7s and C-130s) were used mainly over large nonagricultural flatlands in Morocco only. Small aircraft could make precise applications in more ecologically or economically sensitive areas in each of the afflicted North African countries.

A large-scale pesticide-based control campaign is not without public health and environmental risks. Pesticide use is often associated with accidental intoxication of applicators and unhealthy residue levels on agricultural commodities. Adverse environmental effects are, however, more pervasive and may even be unavoidable, especially when large areas are treated in emergencies. The undesirable environmental effects of pesticides include disruption of the local ecology by injuring or killing nontarget organisms and bioaccumulation of organochlorine compounds in lipid tissue (including mammalian milk). Nevertheless, few studies have examined and identified the impacts of anti-locust pesticides on the African environment (OTA 1990). Tests conducted in Sudan (Dynamac 1989) during the last plague were met with unanticipated difficulties, and the results are widely perceived as inconclusive (AID 1991a).

Recently, a pilot study was completed by the Food and Agriculture Organization (FAO) of the United Nations in Senegal (Everts 1990) that measured the impact of commonly used anti-locust insecticides on nontarget organisms. Terrestrial arthropods and aquatic animals, especially crustaceans, were significantly affected. The long-term effects of these and other pesticides on the environment are not fully understood, however.

Because different pesticides present varying degrees of risk to the environment (Table 13.1), the selection of an effective but ecologically benign pesticide is important. For combatting desert locusts, a very selective insecticide would be ideal when chemical control is required. Use of organochlorinated compounds (BHC, dieldrin, lindane) was discontinued because they are persistent and broad spectrum. Other criteria for selecting anti-locust pesticides include cost, storage stability, availability, formulation, and compatibility with existing application equipment.

Pesticide Impacts and Problems

Humans

Effects of antilocust pesticides on humans have been noted primarily among pesticide handlers and applicators. The most commonly used insecticides during the campaign in North Africa were malathion, fenitrothion, and deltamethrin — all only moderately toxic to humans (TAMS/CICP 1989) — and direct effects of these chemicals on humans were not reported. Direct exposure to these pesticides occurred primarily as a result of improper equipment maintenance, pesticide handling, and application.[11] Safety clothing and other precautions were not always used during spray operations, particularly when farmers conducted treatments without government supervision. Control operations were most often conducted in uninhabited areas or rangeland where public exposure was minimal. Rural populations, including nomads, were cautioned about imminent spray operations in the vicinity, and public warnings were issued against consumption of locusts. This discouraged culinary use of locusts in treated areas; more slow-acting pesticides (malathion), which allowed swarms to move beyond treatment sites before dying, did not appear to harm humans who could have collected them as food, as the mammalian toxicity of such chemicals is relatively low (DAC 1992).[12]

Unfortunately, there were no programs to monitor pesticide exposure, nor were there emergency mobile medical units to treat intoxication cases in a timely manner; this precluded accurate assessment of pesticide impacts on humans in most countries. In Morocco, however, acetylcholinesterase (AChE) levels in blood were regularly measured[13] in control operations personnel: pilots, ground applicators, pesticide handlers/loaders, technicians, drivers, and military personnel. When workers showed AChE serum levels to be 50-75 percent below baseline, they were relieved from spray operations for 15 days and follow-up tests were conducted to assure return to normal AChE titers.

During the campaign, 1,016 persons were removed from spray operations temporarily or permanently (DAC 1992). It may be significant that in Morocco, DDVP, a relatively acutely toxic and highly volatile organo-phosphate compound, was extensively used and may have been responsible for the seemingly large numbers of people so afflicted. About 500 blood samples were taken at random from the general population, but low AChE titers were not detected. Avoidance of populated areas and warnings to the public about spray operations during the campaign were apparently effective protective measures for the general populace.

The Environment

Although locust control was necessary to avoid widespread food shortages, emergency operations are neither economically desirable nor environmentally ideal. By the time a plague has developed, locust populations are large and mobile and tremendous amounts of pesticides must be used. In addition to killing the target pest, large quantities of pesticides will inevitably affect the local ecosystem.

Pesticide applications occurred throughout a gradient of North African ecosystems: xeric desert (a few millimeters [mm] of rain per year); lush coastal hills (more than 1,500 mm of precipitation per year in some areas); fertile Mediterranean flatlands; wetlands; islands; mountains; steppes; wadis; and oases. Information on the flora and fauna of North Africa is not readily available, and little is known about the distribution of endangered species. Habitat destruction from overgrazing, deforestation, and other nonsustainable practices has caused ecological disruption that would be compounded by massive pesticide campaigns.

Some environments are particularly vulnerable to the introduction of toxins (Table 13.2), especially coastal wetlands, which provide critical habitats for migratory avian wildlife in addition to several indigenous species (Showler and Maynard 1988; Potter and Showler 1990). Wildlife is at risk because it cannot be excluded from sprayed areas; at particular risk are insectivorous and predatory birds, both migratory and sedentary (AID 1991a). Aerial pesticide applications can cover hundreds of km^2 per treatment, and in moderate-to-high wind-speed conditions, insecticides can drift far beyond the target area into fragile ecosystems. Nontarget organisms can be exposed to pesticides directly through dermal contact, or indirectly by ingestion of contaminated vegetation or prey.

Although no major environmental perturbations were observed following spray operations against locusts in North Africa, observations indicated that several incidents of animal poisoning may have occurred.[14] It is difficult to ascertain the number of wild animals that may have succumbed to pesticide contamination due to inaccessible terrain and the presence of scavengers (hyenas, fennecs, vultures) that remove carcasses. In several instances nontarget kills included small birds around contaminated water puddles, and reptiles, insects and arachnids in treated areas. Pollinating bee colonies accidentally sprayed (beekeepers were warned to remove or cover their hives prior to spray but some ignored the cautions) were severely weakened or killed (Potter 1988).

Few studies have examined the impacts of anti-locust pesticides on human health and the natural environment in Africa. The most extensive study of pesticide impacts was conducted in Sudan in 1987 on the efficacy and environmental effects of six commonly used anti-locust pesticides. The methods and results of the Sudan experiments have been found to be of dubious quality, however, and are therefore not extensively regarded as reliable. Two recent studies of pesticide effects on the environment, one in Senegal and the other in Morocco, have been conducted. The Senegal study, under the auspices of the FAO, measured the impacts of locust and grasshopper insecticides on nontarget organisms. Terrestrial arthropods and aquatic life, especially crustaceans, were significantly affected. In 1989, the Denver Wildlife Research Center and the government of Morocco began to study the effects of malathion and DDVP on nontarget organisms. The project was accomplished in two phases: the first phase emphasized training in aspects of ecotoxicology, and the second phase consisted of a field study using malathion and DDVP applications on experimental plots in southwestern Morocco. Its aims were to determine mammal, bird and insect mortality using carcass searches, telemetry, and post-treatment observations; the magnitude of ecological disruption; the effects on food habits of mammals and birds, and effects on emigration, mortality, and reproductive success; the effects on brain cholinesterase in mammals and birds; the residue levels on vegetation, insects, and food of nontarget organisms; and droplet deposition, spray drift, and meteorological conditions affecting pesticide application (DAC 1992).

Samples of vegetation from the Agadir and Guelmim provinces in Morocco were analyzed for DDVP, malathion, and fenitrothion residues 2-6 months after the last locust plague had ended. Very few samples exhibited residues (detected residues ranged from about 0.2 ppm to 4.1 ppm on plants). Soil samples had no residues (except in pesticide storage sites). Some water samples taken in October and November 1988 (during the campaign) were contaminated with organochlorine and organophosphate pesticides (DAC 1992). Nevertheless, the extent of pesticide contamination of plants, soil, and water resulting from the locust spray operations in North Africa are not understood well enough to be characterized in general terms.

Unwanted Pesticides and Empty Pesticide Containers

Large stocks of unusable, obsolete, environmentally undesirable or banned pesticides have accumulated in North African countries. These

TABLE 13.2 Vulnerable Habitats in North Africa

Habitat	Vulnerability
Desert/grassland	Pollinators, birds, and other animals. Chemicals are usually applied during brief, moist periods of the day when all biota are active. Such areas are already under pressure from erosion, desertification, overgrazing.
Temporary lakes	Annual fish species, and seasonal bird congregations.
Oases	Fish, birds and mammals, which depend upon oases as their only sources of water.
Rivers and lakes	Pollinators, fish, birds, and biota in nearby cropping systems.
Wildlife reserves	Endangered wildlife species.
Croplands	Beneficial arthropods, including pollinators.

Source: Adapted from TAMS/CICP 1989.

stocks are a problem mostly for two reasons: 1) They are often stored in deteriorating containers such that pesticide spills and leaks are likely to occur in the future; and 2) they may actually be used for pest control when stocks of preferred chemicals are exhausted. Many of these materials are left over from previous locust activities, and include compounds that are both broad-spectrum and environmentally persistent (BHC, dieldrin, lindane). Some of the unwanted stocks have been stored for about 30 years, and in many cases, the origin is not documented and labels are no longer readable. Unwanted pesticide stocks can be quite large and thus present logistical problems regarding proper storage.[15]

In addition to potential environmental and human health risks associated with large stocks of unwanted pesticides, there is the dilemma of dealing with empty pesticide containers — usually 200 liter metal barrels. The primary concern about empty pesticide barrels is the high demand for their use by the general public as water and food storage containers, which, of course, can lead to contamination of the stored consumables. Pesticide barrels are commonly sold on the market despite the fact that this practice is intrinsically unsafe. It is for this reason that used pesticide barrels need to be rendered useless, reconditioned, or decontaminated.[16] There were no reports of human intoxication from spent anti-locust pesticide barrels, but this may be due to the lack of systematic medical monitoring in the general population.

Reducing Pesticide Impacts

Reducing actual and potential adverse effects of pesticides during locust control operations involves prevention. Prevention can, and should, be accomplished within dual contexts: 1) prevention of impacts during plagues; and 2) prevention of plagues (strategic control). Both approaches rely on reduced application of synthetic pesticides and minimized exposure of humans and the environment to pesticides when they are used.

Surveys

Surveys can be conducted in many ways. The aim should be to locate locust population buildups, aggregations, swarms, and egg pod fields in order to intervene prior to the advent of serious outbreaks. Surveillance tools include satellite sensors to obtain vegetation indices and weather patterns, and aerial and terrestrial reconnaissance methods. Egg pod surveys should be conducted to determine the potential magnitude of imminent outbreaks, and so that eggs can be destroyed prior to eclosion. Surveys should be designed such that information can be integrated on a regional scale to facilitate strategic control efforts and, during plagues, maximize preparation time before each control operation. Hasty and often potentially unsafe responses to invading swarms can then be avoided. An ideal surveillance system would require international cooperation and coordination and would be most effective if performed as part of a strategic control initiative (Showler and Potter 1991).

Pesticide Selection and Dosage Regulation

Pesticides appear to be the only option for combatting locust swarms in the absence of alternative control measures. Although synthetic pesticides are generally perceived as detrimental to the environment, there does exist a range of toxicities among the available pesticides (Table 13.1). Judicious pesticide selection can greatly reduce adverse environmental impacts. A relatively short-residual and selective insecticide such as malathion or carbaryl would be less likely to cause serious ecological disruption compared with a broad-spectrum, fat soluble, and environmentally persistent pesticide such as BHC or dieldrin. Insecticides that break down relatively quickly, such as malathion, are also less likely to reach water sources than more persistent chemicals. Still, even the least toxic chemicals (malathion and carbaryl) are highly toxic to insect pollinators and may adversely affect certain vertebrates (OTA 1990). It is sometimes argued that long-residual pesticides are best for locust control because reapplications of short residual pesticides will not be necessary.

On the other hand, it is uncommon for different locust swarms to settle in the exact same location. For controlling adult locusts, then, short-residual pesticides are as effective as long-residual compounds. A stronger argument for using long-residual pesticides involves killing nymphs by applying the pesticide in a strip on vegetation such that successive bands are killed as they cross the sprayed zone. This would result in less chemical being sprayed than if separate chemical applications were made for every band of nymphs.

Fortunately, debate over the most environmentally sound mode of killing nymphs, clearly a choice between "evils," may become moot as alternative control measures are developed; also, bait formulations offer a relatively environmentally benign option for nymph control. During the last campaign, some dissatisfaction with malathion was expressed because it did not immediately immobilize locusts (DAC 1992). Malathion-treated locusts often survive, feed, and fly for hours before dying. The tendency was to repeat applications using malathion or to resort to more toxic pesticides (DDVP) (DAC 1992).

To avoid unnecessary repeat applications, the use of pesticide "cocktails" should be explored whereby a relatively selective slow-acting pesticide (malathion) can be "spiked" with small amounts of a fast-acting quick knock-down insecticide (a pyrethroid). In this way, locusts would be rapidly immobilized, then killed in time by the selective insecticide.

Judicious selection of pesticide formulation is another way of reducing environmental impacts. Baits, the least likely formulation to affect nontarget organisms, would be best suited for use against nymphs.[17] ULV formulations are undiluted and are therefore more potent per unit volume than other formulations. Nevertheless, ULV formulations are applied with micronaire sprayers, which produce droplets 80 microns (μ) or less in diameter at rates of 1 liter/ha or less, a smaller amount of active ingredient than is applied when other more dilute formulations are used. Also, there is no need to mix or prepare ULV-formulated pesticides in the field, which would likely reduce loader/handler exposure.

Precision Application

Appropriate pesticide application techniques, particularly in ecologically fragile habitats, can decrease the likelihood of significant environmental impacts. Large aircraft are more apt to spray beyond the target zone than ground equipment or smaller aircraft.

In order to aerially treat settled locust swarms and crawling bands of nymphs with maximum accuracy, the pilot should have markers or beacons on the boundaries of the target. Application precision is also affected by wind, which can cause spray droplets to drift far beyond the intended target. For this reason it is most prudent not to conduct aerial operations within 1 km of aquatic systems and other fragile or critical habitats (TAMS/CICP 1989).

Training and Public Awareness

Periodic training of crop protection personnel and extension visits to farmers on pesticide safety would help prevent human intoxication. Applicator, loader, and handler exposure to pesticides could be decreased by development and use of protective clothing suitable for hot climates. Systematic AChE tests should be mandatory for workers; affected persons should be removed from contact with AChE-inhibiting chemicals until AChE titers return to normal. Local hospital and medical clinic personnel should be trained in diagnosis and treatment of pesticide intoxication, and antidotes[18] (atropine, for example) should be made available.

The use of many different pesticides in different formulations applied at different dosages (and possibly with different equipment) involves various levels of precautionary measures. While constant training would reduce pesticide-related health problems, standardization of pesticide stocks, application equipment, and procedures would prevent many accidents, especially while working under emergency conditions. Public awareness of local spray operations through the mass media and visits by crop protection service personnel should continue to be a priority in the event of future plagues. An additional safety measure to discourage consumption of pesticide-treated locusts would be to add colored dye to pesticide formulations to mark contaminated locusts.

Economic Thresholds

Economic thresholds are measures of pest populations or levels of crop damage that, if not controlled, will result in unacceptable economic loss to the farmer. Threshold levels can vary with the growth stage of the crop, the relative quantity and species of natural enemies of the pest(s), time of year, cost of control measures, and value of crop yield, among other factors. Determination and use of economic threshold levels for desert locusts would reduce the perceived need to spray insecticides if the locusts are unlikely to cause intolerable damage. Although some attempt has been made to develop economic thresholds for grasshoppers in Africa (Coop 1991), there has been no concerted effort in this regard for desert locusts. For desert locusts, two general types of economic thresholds must be devised — one for swarming locust populations during plagues, and the other for preventive intervention in key breeding areas. The value of developing economic threshold levels for locusts and / or grasshoppers has been characterized using data collected from the last major plague of locusts and grasshoppers in Africa:

> In a comprehensive but preliminary report by FEWS (1987) the best available data were examined. About 3.8 million ha were treated in the Sahel at a cost of $41.7 million dollars. The value of the production in the affected area was valued at $78 million, but $31.9 million of this production was lost anyway. Thus investment of $41.7 million saved production worth $46.1 million, a benefit/cost ratio of 1.1 to 1. In the detailed mid-term program evaluation by A.I.D. (TRD 1989), these conclusions were examined more closely. A change of one FEWS assumption - that the pests if left unchecked would have placed additional production at risk - by 10 percent of the amount actually treated, would change the benefit/cost ratio to 1.3 to 1 (AID 1991a: 28).

Implementation of flexible and realistic economic threshold levels would eliminate the economic and environmental costs associated with unnecessary pesticide applications and could conceivably, if used within the framework of a plague prevention strategy, eliminate the need to treat swarms altogether (Showler and Potter 1991).

Biological Control

In an effort to find environmentally safe alternatives to chemical pesticides, research has been conducted to identify and develop biological control agents that would provide very selective control of locusts and grasshoppers. Several organisms have show some promise as lethal pathogens of acridid pests.[19] The current challenge is to continue to identify and develop suitable microorganisms from a range of possibilities.

Various strains of potentially effective microbes must be developed, field tested against target and nontarget species under various conditions, and the results must be corroborated. Methods to mass produce and apply the biocontrol agents must also be developed and tested. Potentially useful entomopathogens are known to be indigenous to locust/grasshopper outbreak areas; but there are ecological constraints to the spread of pathogens in acridid populations, especially if the organism is introduced to a new area. Also, naturally occurring biological control is insufficient to prevent locust/grasshopper outbreaks, so microbial biological control agents are most likely to be useful if applied repetitively, when necessary, like chemical pesticides. If a "biopesticide" is found to be as effective as chemical compounds, an existing infrastructure for pesticide distribution and application could be used with similarly packaged and applied biopesticides.

Nosema locustae has been formulated in a wheat-bran bait and is sold commercially as "Nolobait" after being developed by the U.S. Department of Agriculture and registered by the U.S. Environmental Protection Agency. The pathogen requires 3-4 weeks to kill only 50-60 percent of tested grasshopper populations, but it can be passed from one generation to the next (OTA 1990). *Nosema* was tested in Senegal, Cape Verde, and Mali against economically important acridids but it has not shown the efficacy of certain other candidate organisms (TRD 1989).

Currently the most promising candidate as a biological control agent is a particular strain of *Beauvaria bassiana*, which has achieved a 98 percent kill rate in African grasshoppers over 7 days (MSU/INIA 1992). There are a number of studies underway, and others are being planned to discover new entomopathogens and develop promising biocontrol agents for use against locusts in Africa.

An advantage of using microbial biological control agents for locust/ grasshopper management lies in minimizing the potential for significant ecological disruption. Considering the time it takes for most known entomopathogens to stop locust swarms and the political pressure for immediate crop protection during outbreaks, it is unlikely that microbial pesticides could halt regional plagues. Nevertheless, a selective and virulent entomopathogen would be an effective and environmentally innocuous acridid population management tactic in a strategic control context.

Non-Pesticidal Chemicals

Extract from the neem tree (*Azadirachta indica*) kernel has been shown to have potential as a feeding deterrent or repellent to locusts and grasshoppers and has served as a traditional crop protection tool for farmers in the Sahel. Experiments conducted at ICRISAT (International Crops Research Institute for the Semi-Arid Tropics) in Niger showed that neem kernel extract was effective against 9 out of 10 species of Sahelian acridids, including *Oedaleus senegalensis* and *Schistocerca gregaria*. Other experiments using neem against acridids, however, have yielded inconclusive results (TRD 1989).

According to the National Research Council (1992), neem extract can cause a reversal of desert locust swarming behavior to solitary behavior — an effect that has yet to be verified by systematic testing. Neem extract may prove to be a useful tool for crop protection or even for dispersing swarms, but it is unlikely that neem will substitute for toxic pesticides during plagues. Similar to most microbial biological control agents, neem extract will probably be most useful for routine crop protection and for managing locust populations in recession breeding areas as part of a strategic control program. Other potentially useful non-pesticidal chemicals in locust/ grasshopper control and management include pheromones, kairomones, and phytohormones. The International Center on Insect Physiology and Ecology (ICIPE) and others are attempting to identify natural pesticides and chemicals that modify locust behavior. Like biological control agents, these chemicals are usually selective and pose less risk to the environment than synthetic chemical pesticides (OTA 1990), and such compounds lend themselves well to innovative, integrated control tactics.

Protected Habitats

Designation of areas to be protected from exposure to anti-locust pesticides would afford some measure of safety to non-target organisms, some of which may be endangered. Formal governmental recognition of protected areas would also help to increase awareness of the need to preserve critical habitats. In addition to providing sanctuary for wildlife, pesticide-free areas may serve as refuge for pathogens and parasites of locusts and grasshoppers, which can help to regulate locust populations (AID 1991a).

Protected areas would include national parks, wildlife reserves, and other land predesignated for the conservation of local ecosystems. Critical habitats would include terrestrial and aquatic systems that are essential to the survival of animal and/or plant species, some of which may already be in danger of extinction. Aquatic systems, in general, are considered critical because contamination could spread into watersheds, lakes, rivers, wetlands, wadis, irrigation schemes, and drinking water. North African wetlands are particularly important to protect because they provide fly-over stops for migratory birds.

It should also be recognized that wadis, oases, and tributary drainage systems in the desert are the sole sources of vital sustenance for many organisms. Contamination of such isolated systems that sustain local life could have particularly long-term and serious effects.

North African countries have expressed the intent to conserve the environment. For example, Tunisia was a signatory nation to the World Heritage Convention (1975), the Ramsar Convention (1976), and the Barcelona Convention (1977), each of which endorses international environmental conservation. A goal of Tunisia's national park program is to conserve an area representing each of Tunisia's major ecosystems; Tunisia has five established national parks, two proposed parks, and nine protected reserves (Potter and Showler 1991). In the case of Tunisia:

> Several pesticide treatments were carried out in or near fragile wetlands and oases during the spring 1988 desert locust invasions. Deltamethrin, a pyrethroid pesticide, was used to control locusts in the al-Faouar oasis near Kebili. There were also treatments on the edge of Ibn Chabat oasis near Tozeur. Effects of these treatments on nontarget organisms are unknown. Tunisia's oasis ecosystems are, however, intensively cultivated and extremely fragile due to a dependence on scarce water sources at the edge of the Sahara. All pesticides used in Tunisia are considered to be toxic to aquatic life, and contamination of irrigation systems could seriously affect the oasis ecosystem productivity. The Tunisian government has, in a prudent policy decision, prohibited future anti-locust pesticide applications in oases (Potter and Showler 1991).

During all major locust control operations undertaken in the future, systematic environmental monitoring of pesticide impacts should be integral to the overall program. Results from these tests should be given careful attention in order to modify operations appropriately.

Strategic Control

Strategic control aims to stop or avoid plagues through intervention at major breeding areas at critical population thresholds to halt or prevent populations from swarming. Plague prevention programs would involve continuous locust survey[20] in recession breeding areas and could conceivably rely on nonchemical means of locust population management to maintain recession conditions indefinitely (Showler and Potter 1991). Nevertheless, "shifting to a preventive approach first requires a reorientation of thinking by African and donor policymakers, followed by corresponding changes in programs and financing" (OTA 1990: 73). Disputes among and between involved countries — and unpredictable weather — will also challenge strategic control efforts.

In 1988 the International Conference on the Locust Peril determined that a "strategic control strike force" is necessary to prevent locust plagues. This concept is endorsed by the United Nations General Assembly (FAO/ECLO 1989) and supported in principle by the Programme de Recherches Interdisciplinaire Français sur les Acridiens du Sahel (PRIFAS) (Duranton et al. 1989). According to PRIFAS (1989), the cost of crop protection efforts during one plague year will equal the cost of 15-20 years of strategic control. A preliminary estimate is $40-50 million for a five-year preventative program. Plans for strategic control by the international community are currently being discussed (FAO/ECLO 1989; Showler and Potter 1991). In conjunction with developing a strategic control program, FAO and the International Development Bank assisted in establishing the Force Maghrébine d'Intervention (FMI), which has been functioning since late 1989. FMI is composed of member countries Morocco, Algeria, Tunisia, Mauritania, Niger, and Mali, which collaborate on survey activities. Its continuation depends, however, on committed funding through FAO and the Commission de Lutte Contre le Criquet Pélérin en Afrique du Nord-Ouest (CLCPANO) (DAC 1992).

Because strategic surveillance and intervention must occur at recession breeding areas, North African countries must depend upon the collective decisions of Sahelian and East African country governments to facilitate and/or implement strategic control efforts.[21] Successful plague prevention strategies would be the ultimate method by which North Africa would be spared the potential adverse environmental and human impacts inherent to massive emergency pesticide spray campaigns.

Pesticide Disposal

The dilemma of how to deal with unwanted pesticide stocks can and should be avoided during future locust control campaigns, even if pesticides are still the sole available control tactic. Immediate pesticide needs could be fulfilled by a "pesticide bank" such as those created by the European Economic Community and the U.S. Agency for International Development during the last plague.

> Pesticide banks consist of agreements to share a common pool of chemicals among separate potential users, either by bilateral or multilateral agreements among the users themselves, or by centralizing the 'bank' in an organization, such as FAO or European Economic Community, that has a broad area of responsibility. Pesticide banks help prevent the buildup of excess pesticides within African countries, by ensuring that a number of potential users have an adequate centralized supply which can be provided on short notice to areas where a need has been determined and verified (AID 1991a).

Unwanted accumulations of pesticides can also be prevented by effective donor coordination and by provisioning pesticides that are effective and least disruptive to the environment, and that could be used for routine crop protection activities. Existing stocks of excess pesticides must always be contained and stored in a safe manner. Surplus stocks can be eliminated by employing one or more of the following approaches:

1. Use the pesticide for a currently accepted alternate use;
2. Reformulate pesticides into products that can be used;

3. Distribute stocks of pesticides to other countries in immediate need of them for registered uses; or
4. Destroy the stocks (DAC 1992).

Destruction of pesticides should only be an option for eliminating banned, unusable, or undesirable chemicals. The only two field-tested methods for pesticide destruction involved incineration. One method used a modified cement kiln in northern Pakistan to incinerate mixtures of organophosphate pesticides and dieldrin (an organochlorine compound).

The results of the pilot test showed that stack emissions met Pakistani environmental protection standards for air pollutants and nearly met U.S. Environmental Protection Agency standards (Huden 1990). The other proven way of eliminating pesticides involved the removal of dieldrin from Niger to the manufacturer in Europe for incineration in facilities designed for that use (AID 1991b).[22]

Because of the potential of unwanted pesticide stocks to leak, spill, or be sprayed in the environment, the issue of pesticide disposal is widely recognized among North African countries and the donor community. Research is being encouraged to find other environmentally acceptable ways of destroying undesirable pesticides that include microbial decomposition, chemical detoxification, and development of environmentally acceptable mobile incinerators. Burial of pesticide stocks or spraying the unwanted chemicals over "barren" areas are not, in general, considered ideal options for environmental reasons.

Conclusions

Pesticides by definition are toxic and adverse impacts on the environment resulting from massive pesticide spray campaigns against regional locust outbreaks are unavoidable. Ideally, synthetic chemical pesticide use should be discontinued; but during the last plague, and for now, pesticides are the only available tactic for locust control. As research efforts yield new tactics that minimize pesticide use in anti-locust campaigns, impacts on the environment and humans can be mitigated. Evolution toward the capacity to combat locust plagues with minimal risk to the environment will depend to a large extent upon the actions of policymakers in North Africa, the Sahel, donor countries, and international development organizations. It is clear they must promote environmental protection and a more tactically integrated approach to desert locust control to reduce or even eliminate pesticide use in regions where the environment is already in grave peril.

Precise delivery of the least environmentally disruptive pesticides and formulations to target areas that are not located in fragile or protected habitats should continue to be the objective during future plagues and when pesticides must be used. Discovery, development, and adoption of nonsynthetic chemical and biological means of locust control would likely replace synthetic pesticide use in many situations and further reduce environmental risks.

Coordinated strategic control, whether using selective synthetic pesticides or non-chemical tactics, would effectively eliminate large-scale crop protection spray campaigns against locusts in North Africa. Implementation of a strategic control program in politically unstable and/or contested areas[23] in remote terrain would require international collaboration across regions. It would entail continuous survey, timely and selective intervention, detailed knowledge of the pest, and long-term financial commitment to the task.

Prevention of locust outbreaks using environmentally friendly intervention tactics in limited areas should be the ultimate goal of strategic control programs and would facilitate the pursuit of sustainable and dependable agricultural production in not only North Africa, but throughout the desert locust's distribution area.

Notes

1. *Phase transformation* is the change from solitary to gregarious behavior in nymphs and flying adults, accompanied by certain morphological changes.

2. As an example of locust damage to crop production: in 1954 locusts caused the loss of $50 million (today's dollar value) worth of crops in only six weeks in Morocco's Sousse Massa Valley (Steedman 1988). In 1957, more than 600,000 ha were infested in Tunisia, and significant damage was done to almonds, dates, olives, and other fruits, vegetables, and grain (Cavin 1988). Precise crop loss data during the 1950-1962 plague is lacking, however (OTA 1990).

3. Tunisia was also invaded by locusts from southwestern Libya, but on only one occasion in mid-May.

4. For example, Tunisia did not receive greenness information while it was infested (Showler 1992).

5. Surveillance includes egg pod surveys to help predict the scale of subsequent outbreaks.

6. Northern Mauritania was mined and Western Sahara was contested territory.

7. Dichlorovos (DDVP) was used most often in Morocco. Less commonly used organophosphate compounds in North Africa include diazinon and chlorpyrifos.

8. Exhaust nozzle sprayers were used mostly for application of ultra-low volume insecticide formulations.

9. Usually malathion or fenitrothion.

10. These aircraft included both fixed-wing aircraft and helicopters. The fixed-

wing aircraft included the Antonov 2, the C-130, the Cessna Ag Wagon, the DC-6, the DC-7, the Dromadaire, the Grumman Ag Cat, the Piper Pawnee, and the Turbo Thrush. The helicopters included the Alouette, the Bell 206, and the Hughes.

11. For example, BHC was used in dust and bait form in Tunisia and Algeria, respectively, particularly when stocks of malathion and other relatively nonpersistent pesticides were exhausted. BHC is known to accumulate in the human liver and fat cells, like DDT, but there were no reports of chronic or acute effects among humans.

12. In Sahelian countries, however, consumption of dieldrin- and BHC-treated locusts apparently resulted in cases of serious illness (AID 1991a). There were also unsubstantiated reports of pesticide intoxication in southern Tunisia where BHC dust was used.

13. Only useful for measuring exposure to organophosphate and carbamate compounds.

14. For example, in Tunisia 30 sheep died after having grazed on BHC-contaminated rangeland; several gazelle deaths were reported (but not confirmed) in November 1988 (Potter and Showler 1990). In Algeria a limited number of sheep deaths were suspected to have resulted from pesticide applications and, in one case, it was rumored that wolves feeding on contaminated sheep carcasses also died from pesticide intoxication.

15. Morocco, for example, had about 768,000 liters (l) of liquid formulation BHC; 711,000 kilograms (kg) of BHC dust; and 380,000 kg of BHC bran bait in early 1992 (DAC 1992).

16. At this time, there is no economical or practical way of decontaminating or reconditioning empty pesticide drums in Africa. Pesticide drum destruction by puncturing and crushing is the only method available. Such drums may be smelted for later use.

17. There is, however, concern about ingestion of baits by livestock (TRD 1989).

18. Antidotes are available for treatment of organophosphate and carbamate intoxication only.

19. Potentially useful pathogens and parasites of locusts and grasshoppers in Africa include the following: the virus *Oedaleus entomopoxvirus*; the protozoa *Nosema cuneatum* and *Nosema locustae*; the nematodes *Steinernema* sp. and *Heterorhabditis* sp.; the bacteria *Bacillus thuringiensis*, *Bacillus sphaericus*, *Enterobacter* sp. and *Serratia marcescens*; and the fungi *Beauveria bassiana*, *Metarhizium anisopliae*, *Metarhizium flavoviride*, and *Entomophaga grylli*.

20. Survey efforts would include searches for egg pod fields.

21. Because southern Algeria harbors recession breeding areas Algerian participation could be critical to a regional strategic control program.

22. The cement kiln test in Paksitan was a USAID and Pakistani effort. Elimination of dieldrin from Niger was accomplished by the Shell Chemical Company; USAID; the German Technical Assistance Agency (GTZ); and the government of Niger.

23. Contested areas include Sudan (civil wars); northern Mauritania (mined); Western Sahara (contested); Ethiopia (civil wars); and most recently, northern Mali and northern Niger (contested).

References

AID (Agency for International Development). 1991a. *Review of Environmental Concerns in A.I.D. Programs for Locust and Grasshopper Control in Africa.* Washington, D.C.: Africa Bureau, Agency for International Development.

———. 1991b. *Report to the United States Congress by the Agency for International Development: Integrated Pest Management and Pesticide Management.* Washington, D.C.: Agency for International Development.

Bois, C., 1944. "Années de disette, années d'abondance; sécheresses et pluies en Tunisie de 648 à 1881." *Revue Pour l'Etude des Calamités* 7:3-26.

———. 1948. "Années de disette, années d'abondance sécheresses et pluies au Maroc." *Revue Pour l'Etude des Calamités* 11:33-71.

Cavin, G. E. 1988. "Desert locust control: Tunisia and Morocco trip report." College Park, Maryland: Consortium for International Crop Protection.

Coop, L. 1991. "Crop loss assessment near Mourdiah, Mali." Oregon State University. Paper presented at Researchers Colloquium on Crop Loss Assessment in Millet in the Sahel. Ouagadougou: Institut du Sahel and the U.S. Agency for International Development.

DAC (Development Assistance Corporation). 1992. *Final Evaluation of the USAID/ Morocco Locust Control Project.* Washington, D.C.: Development Assistance Corporation.

Duranton, J. F., M. Launois, M. H. Launois-Luong, M. LeCoq, and T. Rashadi. 1989. "La lutte préventive contre le criquet pèlerin en Afrique." Montpellier: Programme de Recherches Interdisciplinaire Français sur les Acridiens du Sahel.

Dynamac Corporation. 1988. *Results of the Locust Pesticide Testing Trials in Sudan.* Washington, D.C.: Agency for International Development.

Everts, J. W. 1990. *Environmental Effects of Chemicals in Locust and Grasshopper Control. A Pilot Study.* Rome: Food and Agriculture Organization of the United Nations.

FAO/ECLO (Food and Agriculture Organization of the United Nations/Emergency Center for Locust Operations). 1989. *The Desert Locust Research and Development Register.* Rome: FAO/ECLO.

FEWS (Famine Early Warning System). 1987. *1986 Grasshopper and Locust Infestations.* Washington, D.C.: Agency for International Development.

Huden, G. H. 1990. *Pesticide Disposal in a Cement Kiln in Pakistan: Report of a Pilot Project.* Washington, D.C.: Agency for International Development.

INS (Institut National de Statistiques). 1987. *Annual Report.* Tunis: Institut National de Statistiques.

Khoury, H., C. S. Potter, H. Moore, and A. Messer. 1988. *Technical Mission Report for the Tunisia Locust Control Campaign.* Washington, D. C.: Office of U.S. Foreign Disaster Assistance, Agency for International Development.

MSU/INIA (Montana State University/Instituto Nacional de Investacao Agraria [Cape Verde]). 1992. *Synopsis of 1991 Research on Development of the Fungus Beauvaria bassiana for Grasshopper Control in Africa.* Washington, D.C.: MSU/INIA, Agency for International Development.

National Research Council. 1992. *Neem: A Tree for Solving Global Problems.* Washington, D.C.: National Research Council.

OTA (Office of Technology Assessment). 1990. *Special Report: A Plague of Locusts.* Washington, D.C.: Office of Technology Assessment, U.S. Congress.

Pedgley, D. 1981. *Desert Locust Forecasting Manual.* London: Centre for Overseas Pest Research.

Potter, C. S. 1988. *Environmental Assessment of the Tunisia Locust Control Campaign.* Washington, D.C.: Agency for International Development.

Potter, C. S., and A. T. Showler. 1990. "The desert locust: agricultural and environmental impacts," in I. W. Zartman, ed., *Tunisia: The Policial Economy of Reform.* Pp. 153-166. London: Lynne Rienner Publishers.

PRIFAS (Programme de Recherches Interdisciplinaire Français sur les Acridiens du Sahel). 1989. "Surveillance des acridiens au Sahel: lettre d'information du 7 Juillet 1989." Montpellier: PRIFAS.

Showler, A. T. 1992. "Desert locust, *Schistocerca gregaria* (Forskal) (Orthoptera: Acrididae), campaign in Tunisia." *Agricultural Systems* (in press).

Showler, A. T., and K. A. Maynard. 1988. *Algeria Locust Operations Assessment.* Washington, D.C.: Office of U.S. Foreign Disaster Assistance, Agency for International Development.

Showler, A. T., and C. S. Potter. 1991. "Synopsis of the 1986-1989 desert locust (Orthoptera: Acrididae) plague and the concept of strategic control." *American Entomologist* 37:106-110.

Steedman, A. 1988. *Locust Handbook.* London: Overseas Development National Resources Institute.

Steiner, J. L., J. C. Day, R. I. Papendick, R. E. Meyer, and A. R. Bertrand. 1988. "Improving and sustaining productivity in dryland regions of developing countries." *Advances in Soil Science* 8:79-122.

TAMS Consultants, Inc., and the Consortium for International Crop Protection (CICP). 1989. *Locust and Grasshopper Control in Africa/Asia: A Programmatic Environmental Assessment.* Washington, D.C.: Agency for International Development.

TRD (Tropical Research and Development). 1989. *Africa Emergency Locust/Grasshopper Assistance (AELGA) Mid-Term Evaluation.* Gainesville: Tropical Research and Development (for the U.S. Agency for International Development).

14

Environmental Impacts of Tourism along the Moroccan Coast

Mohamed Berriane

For many years Morocco's coasts remained relatively undeveloped compared with those of its Western European neighbors. With European ingression at the beginning of the present century, Morocco's coastal areas began to experience substantial development. This gained momentum in the 1950s and reached a sustained rhythm during the 1970s. The modern economic sectors of the coastal areas have functioned as a powerful magnet for the inland populations.

International tourism — recently imported to Morocco — has come to strengthen this coastal concentration, at times conflicting with the other economic activities. The majority of foreign visitors are attracted primarily to the seaside, and tour operators prefer to deal in seaside resort packages. This is why, despite the variety of Moroccan touristic products, 69 percent of the total capacity in rated beds and 67 percent of the overnight stays in hotels are concentrated along the coast. The same seaside-resort tropism applies to local tourism, as more than 60 percent of touristic visits made by Moroccan holidaymakers are to the coast.

Unfortunately, Morocco's coastal environments, which are fragile and increasingly threatened, are protected neither by environmental legislation nor by land-use restrictions. Moroccan legislation concerning coastal areas is mute; no legal text can be found that refers to them explicitly. As a result, further environmental degradation can be anticipated.

This chapter examines the environmental impacts of tourism and related urbanization along Morocco's coasts. It focuses particularly on the Atlantic Coast between Rabat and Casablanca, and the Tetouan Coast and

Bay of Tangier on the Mediterranean. Observations from other Moroccan coastal areas have been added. Environmental problems analyzed include pollution, degradation of coastal landforms, overexploitation of freshwater resources, and the general deterioration in the quality of the coastal environment. Other problems considered include the loss of public access to beaches and growing conflicts between tourism and other economic sectors.

The Impact of Urbanization on Coastal Areas

Damage to the natural coastal environment is caused primarily by excessive urbanization, occurring at a rapid and sometimes disorderly pace in the wake of touristic development. Seaside resorts along the coastal axis Rabat-Casablanca, intended for local tourism, and those situated on the coast of Tetouan, established initially to accommodate international tourism, have particularly resulted in extensive urbanization. This urbanization has involved *de facto* privatization of what should be public space. It has also resulted in serious damage to the fragile coastal environment.

The Coastline Between Rabat and Casablanca

The beaches of the southwestern suburbs of Rabat along the Atlantic coast have been popular resort areas since the Protectorate era. These sheltered beaches have been subjected to sustained pressure since the end of the 1960s. This pressure intensified during the 1970s and 1980s. A sea view is highly valued; thus a proliferation of local government subdivisions, private real-estate promoters' schemes, the initiatives of "beach committees," and national urban planning operations have led to heavy coastal construction.

The transformation of the coast into an urbanized environment is limited to a thin coastal band 200-400 meters (m) wide between Highway 222 and the seashore. The contrast is striking between this crowded coastline and the untouched rural land on the opposite side of the road. Beginning from the old core of El Harhoura, urbanization creeping toward Rabat has already reached the beaches of Gay-Ville and Témara in the opposite direction.

These three resorts now form one long, highly developed coastal stretch. After a short interruption one rapidly reaches the Contrebandier-Sidi El Abed coastal complex, now almost saturated. Farther on, dense coastal development resumes along the seashores of Val d'Or and Ech Chiahna. The only exceptions are at the southern point of Sehb Dhab, where development is prohibited by existing land statutes, and around the estuary of Oued Ykem, where swimming is dangerous. Except for these areas, the urbanization of the coast south of Rabat is nearly complete. Urbanization seems to be the fate of all coastlines located within the vicinity of a big city.

Another seaside under even stronger pressure runs north from Mohammedia and the old resort of Pont Blondin, which are just north of Casablanca. Until the mid-1970s only a sparse line of cottages and cabanas from the colonial period was found along the beach (Figure 14.1). From 1974-1975 on, land parceling to the north of Mohammedia was initiated by real estate agencies based in Casablanca and by individual land brokers. Moreover, starting at the older sea resort of Pont Blondin, other land development has extended south toward Mohammedia. These building plots are characterized by their sizable dimensions. That of Monica Plage, parceled out by the "Société Civile Immobilière," spreads over an area of 49,363 square meters (m^2), the average plot being 637 m^2. From 1980 to 1987, the coastline north of Mohammedia was thus rapidly urbanized. Agricultural land along the coast, which used to be extensive, has virtually disappeared.

Such urbanization cannot be explained solely by the demand for sea-resort dwellings. The expansion of the Rabat-Casablanca urban complex and the need for permanent lodging increasingly account for these extensions. Nevertheless, the impetus for urbanization has been the initial nucleus of seasonal seaside residences and the lure of seaside living. Unspoiled spaces are virtually nowhere to be found along the coast between Rabat and Casablanca. A *de facto* privatization of tens of kilometers (km) of land has taken place with dense permanent residential land use having replaced sparse seasonal recreational land use. Public recreational land has been supplanted by private residences that are part of an uncontrolled urban sprawl. Yet this urbanization is completely legal as it has been carried out within the framework of authorized urban town planning and development.

The "Concretization" of the Tetouan Coast

Along the Mediterranean near Tetouan the same coastal urbanization can be found. Here, an attempt to develop international tourism initiated the "concretization" of the seaside. After the noticeable failure of this attempt to attract mass European tourism, development has been taken over by what can be termed "real estate transactions of a touristic nature."

Ten years ago touristic settlements occupied only 10 percent of the Tetouan coast (Berriane 1980). Today, there is a continuous strip of touristic development between the coast and Highway 28 (Figure 14.2). If development of the Tetouan coast continues at its current pace, the entire coastline

244

A. Situation in 1968

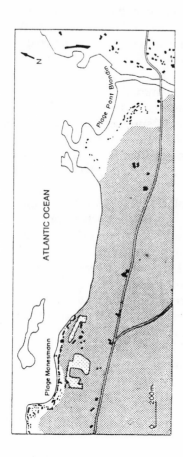

B. Situation in 1987

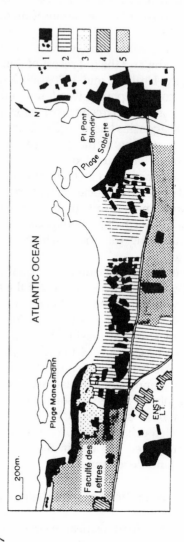

FIGURE 14.1 Urbanization of the Coastal Area Between Mohammedia and Pont Blondin (in shadings, 1 + cottages and villas; 2 = high standard sea-resort land plots, ongoing allotment; 3 = green space; 4 = common infrastructure; 5 = arable land).

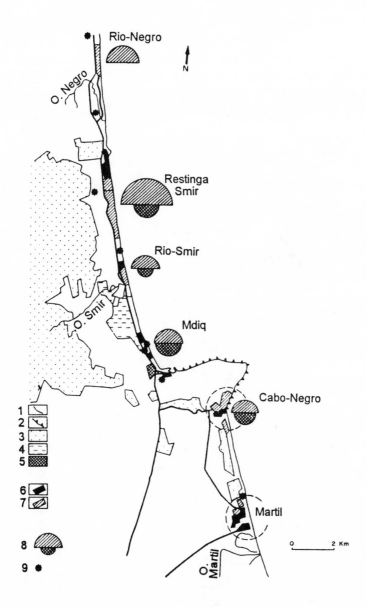

FIGURE 14.2 Touristic Settlements on the Coast of Tetouan (in shadings, 1 = low coast; 2 = rocky coast; 3 = woods; 4 = marshland; 5 = urban center; 6 = existing touristic foundation at end of 1970s; 7 = touristic foundation being filled or already operative; 8 = expected and existing bed capacity; 9 = project)

Source: Data collected by author.

246

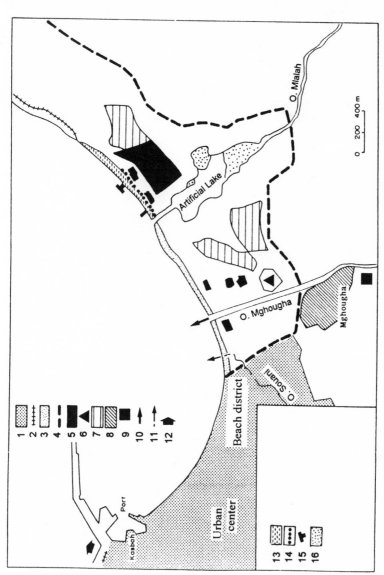

FIGURE 14.3 Tourism and Environment in the Bay of Tangier (in shadings, 1 = urban areas; 2 = cliff; 3 = beach; 4 = limit of the SNABT management office of the Bay of Tangier; 5 = the Bay's touristic units; 6 = camping; 7 = villas; 8 = industrial area; 9 = slaughter house; 10 = industrial waste; 11 = sewage of polluted waters; 12 = drain sewage; 13 = beach in the process of impoverishment; 14 = recently formed rocky beach; 15 = beach protection work; 16 = silting up of the artificial lake)

Source: Data collected by author.

between Mdiq in the north and Fnideq in the south will become urbanized. Progressive privatization of the Tetouan coast is occurring hand-in-hand with urbanization. This is being carried out within a sound legal framework, as that area has been subject to official town plans dating back to the late 1960s. Nonetheless, this privatization is greatly circumscribing public access to what should be public beaches.

Illegal Urbanization Along the Coast Near Tangier

Demand for seaside residences is increasingly oriented toward uncontrolled sites, thereby evading official intervention. In these cases the environmental damage is even greater. In the vicinity of Tangier, there is high demand for vacation sites. This demand is no longer strictly local — it is national in scale. Consequently, heavy pressure is being exercised on the small bays of the Strait of Gibraltar, where unauthorized vacation houses are rapidly appearing.

These bays, sheltered from the southern winds by a succession of capes, until recently harbored a number of pristine beaches. Unplanned urbanization of many of these beaches, located between Cape Malabata and Ksar Sghir, is now well advanced. Enclosed by sea cliffs, these beaches are generally very narrow: 60 m wide in the case of S. Khankouz Beach; 50 m for that of Dar Labrous; and only 30 m for that of Merkala. The oft-haphazard construction of vacation houses is rapidly encroaching on these beaches and other accessible coastal sites.[1]

Thus 100 secondary residences are scattered between Malabata and Ksar Sghir without the slightest official control. Demand is so high that a land-use plan for the coast of the Strait has been deemed necessary. In the interim, local authorities have prohibited any new construction. Nevertheless, due to the remoteness of the sites in question, the lack of effective means of control, and the occasional complicity of officials, construction, even though slowed, has not entirely ceased.

Rampant urbanization of beautiful beaches, *de facto* privatization of the public domain, the intense speculation that will assail the remaining sites, and degradation of the relatively fragile coastal environment — such are the main consequences of the proliferation of seaside dwellings.

Another significant consequence is the disappearance of the limited agricultural land at Ksar Sghir and other areas.[2] The rapid and chaotic multiplication of seaside cottages is occurring at the expense of cultivable land. Development plans for Ksar Sghir call for a resort of individually owned cottages and semi-collective housing. As a result, many land-owning peasants have already abandoned their agricultural activities, turning their lands into recreational property. Farther east, the situation is even worse. In Oued Laou, both the traditional irrigation area and the village center have benefited from certain improvements, including the modernization of the irrigation network and the opening of a road in 1981, which established a direct link with Chefchaouene and transformed Oued Laou's *suq* (traditional market) into an exchange center for the Rif, the coast, and the neighboring towns. However, this road suddenly increased the flow of Moroccan tourists, particularly campers driven off the Tetouan coast. In the beginning problems were confined to a huge disorganized camping site that stretched over several kilometers. Then, progressively, visitors from Casablanca and Rabat began buying plots of arable land and using them to build vacation cottages. Erected in complete anarchy, with no running water or sanitation facilities, several dozen cottages have now been constructed. Arable lands, so rare in these valleys, are gradually being transformed into urban-style real estate.

Pollution and Degradation of the Coastal Environment

Pollution

Pollution is a serious consequence of the heavy pressure by vacationers and campers. Most planning programs intended for local tourism do not include sanitation systems. Projects officially executed (for example, the resorts at Sidi Bouzid, Sidi El Abed, and south of Rabat) as well as those achieved in an unplanned way have provided only for individual sewage or septic pits. With cottages being erected on the beach itself or within immediate reach, rapid pollution of the beach and coastal waters has been occurring. At the resorts located south of Rabat and in Sidi Bouzid, use of septic pits has been justified by the fact that these beaches are meant for visits limited to the summer season. However, many of these resorts are now occupied all year by permanent residents. Extensive pollution is an inevitable consequence.

The idea that the sea plays a role in cleansing and purification is widely shared by visitors. The beach is also considered public property and, consequently, visitors do not take responsibility for keeping it clean. Rubbish and waste accumulate endlessly on the beach, and garbage disposal takes place only meters behind camping sites or houses, usually in hollows between dunes or the beds of dry wadis. Even when local councils attempt to remedy this, they cannot afford to do so because of limited financial resources.

The rural commune of Oued Laou, for example, has considered the collection and disposal of refuse, provision of drinking water, and establishment of a sanitation network. However, the chaotic mushrooming of dwellings has largely transcended local resources, both human and fiscal. Of all kinds of tourism, unorganized camping is the coast's most polluting form. Among the problems are the excessively high density of summer visitors, the shortage of sanitation facilities and drinking water, waste management that is either nonexistent or limited to on-site burial of refuse, dishwashing in the sea, and a pervasive sewer smell.

Degradation of the Beach and the Dune

Polluted because of mismanagement and summer overload, beaches can also be physically degraded when the bordering dunes are harmed. Direct relationships between dunes and beaches have been demonstrated by research on coastal geomorphology (Paskoff 1986). The bordering dune is essential to the beach's dynamic equilibrium because it provides a sand reserve. When dunes suffer from urbanization and trampling by excessive touristic use, the degradation of beaches results.

On the Atlantic littoral the bordering dunes are a much coveted site for rows of cottages (for example, the beaches of Bouznika, Skhirate, Moulay Bou Selham, and Mohammedia) because they offer a panoramic view of the beach and ocean. Concrete retaining walls are often constructed at the foot of dunes to protect seaside dwellings (for example, Moulay Bou Selham and Skhirate). Moreover, legal or illicit use of the sand for building purposes occurs at practically all beaches, as well as leveling off of dunes to create building sites (for example, Sidi Bouzid and Mohammedia). The end result is the depletion of dune sand, preventing the exchange of material with the beach. The latter therefore erodes away. Examples of beaches in the process of sand deprivation are numerous. They include the beaches of the Bay of Tangier and along the Strait of Gibraltar; Moulay Bou Selham; Kariat Arkmane; and Monica to the north of Mohammedia. Existing protective works have only worsened the situation as the attack of sea surge has become even stronger.

The bordering dunes also suffer from heavy trampling and harm by car traffic. Once the vegetation has been destroyed, dunes resume movement, threatening roads, buildings, and agricultural areas.

The Overexploitation of Water Resources

A final impact of tourism on the environment concerns overexploitation of water resources. Touristic areas are often established where water resources are highly limited — for example, the bay of Al Hoceima and Agadir. Nevertheless, the average consumption of water per tourist (including swimming pools and green areas, which require huge quantities of water) can reach up to 10 times the average consumption of a local resident.[3] Overexploitation of scarce resources thus becomes unavoidable. A dwindling underground water table often coincides with the installation of major hotels. Nevertheless, tourist hotels have always been the last to suffer from water interruptions imposed by drought.

Agadir is Morocco's premier example of the conflict between tourism and scarce water resources.[4] Agadir is situated in an arid climate. The water supply in the surrounding Souss Plain is limited to underground water that is already overexploited by motor-pumps for fruit and early vegetable production. Phreatic water is exploited at a rate of 150 million cubic meters (m^3) per year — 60 million m^3/year more than the recharge rate of the aquifer. Despite this acute shortage of water, Agadir is the focus of further tourism development. As Agadir continues to grow and its tourist sector increases, water shortages will become increasingly acute.

Growing Conflicts Between Tourism and Other Economic Sectors

The Bay of Tangier

The city of Tangier occupies a special place within Moroccan tourism, due to the pioneering character of its coastal tourism, the fact that it now claims more than 14 percent of the country's total hotel capacity, and the cachet of its historic status as an international city.

One of the most important achievements of the Three-Year Plan of 1965-1967 was the creation of the *Société Nationale de l'Aménagement de la Baie de Tanger* (SNABT). This company launched an ambitious project to accommodate 30,000 tourists along a beautiful beach (1,000 ha total) in the eastern part of the Bay of Tangier.

Several kinds of lodging (luxury hotels, holiday villages, campgrounds, tourist residences) were to be erected around an artificial lake with a new marina as the project's central focus. For lack of sufficient funds the project goal was soon reduced to 10,000 beds, to be carried out in an area of 350 ha (instead of 1,000 ha).

By the end of the 1970s, only a few more than 2,000 beds had been provided. The reasons behind this failure were numerous. Apart from the crisis of 1973-1974, which probably hampered investment, the reasons often cited were Tangier's limited tourist season, indifference of travel agencies to northern destinations, and withdrawal of the government as direct investor. Insufficiently stressed, in our estimation, were environmental problems resulting from the bay's management plan and from conflicts that emerged between tourism and the city's other economic sectors.

Tourism/Port Activity Conflict and Degradation of the Eastern Beach

SNABT's choice of site was influenced by the quality of the beach (fine sand and smooth coastal waters); its extensive area (1,200 m long and 200 m wide); and its relative remoteness from the city center (4 km). Yet the end result of this location decision was sustained erosion, which has removed much of the beach. Within a few years 3 km of sand beach lying between the mouth of the Souani wadi and Cape Malabata cliffs were virtually destroyed.

The origins of this environmental disaster can be found in poor planning and conflicts between tourism and other economic sectors. The extension of the Tangier harbor pier, necessary because of the steady increase of marine traffic, altered the dynamics of marine circulation, resulting in rapid losses of beach sediment.

Indeed, after the first few winter storms had carried away the beach, waves began to attack the foundations of the Malabata Hotel and Club Med. A protecting wall was erected parallel to the Malabata and Club Med foundations. Unfortunately, this wall soon collapsed. Authorities then embarked on a rock fortification project along the foundations of the hotels. This project proved useless. Schemes to counter the problem continue. However, the harbor pier has permanently altered the dynamics of the bay. Efforts to reestablish a sandy beach (sand is now trucked in) are probably futile.

Tourism/Industrial Pollution Impact

The SNABT site lies below the old industrial zone called Moghagha. This zone comprises 20 industrial units. Some are highly polluting, such as the dye factories. All discharge their effluent directly into Moghagha wadi. There is also a newer industrial zone farther up the road. This second zone has 80 enterprises provided with a sanitation system.

Nevertheless, the system performs poorly and several factories discharge their effluent into the wadi. Thus Moghagha wadi has become an open sewer for all units in the old industrial zone and a portion of those in the newer zone. Moreover, the river receives runoff waters containing solid factory waste, polluted surface waters, and refuse from a public dump located upstream. Opening into the Bay of Tangier where the SNABT's resort area begins, the river brings in enough liquid and solid waste to pollute the beach continuously.

Farther west, outside the SNABT area, Lihoud wadi also ends up in the sea after collecting other kinds of refuse, including part of Tangier's sewage. For this reason, Merkala Beach is so polluted that it presents health hazards. This pollution has spread throughout the eastern side of the bay. Pollution of the beach and nearby bay are a second reason for the failure of the SNABT project.

Conclusions

In comparison to other Mediterranean countries, such as Spain or even Tunisia, Morocco does not appear to have particularly strong touristic pressure. Indeed, plotted against Morocco's total population and area, the intensity of touristic activity appears relatively low. Nevertheless, this overall impression is misleading. Some resorts have started witnessing heavy concentrations of visitors. The touristic intensity rate (the number of whole nights spent annually per 100 inhabitants) reaches 470 in Tangier, 2,515 in Agadir, and 3,427 in Mdiq. Moreover, these intensity rates take into account only the number of recorded overnight stays at rated establishments, which reflects only international visitors. *Tourism* applies not only to international tourism but to national tourism as well. Seaside resorts are becoming more and more frequented by Moroccans.

A lengthy debate has been going on since the beginning of the 1970s between those who think that tourism offers economic opportunities for developing countries — creation of jobs, infrastructure development, circulation of people and goods — and those persuaded that tourism results in dangerous exploitation and stereotypification of a country's people and environment. In Morocco as well as in Tunisia, tourism has become an absolutely essential economic activity.

Nevertheless, the examples presented in this chapter are representative of the outcome of a touristic policy unconscious of its negative impacts on the environment. Although tourism's contributions to governmental finances are unquestionable, the pressure exerted by tourism on the coastal milieu is far from innocuous.

Unfortunately, Morocco's coasts do not benefit from any kind of protection. Urgent steps must be taken to protect what remains of these coasts. Such steps should be based on comprehensive studies and a master plan for coastal management. It is urgent to designate "reserved" zones where building is prohibited. For example, the time has come to prohibit building on the littoral south of Rabat to preserve remaining undeveloped areas from urbanization. Legislation giving the coast special protection must be established. It should be specific to this natural setting and formulated to distinguish protection of the coastal environment from protection of the environment in general.

Finally, it is imperative to reconsider the geography of tourism development. Coastal development should be de-emphasized in favor of tourism development at promising sites in Morocco's interior.

Notes

1. One of the most noticeable signs of encroachment is the increasing number of fences made of barbed wire and enclosing walls built on coastal slopes, which, until the last few years, were valueless.

2. After the crops have been harvested the peasants of the coastal valley of Ksar Sghir often rent their land to campers. They also sell well water and fresh vegetables to these vacationers. Intervention of urban brokers sometimes entices peasants to relinquish plots of arable land, which are then sold to urbanites.

3. The average consumption per tourist per day is roughly 300 liters. A large holiday resort uses 380-400 m^3 of water daily.

4. There has been a dramatic rise in the city's water needs — 390 l/s in 1977 and 710 l/s in 1985. The Abdelmoumen Dam on the Issen River, intended at first to supply the threatened irrigated area of Oulad Teima, has had to be diverted to provide for the city's ever-increasing need for drinking water.

References

Berriane, Mohamed. 1992. *Tourisme National et Migrations de Loisirs au Maroc.* Rabat: Publications de la Faculté des Lettres et de Sciences Humaines.

————. 1986. "Tourisme et environnement dans la baie de Tanger (Maroc)," in *Contemporary Ecological Geographical Problems of the Mediterranean.* Pp. 61-68. Palma de Mallorca.

————. 1980. *L'Espace Touristique Marocain.* ERA 706. Urbanisation au Maghreb, C.N.R.S., Université de Tours.

Bugnicourt, J. 1975. *Le Tourisme en Afrique: Moteur ou Entrave pour le Développement.* Dakar: ENDAA (ronéo).

Chapoutot, J. 1973. *L'Eau et le Tourisme dans la Région de Hammamet Nabeul.* Mémoire de Maîtrise. Université de Paris VII.

Paskoff, R. 1986. *Les Littoraux: Impact des Aménagements sur Leur Evolution.* Paris: Géographic Masson.

15

The Internationalization of North African Environmental Concerns

Pamela Chasek, Lynn Wagner, and I. William Zartman

Most environmental concerns are international. Rarely are the causes of climatic, terrestrial, maritime, or habitat degradation or the scientific knowledge needed to deal with these environmental concerns limited to a single country or confined by borders. International cooperation is necessary to address these concerns. But by the same token, whatever their needs for cooperation, not all cooperating states have the same interests in the face of a shared environmental problem. While there may be a few instances where international cooperation can occur without conflict of interests (Thatcher 1992; MacNiel et al. 1991), almost invariably "cooperation" is beset with conflict.

This chapter focuses on the interests and behavior of the North African states in three different international fora addressing the environment and the way in which these states have used these fora to achieve their goals — individual and cooperative.[1] The fora presented different opportunities and occurred at different points along the path of increasing environmental awareness. The first forum was ad hoc — a series of meetings convened between 1975 and 1977 to explore and establish a Mediterranean Action Plan to control pollution among the riparian states. The second was the United Nations' Conference on Environment and Development (UNCED) in Rio de Janeiro in June 1992 and its Preparatory Committee meetings over the previous year — which subsequently gave rise to an array of continuous institutionalized processes (Spector, Sjostedt, and Zartman 1994). The third is the ongoing regional cooperation initiative, the Maghreb Arab Union, which dates back to 1989.

Parties can play a number of different roles in such fora. The possibilities are infinite. Nevertheless, Sjostedt has identified the most important roles on the basis of the power of each party and its interest in the issue at hand (1993). According to this schema, parties can Drive, Conduct, Defend, Brake, or Cruise. Drivers try to produce an overall agreement that is consonant with their interests. Conductors also seek to produce an agreement but from a neutral position, with no interest axe of their own to grind. Defenders are single-issue participants, concerned more with incorporating a particular measure or position in the agreement than with the overall success of the negotiations. Brakers are the opposing or modifying resistance who attempt to block progress being made on either the broad regime or on specific issue items. Cruisers are filler, with no strong interests of their own, who are available to act as followers.

Sjostedt's schema provides a useful way to analyze the behavior of states. This chapter uses this schema to identify and explain the roles played by the North African states in the three previously identified fora. It is intended to provide insights into the past and future positions of each of the North African states on environmental issues.

The Fora

The Med Plan

Rising world concern over environmental problems led to the convening of the United Nations' Conference on the Human Environment (UNCHE) in Stockholm in June 1972. Delegates from 113 countries approved a Declaration on the Human Environment, an Action Plan, and a proposal to the UN General Assembly for new institutional and financial means to pursue the Plan. As a result, the United Nations Environmental Program (UNEP) was created, and other initiatives resulted.

The Mediterranean Action Plan (Med Plan) was an early result. Beginning in the 1960s, increasing pollution in the Mediterranean Sea attracted international concern. Riparian states held various meetings and proposals for action were put forth during the 1960s and early 1970s, but the states did not have enough information about the extent of pollution to create consensus on the way to approach the problem. The first and second meetings of the UNEP Council asked the UNEP Executive Secretary to stimulate regional agreements for controlling ocean- and land-based pollution and called for regional activities for the protection of the marine environment, respectively.

The resulting Med Plan was drawn up by a group of technicians at an Intergovernmental Meeting on the Protection of the Mediterranean held 21 January-4 February 1975. It was codified as a legal instrument at a Conference of Plenipotentiaries of the Coastal States of the Mediterranean Region for the Protection of the Mediterranean Sea at Barcelona on 2-16 February 1976 by 16 Mediterranean governments (UNEP 1992). The Med Plan consists of four interconnected components: regional treaties; coordinated research and monitoring; integrated planning; and administrative and budgetary support. Protocols have since been passed, providing details on how the components are to be achieved. Morocco, Tunisia, and Libya signed the Barcelona Convention within the year and it came into force on 12 February 1978. Algeria acceded to the convention and protocols in 1981. The following analysis of this negotiation highlights the role that these North African states played in drafting the Med Plan and its convention and protocols.

UNEP played a very active role as the Secretariat for this series of negotiations, among other things ensuring that foreign ministry representatives would remain involved and fund the Med Plan. The principle of "geographic distribution" was adopted to reward countries for participating. The North African states' rewards indicate their level of involvement in the negotiation and interest in developing capacity to address the issue of marine pollution. Regional Activity Centers (RACs) were developed to assist UNEP and coordinate projects of the Med Plan Coordinated Pollution Monitoring and Research Programme (Med Pol). Tunisia was named host to one of the five RACs.

Prestigious lead laboratories for monitoring and research were set up in seven countries, one of which was Algeria. Morocco was not named host to a laboratory, although it participated in the negotiation and introduced some resolutions to the agreements. Libya did not actively participate, and it did not even attend three of the 13 major Med Plan intergovernmental meetings between 1975 and 1984. Libya also did not receive any tangible reward (Haas 1990).

Most areas of contention arose along North-South lines between developed and developing countries. France and Italy, and Algeria and Egypt were, respectively, the most assertive spokespersons for each position. Disagreements focused mainly on the developing countries' desire not to hamper their opportunities for economic development with pollution control regulations, in light of their small share in the responsibility for the present state of the Mediterranean. The developing countries also wanted a program that would improve their science capabilities. The developed countries were concerned with choice of pollutants to be covered and pathways by which they are transmitted; they wanted to limit financial responsibility for transfers to the southern shore, a subject that put France in opposition to the Maghreb. France especially argued for using existing EEC directives as a guideline (Haas 1990).

Although certain disagreements did emerge along these (for the most part) North-South lines, the negotiation process over the Med Plan has been characterized as a problem-solving exercise as opposed to a bargaining session of interests (Thatcher 1992). Scientists, mostly under the coordination and direction of UNEP, played an important role in laying out the issues and developing a plan of action. Many of the scientists did not receive any instructions from their foreign ministries prior to serving as delegates to the Med Plan meetings.

The Algerian, Egyptian, and Greek scientists enjoyed such a free hand. The French scientists, in contrast, received detailed instructions from their foreign ministry (Haas 1990). Access to and sources of scientific data proved to be important issues in the development of a consensus on what was to be done in the Mediterranean. Few countries had pollution specialists at the beginning of the negotiation process. Consensus on the issues was facilitated as the North African (and other) states became more versed in the technical aspects of the negotiation, in response to education by UNEP and especially through the development of domestic scientific expertise under the impulsion of the international process (Haas 1990).

The Barcelona Convention, the umbrella Convention for the Protection of the Mediterranean Sea Against Pollution, was signed in February 1976 along with the *Protocol for the Prevention of Pollution of the Mediterranean Sea by Dumping from Ships and Aircraft* and the *Protocol Concerning Cooperation in Combating Pollution of the Mediterranean Sea by Oil and Other Harmful Substances in Cases of Emergency* (Haas 1990). This part of the negotiation dealt with relatively uncontentious forms of pollution, and UNEP played a minor role as a result.

One issue of disagreement, however, was Morocco's proposal for the creation of an Interstate Guarantee Fund to compensate states for the costs of cleanup during emergencies. France opposed this proposal because it foresaw difficulties in determining whether countries should be compensated for deliberate, accidental, or background cases of pollution. The Interstate Guarantee Fund was adopted by the conference as a resolution, with the reservation of France, rather than being included in the framework convention (Haas 1990).

The Land-Based Sources Protocol, which was signed in Athens in May 1980 and entered into force in 1983, is the most important part of the Med Plan. It sets limits on industrial, municipal, and agricultural emissions into the Mediterranean, and it controls wastes transmitted by rivers and through the atmosphere. These were the most contentious issues negotiated, and UNEP was very active in drafting the protocol and supplying information to delegates in order to persuade them to support it (Haas

1990). Negotiation on the text was conducted by legal representatives from foreign affairs ministries in October 1977 in Venice; January 1978 in Monaco; June 1979 in Geneva; and by the Conference of Plenipotentiaries in May 1980 in Athens (Haas 1990). Disputes concerned the channels of transmission and nature of installations to be covered, and the use of ambient or emission standards. France and Italy were committed to following the existing EEC directives designating the emissions to be treated and the substances whose emission was banned. The developing countries were concerned that the protocol would constrain their economic development. In addition, Turkey and Algeria were worried that the protocol would become a nontariff trade barrier. During a February 1978 meeting in Monaco, Algeria objected to every paragraph to slow the discussion and make delegates justify the compromises they had made (Haas 1990). The biggest disagreement was over the use of emission controls, as preferred by the Europeans, or ambient standards, as advocated by the South.

The text called for certain substances to be eliminated (black list) and others to be strictly limited (gray list). The developing countries were concerned about the possible economic effects of banning the emission of certain substances from their industries. They also argued that their coasts had historically experienced less pollution and would be better able to assimilate emissions. The industrialized nations had greater coastal pollution and called for emission standards. The resolution of this disagreement was achieved by applying emission standards for the black list and ambient standards for the gray list, based on suggestions by the UNEP secretariat (Haas 1990). At the 1979 meeting in Geneva, Libya, Tunisia, Morocco, Lebanon, and Turkey added the words "and implementing" to the phrase "formulating...programs of assistance to developing countries," thus approaching a major goal of receiving technical assistance. France, however, set back this goal when it converted Morocco's proposal for technical assistance "provided on a favorable financial basis" to the provision of "appropriate equipment on advantageous terms to be agreed upon among the Parties concerned" (Haas 1990: 114). The technical annexes, which identified specific substances to be controlled, were discussed by scientists at concurrent meetings and were less contentious than the political talks. UNEP supplied scientific information, which facilitated early agreement on the substances to be covered. At the June 1979 Geneva meeting, the scientists had effectively completed the technical annexes (Haas 1990). Algeria, Egypt, France, Monaco, Tunisia, Turkey, and the EEC quickly ratified or acceded to the protocol, and it entered into force in June 1983; Morocco ratified it in 1987.

Integrated management is the least successful component of the Med Plan. This approach was UNEP's idea and goal, and was never as fully accepted as the other components, especially by the scientific community. On previous components the scientific community had been instrumental in convincing the foreign office executives that agreement was important for the fate of the Mediterranean, but the scientists did not play a similar role for the integrated management component (Haas 1990). France played the main state role in this component.

In 1975, the French offered to prepare a "Blue Book," which would be an operational plan for the integrated planning section of the Med Plan. France thus captured the lead in the integrated management component by drafting the document, and later by supporting the RAC for this component (Haas 1990). An operational document, called the "Blue Plan," was sent to UNEP in early 1976. In January and May, discussions on the plan were held among national experts. The Blue Plan was submitted to governmental representatives in Split, Yugoslavia, in February 1977 (Haas 1990). It was agreed that the Blue Plan would involve cross-disciplinary sectoral studies, to incorporate development concerns with their environmental consequences. How the sectors were to be chosen and how they would be integrated was not agreed upon.

Prior to the Split meeting, Mostapha Tolba, the executive director of UNEP, noted that there were two diverse groups of interests in integrated planning. The French, and to a lesser degree the Italians, were interested in the Blue Plan. But the Plan was too abstract for the developing countries' preferences; they were more interested in projects that would be directly applicable to their development efforts. Tolba separated the Blue Book into two components: an integrated management approach following the French proposal, and Priority Actions Programs (PAP) to study projects of immediate interest to the delegates. At Split, 15 governments approved both components (Haas 1990). The subsequent selection of PAP projects resulted in high percentages of the North African states' priority projects being adopted (100 percent for Morocco and Libya, 86 percent for Tunisia, and 83 percent for Algeria) (Haas 1990).

The Earth Summit

The United Nations Conference on Environment and Development (UNCED) — also known as the "Earth Summit" — was held in Rio de Janeiro in June 1992 on the twentieth anniversary of the Stockholm Conference on the Human Environment. UNCED enabled heads of state and development and environmental specialists to take stock of the past two decades and to identify new strategies for dealing with environmental issues that are inseparable from social and economic development.

When the United Nations General Assembly adopted Resolution 44/228, which articulated the broad goals of the Conference, the world body made it clear that the linkages between development and the environment must be tackled through a fresh international consensus on global issues — in particular the revitalization of development in developing countries on an environmentally sound and sustainable basis. The specific issues to be addressed included protection of the atmosphere; protection and management of land resources; conservation of biological diversity; promotion of environmentally sound use of biotechnology; protection of the oceans, seas, and coastal areas; protection of the quality and supply of freshwater resources; and environmentally sound management of wastes and toxic chemicals.

In establishing UNCED, the United Nations underscored a number of critical issues that need to be addressed at the international, national, and local levels. These include the transfer of environmentally sound technology to developing countries; a concerted attack on poverty; economic instruments and institutional arrangements; and development patterns in various economic sectors, including energy, agriculture, and forestry. Finally, UNCED was asked to deal with the financial needs of developing countries so that the current net outflow of resources from the poor to the rich nations is reversed, and new and additional financial support is provided to revitalize developing country economies in an environmentally sustainable manner.

In the early 1990s the UNCED Preparatory Committee (PrepCom), chaired by Ambassador Tommy Koh of Singapore, was responsible for carrying out the preparations for the actual conference in Rio. The PrepCom, consisting of all interested members of the UN General Assembly and some nonmembers (for example, Switzerland), was responsible for negotiating the agreements to be completed and signed in Rio. The PrepCom met four times: August 1990 in Nairobi, Kenya; March 1991 and August 1991 in Geneva; and March 1992 in New York.

The UNCED Secretariat and other UN officials planned for at least five documents to be signed in Rio: Agenda 21, an "Earth Charter," a statement of forest principles, a framework convention on climate change, and a convention on biodiversity.

Agenda 21 is a framework for action in the twenty-first century on international environmental laws and a range of cross-cutting issues, including financial resources, transfer of technology, human settlements, poverty, health, and education. The Earth Charter, which was supposed to lay the ethical groundwork for Agenda 21, is a document stating the principles by which people should conduct themselves in relation to one another and to the environment. The statement on forest principles came about as a result of a need for an international convention on forests. At PrepCom II the developing countries, led by Malaysia, vetoed any negotiations on forests outside of the UNCED process and expressed strong reservations about trying to reach any forest agreement in time for June 1992. Instead they agreed that the PrepCom is to examine a "nonlegally binding authoritative statement of principles" on the forests, either to be included in the Earth Charter or to stand separately.

In a separate forum, the International Negotiating Committee for the Framework Convention on Climate Change (INC), formed by the UN General Assembly in December 1990, negotiated an agreement on an international structure for controlling greenhouse gas emissions. The INC, which included delegates from more than 116 nations, met five times between February 1991 and May 1992 before it adopted the framework convention signed in Rio. In yet another forum, the Intergovernmental Negotiating Committee for a Convention on Biological Diversity, established in November 1988, negotiated a convention aimed at conserving the maximum possible biological diversity for the benefit of present and future generations.

The Maghreb Arab Union (UMA)

The *Maghreb Arab Union* (UMA) was established in February 1989 at Marrakesh at a summit of five North African states — Mauritania, Morocco, Algeria, Tunisia, and Libya. It has no relation to the series of environmental institutions but is to foster policy harmony and integration among the members, replacing regional disputes with cooperation among the neighboring states. It works through its ministerial committees and its sovereign presidential council of all heads of state, deciding (since September 1991) by majority vote.

Five summits have been held since Marrakesh — 22 January 1990 in Tunis; 22-23 July 1990 in Algiers; 10-11 March 1991 in Ras Lanuf (Libya); 15-16 September 1992 in Casablanca; 3-4 October 1992 in Nouakchott (after the Lockerbie extradition affair had cooled slightly); and 2-3 April 1994 in Tunis after a long interlude resulting largely from Algerian internal paralysis. The second and fifth summits were concerned with institutional matters; the third issued various agreements on an agricultural common market, investment guarantees, phytosanitary coordination, elimination of double taxation, and transit and transport; and the fourth focused on the creation of a free trade area by 1992 and a common market by 1995, two deadlines that have been ignored (Deeb 1992; Zartman 1993). The sixth summit was dominated by economic matters and signature of 11 agreements on customs, trade, insurance, agriculture, telecommunications, publishing, film, banking, a transregional highway, and, again, the creation of a free-trade zone.

A proposed North African Environmental Charter was elaborated following the third summit. Unexceptional in its principles, it took the form of a framework law or action plan, requiring thorough legislative coordination among member states. Adopted by the fifth interministerial committee on 20 November 1991, it was accepted by the fifth summit at Nouakchott in October 1992. Two years later it still awaited ratification by the members.

North African Concerns Within the Fora

The Mediterranean Action Plan resulted from a process that was very much of a problem-solving exercise rather than a bargaining session among interests. This is because the convention was worked out by technicians and followed a course of identifying problems and assigning answers, with little concern for specific national positions and priorities (Thatcher 1992). Even the financing was settled by agreement among government representatives in Split in February 1977 on the basis of a UNEP proposal for financing of half the budget by the member states and the rest by UNEP and other international institutions. Allocation of state shares does not seem to have raised problems noticeable elsewhere, possibly because of use of an established UN formula.

Leadership for the Med Plan negotiations was provided by UNEP, although this role was played out more as that of a Driver than as the "procedural conductor" or "disinterested leader" that might be expected of leadership in environmental negotiations (Zartman 1992).

UNEP was very active in drafting the document that was discussed, encouraging resolution of conflicting positions and forging "transnational alliances with regional scientists who then provided advice to their governments consistent with UNEP's own preferences" (Haas 1990: 78). This last action was carried out in part through providing financing for research activities, under the guiding philosophy that governments would respond best to domestically generated scientific data. The Maghreb states were among the nations that took advantage of UNEP assistance for scientific research.

The North African delegations' strategy was generally one of a Defender, modifying or trying to slow down the effect of a drive, to ensure that their interests were represented (Sjostedt 1993). The developing countries used bargaining techniques to stall until they had developed domestic evaluations of their pollution problems. For example, Tunisia originally opposed placing fluorides and phosphorous on the gray list. Tunisia conducts phosphate mining along the Mediterranean coast and thought that regulations on these chemicals would affect this industry.

Following evaluation of information from UNEP, however, Tunisian scientists were convinced of the environmental need to control these substances, and they in turn convinced their foreign ministry officials to accept their inclusion in the protocol (Haas 1990). The North Africans used the negotiation to obtain resources to enhance their domestic scientific capabilities, which enabled them to participate more fully and effectively in the process. In some instances, the North African strategy resembled that of "compensation" — trading acceptance for inducements and side-payments — or even "exit" through the use of exceptions and derogations (Sjostedt 1993).

The North African states wanted to set standards that would require the Mediterranean's North Shore states to control their emissions yet allow the South Shore to continue to pollute up to a higher threshold. They also desired to include technical assistance in the agreement (Haas 1990).

As their delegations became familiar with the technical aspects of the problems, however, their approach focused on the environmental necessity for action, while still modifying proposals to represent their needs in addressing these issues. One issue of interest is that in several instances it appears as though the North African delegations were not strictly tied to following foreign ministry guidelines.

This was the case during the initial meetings when the Algerian science delegation had a relatively free hand (Haas 1990). This also appeared to be the case when a Tunisian delegate to the Med Plan meetings was outspoken in making known his country's interest in the Specially Protected Areas Protocol and being named host to its RAC, even though he had no political base within his administration to alter national policies (Haas 1990).

At the beginning of the negotiations Algeria's strategy was to use a braking policy by opposing the issues under discussion. In the early 1970s Algerian president Houari Boumedienne had been openly antagonistic to environmental protection. At one point he announced that "if improving the environment means less bread for the Algerians, then I am against it," (NOVA 1980, as quoted in Haas 1990: 72), and in the first 10 years of the negotiations Algeria missed two of the 13 major meetings.

Yet among the developing countries at the negotiations, the Algerians had the strongest delegations and often held strong positions in opposition to the Med Plan (Haas 1990). An issue of particular importance was the Algerians' frequently asserted position that the biggest polluters should pay the most for the support of the Med Plan. The Algerians were also dubious about the quality of externally generated scientific data (Haas 1990). Beginning in the 1980s, however, following the production of domestic scientific data on marine pollution and changes in the status of the marine science community within the administration, Algerian scientists gained the ear of the government, and Algeria became an active supporter of the Med Plan, playing the role of Defender in the negotiations (Haas 1990).

Algeria supported the Med Plan in the end because its officials finally agreed that land-based sources of pollution required treatment and came to believe that the country would benefit materially from participation in other Med Plan projects (Haas 1990). Tunisia too became more enthusiastic after 1979, whereas Morocco has generally kept a low profile and has taken few national measures (Haas 1990). Although the North African states participated in all of the UNCED negotiations, five environmental issues were of particular concern: freshwater resources, oceans/seas, hazardous wastes, desertification, and agriculture. The following briefly summarizes the treatment of these issues within the UNCED negotiations.

Freshwater Resources

The North African states face the prospect that all available fresh surface and groundwater supplies will be fully utilized in 10-20 years. Although Morocco has made serious efforts in the water and sanitation sectors, it still faces the prospect of a declining water supply beyond the year 2000, when its population is projected to grow to 31 million. Algeria is already facing a "water barrier" requiring accelerated efforts, investments, regulations, and controls just to keep apace of spiraling populations. Tunisia is the only North African country that has instituted tariff systems for municipal and industrial water use.

Substantive negotiations on protecting the quality and supply of freshwater resources were launched at PrepCom III in August 1991. Although some progress was made at this session, many of the more technical questions were put on hold pending the outcome of the International Conference on Water and the Environment, held in Dublin in January 1992.

Thus when PrepCom IV began, the delegates began negotiating anew, taking into consideration the recommendations of the technical experts at Dublin. Their call for action at local, national, and international levels was based on four guiding principles:

1. Fresh water is a finite and vulnerable resource, essential to sustain life, development, and the environment;
2. Water development and management should be based on a participatory approach, involving all the users, planners, and policymakers at all levels;
3. Women play a central part in the provision, management, and safeguarding of water; and
4. Water has an economic value in all its competing uses and should be recognized as an economic good.

During the negotiations at PrepCom IV a number of contentious issues emerged. These concerned the environmental effects of dam construction and channeling of water; the need to consider water to be a social as well as economic good; the management of transboundary water resources; and the need for target dates for water resources assessment and sustainable urban development.

The North African states for the most part aligned themselves with the G-77 and the African Group during the negotiations on freshwater resources. They supported the G-77 in its consistent opposition to water tariffs, on the grounds that such tariffs would redirect water resources toward those who can afford to pay and force the poor to use impure water.

There were several instances, however, where one of the North African states spoke out in a Defender role. For example, at PrepCom III Tunisia stated on behalf of 28 developing countries that unless each program area had a section on implementation clearly identifying the need for new and additional financial resources and transfer of technology, the entire document would have to be bracketed. This issue not only affected the negotiations on freshwater resources, but Agenda 21 as a whole. As a result of this intervention the Secretariat worked between sessions to add a section on means of implementation to every chapter of Agenda 21.

During PrepCom IV, Morocco stressed the need for the integration of rural and urban development in the management of freshwater resources. Libya, reflecting a problem inherent in many desert states, stressed the need to address desalinization and other means of increasing available freshwater resources. The resulting Agenda 21 chapter, titled "Protection of the quality and supply of freshwater resources, application of integrated approaches to the development, management, and use of water resources," contains seven program areas:

1. Integrated water resources development and management;
2. Water resources assessment;
3. Protection of water resources, water quality, and aquatic ecosystems;
4. Drinking water supply and sanitation;
5. Water and sustainable urban development;
6. Water for sustainable food production and rural development; and
7. Impacts of climate change for water resources.

Oceans/Seas

Only Morocco of the North African states has both an ocean coastline and a share of the resources and the pollution of the Mediterranean Sea. With this in mind the North African states, led by Tunisia, insisted throughout the UNCED Preparatory Process that regional and enclosed seas be included in the Agenda 21 chapter on oceans. The oceans chapter, titled "Protection of oceans, all kinds of seas including enclosed and semienclosed seas, coastal areas and the protection, rational use and development of their living resources," is the longest and one of the most complex chapters of Agenda 21.

Program areas include integrated management and sustainable development of coastal areas; marine environmental protection; living marine resources; dealing with critical uncertainties/climate change; strengthening international institutions; and sustainable development of islands.

One of the most contentious issues was land-based sources of marine pollution. Although many ocean advocates and environmentalists supported an international treaty aimed at controlling pollution from land-based sources, now recognized as the single greatest threat to the world's oceans, few countries support such a treaty. Developed countries remain reluctant to enter new, broad environmental treaties. Developing countries fear that a global treaty would require them to meet pollution control standards without providing for the technical or financial assistance they will need to comply.

Other than ensuring that the Mediterranean Sea was included in the Oceans chapter, the North African states generally aligned themselves with the G-77 position on the other oceans issues: whales and small cetaceans; relation of the Law of the Sea Convention to UNCED; capacity and institution-building and technology transfer; inadequate attention to development; polar regions; land-based sources of pollution; sustainable use of living resources on the high seas; marine biodiversity; the need to support regional approaches; and the Global Ocean Observing System (GOOS). During PrepCom IV, Tunisia expressed concern about the need to cooperate with subregional, regional, and global intergovernmental fisheries bodies.

Desertification

The problem of desertification, particularly in Africa, has been exacerbated by repeated droughts that have stunted the development efforts of the continent. Before PrepCom IV, many developing countries, including the North African states, said that desertification had been the neglected issue on the UNCED agenda. Due to problems with document availability and translation at PrepCom III and a preoccupation by the working group with other issues, especially atmosphere and forests, this agenda item had been denied critical attention. At the insistence of the African countries, it was decided that Working Group I would put this issue at the top of its agenda at PrepCom IV.

At the end of PrepCom III the francophone African countries, including Tunisia, Algeria, and Morocco, threatened to hold other negotiations hostage unless desertification was given critical attention. For example, at the end of 10 days of negotiations on the Statement of Forest Principles the Africans insisted that the entire document be bracketed as negotiations took

place in English on an English text and there was no simultaneous interpretation available. Thus, they said, they were unable to participate to the fullest
extent possible due to translation problems. The fact that most of the delegates
spoke fluent English was not pointed out. The North African states aligned
themselves with the African group throughout these negotiations.

During PrepCom III the African countries expressed their concern that
the issue of poverty be appropriately addressed within the context of the
debate and urged that the allocation and flow of resources in desertification
control address biomass and energy problems, modification of lifestyles,
and, where needed, protection of species and fragile ecosystems. Algeria
stated that the root cause of land degradation is the lack of economic
development and that this issue needs to be integrated into the chapter on
desertification. Tunisia proposed, with support from Mauritania, to promote and strengthen integrated development plans for those regions prone
to desertification and drought. Tunisia further argued that there was a
need to deal with the social, economic, and ecological impacts of desertification and to organize a monitoring system on fragile ecosystems.

The one issue that caused some contention at PrepCom IV was the
African request for an International Convention to Combat Desertification,
particularly in Africa. Some developed countries resisted this and supported a counterproposal that would initiate an intergovernmental process to examine the most effective means and mechanisms to combat
desertification. Several African delegates said privately that they would
insist on an agreement before approving other documents to be signed in
Rio. As PrepCom IV came to a close, although a number of developed
countries voiced their support for this proposal the paragraphs dealing
with a Desertification Convention remained in brackets (still under negotiation) while many of the developed countries consulted with their
capitals before approving such a measure. The debate highlighted the
importance of the African Group and its leverage on desertification, by
threatening inaction on other issues under negotiation.

Agriculture

Many nations have begun to focus on questions of sustainable agriculture in light of the link between environmental degradation in agriculture
and the problems of hunger, oversupply, and trade and price supports.
Sustainable agriculture is the

> management and conservation of the natural resource base, and the orien-
> tation of technological and institutional change in such a manner as to ensure
> the attainment and continued satisfaction of human needs for present and
> future generations. Such sustainable development (in the agriculture,

forestry and fisheries sectors) conserves land, water, plant and animal genetic resources, is environmentally sound, technically appropriate and economically viable and socially acceptable (FAO Conference on Sustainable Agriculture, April 1991).

The issue was of major concern to the G-77 and the African Group, and it met little resistance from the developed countries (except on the issue of trade). The program areas in this Agenda 21 chapter, "Promoting Sustainable Agriculture and Rural Development," include:

1. Agricultural policy review, planning and integrated programming in light of the multifunctional nature of agriculture, particularly with regard to food security and sustainable development;
2. Ensuring people's participation and promoting human resources development for sustainable agriculture;
3. Improving farm production and farming systems through diversification for farm and nonfarm employment and infrastructure development;
4. Land resources planning information and education for agriculture;
5. Land conservation and rehabilitation;
6. Water for sustainable food production and sustainable rural development;
7. Conservation and sustainable utilization of plant genetic resources for sustainable agriculture;
8. Conservation and sustainable utilization of animal genetic resources;
9. Integrated pest management and control in agriculture;
10. Sustainable plan to increase food production;
11. Rural energy transition to enhance productivity; and
12. Evaluation of the effects of ultraviolet radiation caused by the depletion of stratospheric ozone layer on agriculture.

Hazardous Waste

North-South hazardous waste shipments increased through the 1980s, and unsafe and illegal waste dumps were discovered in several developing countries. In 1988 the Nigerian government discovered that wastes had been exported to Nigeria illegally by Norway, and Guinea Bissau had been offered a $500 million contract to accept up to 50 million tons of hazardous waste. In May 1988, at the annual OAU Council of Ministers Conference in Dakar, Senegal, the OAU condemned the "dumping of nuclear and industrial wastes in Africa as a crime against Africa and the African people."

It also urged African countries to participate in the negotiations that resulted in the 1989 Basel Convention on the Control of Transboundary Movements of Hazardous Wastes and their Disposal and adopt a common position. The main aims of the Convention are to reduce generation and transboundary movements of hazardous wastes to a minimum, to ensure environmentally sound management of hazardous wastes, and to subject such transboundary movements as are permissible to strict control measures. Throughout 1990 the Organization for African Unity (OAU) also prepared an African Convention on the Ban and Import of All Forms of Hazardous Wastes into Africa and the Control of Transboundary Movements of Such Wastes Generating in Africa, to be known as the "Bamako Convention."

Within UNCED the most contentious issue in the hazardous waste debate was over whether to use the Basel Convention or the Bamako Convention as the basis for standard-setting, and whether hazardous wastes should be exported to countries that ban their import. The African countries, including the various North African states, supported the Bamako Convention's wording for a total ban on the transboundary movement of hazardous wastes. The final language was a compromise: "to adopt a ban or prohibit, where appropriate," without the teeth that the G-77 and the African countries wanted.

UNCED formally opened on 3 June 1992 after two days of preconference consultations, during which conference officers were elected, rules of procedure adopted, and the agenda approved. The Conference itself was divided into two main bodies — the plenary and its subsidiary body, the main committee. The plenary was the forum of the general debate, which consisted of 204 country statements delivered at the ministerial level on 3-11 June. Thereafter the summit portion of the conference began and for two days, heads of state and government addressed the world for seven minutes each.

By contrast, the main committee was the site of the actual political negotiations, in essence, a "PrepCom V." Not only were many of the negotiators the same as in the PrepCom, but the Conference elected Singapore's Ambassador Tommy Koh to chair the committee. The mandate of the main committee was to finalize the products of UNCED: Agenda 21, the Statement on Forest Principles, and the Rio Declaration on Environment and Development. Topics in need of substantive negotiations were negotiated by the committee itself or forwarded to contact groups established by Koh and his Bureau on atmosphere, biodiversity/biotechnology, institutions, legal instruments, finance, technology transfer, freshwater resources, and forests. In most cases Koh asked the PrepCom coordinator for the specific issue to hold informal consultations; but on some issues, such as the proposed desertification convention, Koh conducted the consultations himself.

During the seven days of intense negotiation the mood oscillated dramatically from issue to issue and day to day. The entrance of ministers and other high-ranking politicians into the negotiations alternatively improved the pace, as they were able to make the necessary decisions, and impaired the process as they were often unaware of the history of the issue within the UNCED context. When the main committee ran out of its allotted time at 6 A.M. on Thursday, 11 June, three issues still had not been resolved: forests, finance, and atmosphere. These issues went to the Plenary for further negotiations at the ministerial level where, at the eleventh hour, agreement was finally reached.

The North African delegations, like most delegations, were considerably larger at the Earth Summit than they were at the Preparatory Committee. The size of the delegation and the high level of the heads of delegation shows that the Summit was taken seriously by these countries. Unlike many other countries, however, not all of the North African countries were represented by heads of state. Mauritania sent 15 delegates headed by Prime Minister Sidi Mohamed Ould Boubacar. Libya was represented by 9 delegates headed by Mr. Jadallah Azuz Attalhi, Secretary of the Strategic Industries. Morocco's delegation had 35 members headed by Crown Prince Sidi Mohamed. Algeria sent 14 delegates headed by Prime Minister Sid Ahmed Ghozali, and Tunisia sent 12 delegates headed by Foreign Minister Habib Ben Yahia. In the main committee the North African states played a minor role in the negotiations. Most of the issues of greatest concern (as outlined above) had been resolved at the fourth session of the Preparatory Committee. Several observations, however, can be made about their role and activities during the negotiations in the main committee.

During the two days of consultations that preceded the Conference, one item on the agenda was the election of officers. When the African Group put forward its list of 11 nominees for the Plenary Bureau, the delegate from Mauritania immediately expressed his displeasure that his country had not been nominated and insisted that it be added to the list. The African Group later met to decide how to settle this dispute, having 12 nominations for 11 seats on the Bureau. The problem was eventually solved when the Latin American Group offered to give a seat to the Africans, provided that this was not a precedent-setting move.

On the issue of atmosphere the North African countries were put in a difficult position. The Arab Group had insisted at the conclusion of PrepCom IV that the entire chapter of Agenda 21 on atmosphere be bracketed for further discussion at Rio. The Arab Group maintained that the chapter not only was duplicative of the work of the Climate Change negotiations, but overemphasized energy efficiency and conservation. Saudi Arabia took the lead, calling for deletion of references to new and renewable energy sources. In Rio, Saudi Arabia, strongly supported by its political allies, Kuwait and Morocco, held out until the eleventh hour before finally agreeing to compromise text with reservations that it repeated in the closing session. Because Agenda 21 is not a legally binding instrument but a statement of policy, the Saudis' formal reservations to the chapter have no substantive implications.

Of the issues of prime concern to North Africans, desertification and drought were the most contentious. After a series of private consultations Ambassador Koh announced at the final session of the Main Committee that compromise language had been agreed upon, requesting the General Assembly to establish an Intergovernmental Negotiating Committee (INCD) for the elaboration of an international convention to combat desertification. Much to everyone's surprise, the European Community suddenly announced that it could not accept this text. This resulted in a flurry of statements from developing and developed countries alike offering their support for the compromise text. Among the North African states, Mauritania and Algeria took the lead in calling for EC acceptance. After a 45-minute break, during which members of the EC met with members of the African Group, the EC announced its agreement.

The INCD met in Nairobi on 24 May-3 June 1993, in Geneva on 13-24 September 1993, in New York on 17-28 January 1994, and again in Geneva on 21-31 March 1994 and on 6-17 June 1994 for the adoption of the Convention and four regional protocols (Bernstein, Chasek, Goree, and Mwangi 1993-94). Postsignature negotiations continued at the sixth INCD session in New York on 9-20 January 1995. North Africa played a particularly important role in the proceedings of the Committee, in that one of the two working groups, WG-1, was ably chaired by Ahmed Djoghlai of Algeria, former rapporteur of the UNCED PrepCom. WG-1 was responsible for sections on commitments, action program, capacity building, resources, and cooperation.

From the beginning Algeria submitted a 40-page national report on measures to combat desertification, one of the major inputs into the drafting of the final convention. The final convention and its African annex (covering North Africa as well) was a mitigated triumph for the African Group, focusing attention on the area around the Sahara and other deserts although with less commitment of resources than desired.

Within the UMA the story is short. The North African Union has not been mobilized effectively to look at environmental concerns. Much of its activity has been dominated by institutional concerns, but there has been considerable planning of economic integration as well, even though the implementing measures have not yet been enacted. The one area where the UMA has been the framework for cooperation concerns internal security against the Islamicist threat.

The paralysis of the organization due to the Saharan conflict and the Lockerbie affair have not prevented lower-level committees from meeting on specific sectors; but it has kept the highest decision-making body from giving the political or institutional impetus to advancing cooperation.

Exceptionally, the UMA did testify, along with its member states, at the first INCD session, but that activity merely highlights its absence elsewhere. There is an unused forum available for coordination of interests and activities that would at the same time make a special contribution to the life of the new institution itself.

That is problem enough, but the main problem is not there. There is a weak "Environmental Charter" on the table awaiting ratification by the national legislatures, not by the regional body that accepted it. But ratification of the Charter would bring a commitment to greater cooperation among the members of the Union than they are able to envisage in the mid-1990s. Even the Tunisian president during the first half of 1994 was unable to mobilize regional cooperation and harness it behind the obvious benefits to be gained by all members through collaboration to save the regional environment.

Conclusions

The North Africans are skilled negotiators who move in and out of their groupings depending on issue convenience. The North African countries are members of the Group of 77, the African Group, and the Arab Group. As in their general foreign relations, they played their triple membership skillfully during the UNCED process, working as Arabs when it best fit their interests and as Africans at other times. For the most part they did not break ranks with the G-77. On many of the issues under negotiation, the North Africans were primarily Cruisers. Regarding matters such as biodiversity, biotechnology, technology transfer, finance, and radioactive wastes, to name a few, the North Africans accepted the positions of the G-77. Even on some of the issues of particular concern to them, including freshwater resources, hazardous wastes, and sustainable agriculture, the North African countries aligned themselves with either the general G-77 position or the African Group's position.

Within the negotiations on oceans and desertification the North Africans played a stronger role. Tunisia, in particular, was a Driver in ensuring that the Mediterranean Sea was specifically included in the Agenda 21 chapter on oceans. On desertification, the North Africans worked closely with the other members of the African Group who were the Drivers in calling for a framework convention on desertification and drought. Algeria acted as both Conductor and Driver in the INCD as chair of one of the two working groups and obtained a result that was close to its own positions. Skillful politicking that secured the Algerian delegate the procedural post of rapporteur, which he executed capably, positioned him to occupy the more substantively important chair on desertification. On the other hand, the

North Africans were often the Brakers. Morocco supported Saudi Arabia in braking on energy conservation. Tunisia broke ranks with the G-77 in the negotiations on atmosphere at the end of PrepCom IV when it called for a paragraph that would set per capita levels for CO_2 emissions. This amendment, which would have conflicted with the mandate of the ongoing Climate Change Convention negotiations and was strongly resisted by the United States and Canada, was not supported by the G-77. Algeria began as a Braker on the Med Plan and then turned into a Defender, occasionally accompanied by Tunisia.

Tunisia is known within UN circles for having a preoccupation with procedure. Procedural wrangling, often instigated by Tunisia or Mauritania, delayed many of the negotiating sessions at PrepCom III before UNCED. There was much less of this at PrepCom IV, due in part to behind-the-scenes pressure exerted on the Tunisian delegation by other countries, notably among the G-77. One area where the Tunisians did not back down at UNCED was on the issue of formation of committees and proliferation of meetings. At PrepCom III Tunisia opposed language in the resolution establishing rules of procedure for the Rio Conference that could be implied to mean that a number of negotiating committees would be set up.

Tunisia was also in the forefront of the debate, which led to the "two meeting" rule at PrepCom III — no more than two meetings could take place simultaneously. Mauritania and Tunisia held up the progress of the negotiations on a number of occasions by insisting that no more than two meetings take place at any one time, rewording rules of procedure, and insisting that there be a prohibition on the participation of nongovernmental organizations in both the Preparatory Committee and the Conference itself. All of this procedural wrangling was supposed to ensure the fair and equal participation of developing countries in the UNCED negotiations. The issue came up again at PrepCom IV — it didn't matter that it was 4:00 A.M. Tunisia argued with PrepCom Chair Koh for more than 15 minutes on language referring to subgroups and committees in Rio. Tunisia again repeated its concern about the proliferation of meetings during the first session of the Main Committee and then finally dropped the issue.

Tunisia and Mauritania were Drivers in the fight to prohibit nongovernmental organizations (NGOs) from participating in the UNCED preparatory process and the conference itself, a procedural issue with substantive implications that did not appear in the other fora. Although there have been many rumors as to why this was their position (concern about the Polisario's participation as an NGO, concern about opposition groups within their own countries participating in UNCED, opposition to democracy and transparency of the UNCED process), the real reason is not clear. Nevertheless, since PrepCom I in Nairobi these countries have opposed NGO participation.

The size of the North African delegations to the UNCED and its Preparatory Committee — Libya (5); Tunisia (7); Mauritania (7); Morocco (11); Algeria (7) — shows that they have taken this process quite seriously and that it is important to them. Moreover, Tunisia and Mauritania were Vice Chairs of the PrepCom; the PrepCom rapporteur and INCD working group chair was from Algeria.

Similar evidence of environmental awareness is unlikely to be found in the Barcelona Convention negotiations, which came 15 years earlier, in the midst of the United Nations Conference on the Law of the Sea (UNCLOS) to which North African states attached great importance. Also, much of the work on the Barcelona Convention took place at the technical level and most of the research institutes were located on the Mediterranean's northern shore.

With such good and growing experience, what explains the absence of regional North African cooperation on an issue where interests are so similar, such as the environment? As seen, North African cooperation on anything except regional security has been blocked by the politics of conflict — the fear of establishing too strong a dependency and cooperation that might hinder pursuit of the conflict when required. When the impulse is given by others within an international framework, the North African states play the game well; but among themselves, there is no one to lead the process.

In the negotiation context, they are skillful at the roles of Cruiser and Defender, or even Braker, appropriate roles for the states of the South in broad multilateral negotiations. But these roles are not good training for achieving regional cooperation. In the final analysis, environmental cooperation is foreign policy. In global or Mediterranean negotiation the adversary is the North, promoting North African regional cooperation; but in regional negotiation the adversary is within, hindering cooperation.

Note

1. The "North African" states included in this analysis are Morocco, Algeria, Tunisia, Libya, and Mauritania.

References

Bernstein, Johannah, Pamela Chasek, Langston James Goree VI, and Wagaki Mwangi. 1993-1994. *INC for the Elaboration of an International Convention to Combat Desertification* 4 (various numbers). Winnipeg: International Institute for Sustainable Development.

Deeb, Mary Jane. 1992. "The Maghrib Arab Union." Unpublished paper.

Haas, Peter. 1990. *Saving the Mediterranean: The Politics of International Environmental Cooperation*. New York: Columbia University Press.

MacNiel et al. 1991. *Beyond Interdependence*. New York: Oxford.

Sjostedt, Gunnar. 1993. "Negotiating nuclear accident agreements, in *International Environmental Negotiations*, G. Sjostedt, ed. Newbury Park, Calif.: Sage.

Spector, Bertram, Gunnar Sjostedt, and I. William Zartman, eds. 1994. *Negotiating International Regimes: Lessons from UNCED*. London: Graham & Trotman.

Thatcher, Peter. 1992. "The Mediterranean Action Plan." *Ambio* 6:309-312.

UNEP. 1982. *Convention for the Protection of the Mediterranean Sea Against Pollution and Its Related Protocols* and *Mediterranean Action Plan and Convention for the Protection of the Mediterranean Sea Against Pollution and Its Related Protocols*.

Zartman, I. William. 1992. "International environmental negotiation: challenges for analysis and practice." *Negotiation Journal* 2:113-123.

―――. 1993. " The ups and downs of Maghrib unity," paper presented to the Georgetown Center for Contemporary Arab Studies Conference, Washington, D.C.

Appendix

TABLE A.1 Endangered Animal and Plant Life in North Africa

Country	Known Mammalian Species	Threatened Mammalian Species	Known Avian Species	Threatened Avian Species	Number of Plant Taxa	Threatened and Rare Plant Taxa
Algeria	97	12	X	15	3,145	144
Libya	76	12	X	9	1,700	58
Mauritania	61	14	550	5	1,100	3
Morocco	108	9	X	14	3,550	194
Tunisia	77	6	X	14	2,160	26

Source: World Resources Institute 1992. World Resources 1992-1993. A Report by the World Resources Institute in collaboration with the United Nations Environment Programme and the United Nations Development Programme (New York: Oxford University Press).

Index

Afforestation of maritime dunes in Tunisia, 95

Agadir, problems of touristic development in, 249-250

Agdal, role of, in managing grazing resources in Middle Atlas, 46-47

Agricultural mechanization: and crop yields, 22; and drought vulnerability, 28; government incentives for, 22

Agricultural production, efforts to increase in Algeria, 29

Agricultural reforms in 1980s, 26-27

Agriculture: cultivation of marginal lands in Tunisia, 101; land under cultivation in Tunisia, 95-96, 102; plowing process for cereal production, 21; traditional technology, 21-22; sustainable, UNCED negotiations concerning, 268-269

Agropastoralism: and the Beni Guil, 124-125; changes in, 48-51; traditional system of, 40-47

Ait Arfa, 38-50

Animal husbandry: changes in, in Middle Atlas, 47-48, 52n.2; limits to, in Middle Atlas, 40; as part of agropastoralism in Middle Atlas, 41. *See also* Agropastoralism; Pastoralism; Grazing; Overgrazing

Arable land: in Algeria, Morocco, and Tunisia, 5; factors in location of, 5

Barley: and drought resistance, 25-26; production of, 31n.11

Barrage vert, 80

Beaches, degradation of, in Morocco, 248-249, 251-252

Beni Guil: classical pastoral pattern of, 121; expansion of cultivation by, 124-125; privatization of communal land by, 122-124; territory, physical characteristics of, 120-121

Bidonvilles. See Squatter settlements

Biological control of locusts, 230-231, 237n.19

Cantonnement of tribal lands for colonization, 24

Carrying capacity in Middle Atlas, 43, 48

Cash crops replacing rangeland in Middle Atlas, 48

Cedar in Middle Atlas, 43, 179-180, 185

Cereal crops: expansion of, in Tunisia, 101; historical production methods for, 23; as percentage of total cropland, 20; and price controls, 27; rainfall needs of, 20; timing of rainfall and yields, 21-22; traditional production of, 21; wheat versus barley, 25-26

Cereals: imports of, in 1980s, 26; as percentage of daily caloric intake, 20

Chergui, 56-57

Clear cutting. *See* Forest management

Climate change: in Algeria, 84-85; in North Africa, 144-146. *See also* Global warming

Climax forests. *See* Forests

Coastal plains: arable, in Morocco, Algeria, and Tunisia, 4; average rainfall of, 5; defined, 12n.2

Coasts, touristic development of, in Morocco, 241-252

Colonization: and dislodgement to marginal lands, 24; and effects of land concentration, 23-24; effects of, on rangeland in Mauritania, 110-111

Conflict and international environmental policy, 255-275

About the Book and Editors

Deforestation, soil erosion, desertification, air and water pollution, loss of wildlife habitat, and declining biodiversity are interrelated manifestations of a growing environmental crisis in North Africa that has received relatively little attention from government policymakers and is poorly understood by North African peoples, the international development community, and scholars. In this book a multidisciplinary group of scholars explores the broad range of human activities causing the deterioration of North Africa's fragile environment, including population pressure and poverty, rapid urbanization, intense competition for land and water, and mismanagement of natural resources. The contributors examine in particular the conflict between economic development and environmental sustainability. They analyze the historical roots of current environmental problems, the underlying socioeconomic causes, potential solutions, and differences in environmental policies among various countries. This is an insightful portrait of a developing region attempting to reconcile traditional methods of land use with growing demands for resources, the exigencies of economic development, and the limitations of its natural resource base.

Will D. Swearingen is research associate professor in the Earth Science Department at Montana State University, Bozeman. He is author of *Moroccan Mirages* and numerous articles on agriculture, food security, and drought in North Africa. **Abdellatif Bencherifa** is professor of geography and vice dean of the Faculté des Lettres et des Sciences Humaines at the Université Mohammed V, Rabat, Morocco. He specializes in the study of land-use practices in mountain and oasis environments in Morocco and has published widely on these topics.